T0305796

From Failed Communism to Underdeveloped Capitalism

From Failed Communism to

Underdeveloped Capitalism

Transformation of Eastern Europe,
the Post-Soviet Union,
and China

Adam Zwass

With an Epilogue
by Robert Schediwy

Routledge
Taylor & Francis Group

LONDON AND NEW YORK

First published 1995 by M.E. Sharpe

Published 2015 by Routledge

2 Park Square, Milton Park, Abingdon, Oxon OX14 4RN

711 Third Avenue, New York, NY 10017, USA

Routledge is an imprint of the Taylor & Francis Group, an informa business

Library of Congress Cataloging-in-Publication Data

Zwass, Adam.
From failed communism to underdeveloped capitalism :
transformation of Eastern Europe, the post-Soviet Union, and China /
Adam Zwass.
p.   cm.
Includes bibliographical references (p.   ) and index.
ISBN 1-56324-461-6 (cloth)
1. Former Soviet republics—economic conditions.
2. Europe, Eastern—Economic conditions—1989–
3. China—Economic conditions—1976–
4. Post-communism—Former Soviet republics.
5. Post-communism, Europe, Eastern.
6. China—Politics and government—1976–
I. Title.
HC336.27.Z83   1995
338.947—dc20   94-48187
CIP

ISBN 13: 9781563244612 (hbk)

This book is dedicated to my wife, Friederike,
my children, Vladimir and Alicia, and my grandson, Joshua

Contents

Preface

A social order whose stability had been its most admired characteristic collapsed without a war or resistance. Soviet-style socialism is no more. A nontraditional road to capitalism is being paved. Instead of leading from feudal socage through the early manufacture plants, this road originated with state-owned economies whose declared primary objective was equality. Recent developments make an excellent reason for this economist, who studied the Soviet system for many years, to investigate the sources of the implosion and the prospects for the future.

We shall explore several essential questions. We shall discuss the relationship between the velvet revolutions in the outer ring of the Soviet empire and the collapse of the empire itself under its own weight. We shall investigate why the euphoria of the emergence has been followed by apathy and discontent. Did this have to be?

The blurry outlines of the system that was to take the place of the *ancien régime* and the various roads to it were defined variously as: "as quickly as possible, back to capitalism" (by Jozsef Antall of Hungary), "market economy without any buts" (according to Vaclav Klaus of the then-Czechoslovakia), and "back to civilization" (according to Boris Yeltsin of Russia). These "programs" were not easy to realize. The load-bearing layer of the bourgeois revolutions, the layer of private entrepreneurs, had been destroyed and is not easy to reconstitute. The lofty ideals of the Enlightenment, in decline in the West, were of no help to the recent revolutionaries. The revolutions in Eastern and

Central Europe were driven by the hatred of the totalitarian system and by a fascination with the Western way of life. The outlines of the future system, to replace the one in many respects egalitarian, even if in other respects the declarations of egalitarianism sounded hollow, were much less clear.

We shall try to show how rapidly planned economies are being converted into market economies and how quickly the one-party regimes were replaced by pluralistic multiparty systems. At the same time, we shall discuss the considerable costs that have accompanied the attempt to bridge the great chasm between the existing institutional frameworks and a modern economic and political system with shock therapy. The living standard has come down drastically and the envisaged pluralistic democracy manifests itself in a great variety of parties and political groupings, almost all of them without a wider popular support.

The results of the systemic change in each of the involved countries will be analyzed. We shall see the deep cleft between Central Europe, where the end of economic decline can be seen, and the former republics of the defunct Soviet Union, where the deepening chaos in the economy has had a devastating effect on the population.

Communism in Eastern and Central Europe is dead. The ex-communists who are coming back to power have no intention and no wherewithal to bring it back. Yet, communism is still the state doctrine in China. The state, however, is gradually being driven out of the economy and the grip of ideology on people's minds is weakening, as the author could observe during his recent extensive speaking tour of the country. As opposed to the situation in Eastern Europe, the reform in China is accompanied by continuous economic growth.

Questions are many and answers are few. However, if the reader will gain an insight into the issues and an understanding of the developments in these countries, my task is done.

The past role of the West in the developments and its potential future role in assisting the reconstruction of the regions will be discussed in the epilogue by Robert Schediwy of Webster University in Vienna.

The author wishes to acknowledge the interest and support of General Director Adolf Wala and Vice President Heinz Kienzl of the Austrian National Bank. Charlotte Mally provided invaluable secretarial assistance. My wife, Friederike, my son, Vladimir, and my grandson, Joshua, helped in many ways.

From Failed Communism to Underdeveloped Capitalism

Chapter 1

From Semifeudal Russia through Soviet "Real Socialism" to the CIS and Real Capitalism

The year 1991 saw the demise of an economic, political, and social system that had endured for three-quarters of a century. It also marked the end of a 300-year-old empire founded by Peter the Great and expanded by Catherine II and Joseph Stalin.

There is much dispute over the causes of the collapse, even if some reasons for it are clear enough. The Soviet Union was simply unable to keep pace economically with the industrial states of the West, yet its leaders not only were determined to maintain military parity with the world's number one economic power, but even aimed for military superiority. Recent statistics have revealed that the Soviet national product, chronically exaggerated by the Soviet government as well as by CIA experts, was only about 28 percent that of the United States. And, while Soviet defense spending was about the same as U.S. defense spending in absolute terms, relative to the national product it was four times as much. The Soviet Union built military bases on all continents of the world until it finally bled itself to death economically in Afghanistan, its Vietnam.

"Fraternal" aid to state leaders such as Ethiopia's Mengistu Haile Mariam, a cruel and petty dictator, had but one purpose, to which fraternity was utterly irrelevant—to extend the Soviet Union's military presence. The abuse of Marxism and revolutionary rhetoric used by such personages to mask tyranny dealt the final blow to the official, proclaimed ideology of proletarian internationalism. And, further enhancing the irony, owing in part to Soviet pressure, Western colonialism was at the same time being relegated to history.

This fraternal aid was also prohibitively expensive for the Soviet Union's ailing economy. Soviet economist Boris Sergeev gives figures for "politically motivated economic aid and loans": $11.2 billion to Syria, $6.2 billion to Iran, $5 billion to Afghanistan and $4.7 billion to Ethiopia.[1] Subsidies through payment of higher prices in foreign trade were politically motivated: Cuba's sugar was bought at seven to nine times the price on the world market, which meant an annual subsidy of $2 billion. Richard Nixon quoted politically motivated Soviet subsidies at $15 billion per year.[2]

The deputy prime minister of the former Soviet Union, Kamentsev, stated that at least half the loans granted, most of which went for arms (85 billion rubles), were nonrecoverable. Meanwhile, the nation's economic performance was steadily deteriorating.

After the failure of Lenin's War Communism (1919–20), during which economic activity declined by three-fourths compared with its pre–World War I level, and after the New Economic Policy (NEP) (1921–25), which was very successful but was prematurely suppressed, Stalin devised his command system. But in the end, the Stalinist system also proved unsuited to achieve the Soviet Union's manifest aim of catching up with the West.

Equality remained unattainable. Although the income and power pyramids may have been attenuated slightly for the mass of the population, power and income both tended to be concentrated at the top. Broad layers of the population benefited from more equitable incomes, but only with a net downward shift in the standard of living—a weaker incentive, certainly, for improving economic efficiency than production for profit and access to ever greater personal wealth. Work and the fear of losing one's job seem after all to be a much stronger incentive to produce than is job security—that is, the certainty of not losing one's job regardless of either productivity or how the economy is performing.

The extremely hierarchical social system, inspired by fear and terror, which Stalin erected in the 1930s, was no place for Marx's dream of the new man who would spontaneously behave so as to be useful to himself as well as to others, or, as Engels put it, a society where people behave in such a manner that no regulations are necessary, or, as Trotsky hoped, a system in which the man will become the equal of Aristotle, Goethe, and Marx.

The United States' "architects" were much more successful in orienting the relations of production in the new society not to the "nobly behaved" human being of their dreams but to a human being who behaved "humanly." If human beings were angels, remarked James Madison, government would be superfluous.

As it turned out, the idea that an economy administered by a state planning authority would be more productive than a market economy was a presumptuous illusion. The "invisible hand" of the market—the economic mechanisms shaped by the collective wisdom of countless human generations—is, after all, more consonant with human purposes than are the commands of a central economic bureaucracy. Competition among producers to secure a place on a buyers' market is better geared to the production of good-quality goods than are the production and distribution relations previously on the sellers' market of a planned economy.

Defeat in competition with the industrial countries of the West was a foregone conclusion once the latter had learned the art of Keynesian deficit spending to mitigate the effects of cyclical crises. The terminology may have fallen out of fashion in an age of monetarism, but deficit spending was in fact still in operation in Reaganomics. In contrast, top–down reforms in the planned economies were never carried through consistently, and in fact were obstructed to the very end by the formidable Soviet bureaucracy.

The endeavor to fulfill the central plan made use of some special and indeed original techniques, intended more to satisfy the authorities in the hierarchy than to meet human needs. Economic performance came to be measured in terms of resource input and not of buyer demand for goods—what counted was the gross product. The ratio of resource input to the gross product was, as Mikhail Gorbachev continually reiterated, twice as high as in the Western industrial nations. Behind the repeated assurances of achievement by factory managers and economic ministries stood, as economist Vasilii Sel'iunin wrote, "phantom statistics," which were far removed from actual performance.

Even though the ratio of the Soviet Union's inventories to the national product was two to three times higher than in, for instance,

Japan, supply shortages were chronic. The deposits of raw materials and fuels near the industrial centers of the Urals and the European Soviet Union were rapidly depleted; as a result, these vital resources had to be extracted at enormous expense in Siberia and the Far East and transported or piped over long distances to the industrial zones.

Forced Collectivization: The Prime Reason
for Mass Terror and Shortages

Even more devastating than forced industrialization and the unbounded growth of a bureaucracy wielding absolute control over the economy was the enslavement of the peasantry, begun in the early 1930s. Forced collectivization was achieved with an unprecedented brutality against the "class enemy," with millions of victims. In a second stage, the Great Terror of 1936–38, Stalin turned against the regime's supporters. The liquidation of the Revolution's old guard cemented Stalin's one-man dictatorship. The following figures will give an idea of the magnitude of the consequences of collectivization: before World War I, Russia had been literally the bread basket of the world, accounting for 30 percent of the world's grain exports; in the 1930s it became the world's leading grain importer, at a rate of 30 million tons per year.

Shortages became chronic. The bizarre ideal that forced requisitions of agrarian products could serve as a source of "primitive accumulation" to finance forced industrialization reduced agricultural productivity to a level that placed the very subsistence of the population at risk.

The 1990 grain harvest was smaller than that of 1913. "The Bolsheviks," wrote Aleksandr Yakovlev, the ideologue of perestroika, "behaved in their peasant countryside like foreign conquerors. . . . the peasant was alienated from the products of his labor and from the soil . . . that most important means of production of all."[3] The peasants were permitted no identification papers and were bound to their collective farms. Under Stalin, the peasants' small private plots were ruined by taxes; landlessness under Nikita Khrushchev and the prohibition on selling the products of one's own labor under Brezhnev finished the process. The peasants were so thoroughly enslaved that even today they are reluctant to make themselves independent by leasing land or by some other form of personal possession.

The state monopoly on foreign trade and absolute control over the economy had grave consequences: after 1918, firms producing for export were totally cut off from the world market. Industrial enterprises traded goods produced for export or goods imported from abroad at domestic ruble prices with the state foreign trade organizations, which served as clearing houses. Accordingly, industry had no notion of the relationship between domestic and foreign costs of goods sold or acquired abroad. The official exchange rate was used only as a conversion rate or for statistical purposes; moreover, for reasons of prestige, it was always set higher than buying-power parity warranted. No practicable cost–benefit analysis was therefore possible. Ricardo's "comparative cost advantage" ceased to function as an incentive to foreign trade.

And thus as well, foreign trade ceased to exercise its function of promoting growth and quality, as it traditionally had done in a competitive market economy. Foreign trade degenerated into a crude stopgap mechanism for an autarkically inclined domestic economy. Goods were imported to fill gaps in supply and exported to finance indispensable imports. In 1939, foreign trade turnover accounted for no more than 12 percent of the 1913 volume, and in the postwar years it was no more than 5 percent of the national product.

According to GATT statistics, the former Soviet Union exported goods worth a total of $78 billion in 1991—that is, less than Hong Kong ($98 billion) and only slightly more than Taiwan ($78 billion), China, and South Korea (each $78 billion). These figures were a long way from the export volumes of the world's largest exporters: the United States—$422 billion; Germany—$403 billion; and Japan—$315 billion.

Shielded from the competitiveness of international markets, Soviet firms consistently produced low-quality goods and reduced the foreign trade of the world's number two superpower to the level of the developing countries. Eighty percent of Soviet exports were raw materials and fuels, while manufactured goods, principally high-tech goods that the domestic economy was unable to produce, were imported.

The Soviet Union created a similar structure for trade with its CMEA (Council of Mutual Economic Assistance) partner states. Despite the conclusion of a treaty of October 23, 1963, on "multilateral clearing in the newly created CMEA currency (the transferable ruble) and the establishment of the International Bank for Economic Cooperation (IBEC)," the multilateralization of trade relations never became a reality. Accounting was multilateral but trade remained bilateral.

Goods quotas continued as before to be bartered at equivalent value, and quota overhangs were accounted for in monetary deposits or credits, which, however, ultimately had to be settled in goods.

The CMEA was permanently dissolved in 1990. It had never succeeded in making the transferable ruble even partly convertible. CMEA trade continued to be shut off from the rest of the world just as it had been prior to 1964. Because prices within the CMEA countries varied, the CMEA was unable to create its own internal price basis. A five-year average of world market prices was therefore used instead. Prices calculated on this basis differed from prices within the member countries as well as from the current world market prices. After the abrupt rise in the price of crude oil in 1973, a sliding, annually adjusted price structure was adopted, but it continued to be based on a five-year average of world market prices.

One cause of the collapse of the Soviet system was, of course, that the Soviet leaders obstinately pursued their aim of achieving superiority over the West in the arms race, even though the Soviet system was unable to compete economically with the West. But a second factor was the system's perversion of proletarian internationalism into a policy of conquest.

At the time the architects of the October Revolution were preparing the theoretical foundations of a multinational socialist state, they wholly disregarded Karl Marx's view of Russia. Marx regarded Russia as a prison of nations and anyone who contradicted this opinion, whether it be the king of Prussia or the British prime minister, he branded as Russian agents.

Stalin wrote his pragmatic pamphlet "Marxism and the National Question" in Vienna in 1913. In it he rejected categorically the federalist concept of the Austro-Marxists Otto Bauer and Karl Renner. The nation was sovereign, asserted the "wonderful Georgian" (as Lenin described him), and had the right of self-determination and succession.

After the victorious Revolution, however, Lenin and Stalin (whom Lenin had appointed commissar for nationality questions) were loath to give up even one small bit of Great Russia's territory. They used military force to crush the resistance of the "Bashmati" of Central Asia (1917–26), the Menshevik (Social Democratic) government of Georgia, the liberation struggle in the Ukraine, and others. Thereafter, not one republic ever made use of the constitutionally guaranteed right to secede from the union: they knew what was in store for them if they tried. Later on, whole nations together with their political establish-ments (the Crimean Tatars, the Kalmyks, the Chechen-Ingushi, the Volga Germans, to name a few) were forcibly removed from their homelands and resettled in distant regions on suspicion of collabora-tion with the Germans. There were no open nationality conflicts in the Khrushchev and Brezhnev eras. The brutal reprisals were too fresh in people's minds for them to dare a struggle for freedom.

Sixty million Soviet citizens lived outside their national homelands, Gorbachev reported to the CPSU Central Committee on September 20, 1989. Russians, often the pawns of forced migrations, made up 33 percent of the population of Latvia, 38 percent in Estonia, 9 percent in Lithuania, 21 percent in Moldavia, 8 percent in Georgia, 41 percent in Kazakhstan, 13 percent in Turkmenia, 11 percent in Uzbekistan, and 10 percent in Tajikistan.

Many Russians living in other republics have assimilated into their new homelands, even though they were often concentrated in kinds of ghettos around industrial enterprises. Now, however, they have be-come the particular targets of the renascent nationalism that is sweep-ing over the union's former republics. In Estonia, for instance, Russians are regarded as foreigners and treated accordingly. In Moldavia they established the Dnestr republic, which is now embroiled in a conflict with independent Moldova, which regards itself as Roma-nian. For reasons still unknown, Stalin awarded Nagorny-Karabakh, populated by Armenians, to Azerbaijan, and so set the stage for an endless conflict there that has now escalated into open warfare.

On the three-hundredth anniversary of the Ukraine's incorporation into Great Russia (Pereiaslavskaia Rada, 1654), Khrushchev awarded to the Ukraine the Crimean peninsula, with its military ports for the Black Sea fleet and the best resorts in the country. No one at the time could have dreamt that this would lead to the current conflict between Russia and the newly independent Ukraine.

It would, of course, be wrong to equate the Soviet empire with the great Russian empire. Differences in economic development across the vast territory had been somewhat mitigated, but even now, after the end of the Soviet regime, these differences have far from disappeared. The 1989 *World Almanac* statistics for per-capita social product of the republics of the former Soviet Union clearly show how far below the Soviet average the Asian republics were. At 2,138 rubles per capita, only Kazakhstan, with its huge reserves of raw materials and fuel, approached the union average of 2,358 rubles. (This average is itself only a fraction of the per-capita national product not only of the leading EC countries, such as Denmark [$25,500], Germany [$23,700], and France [$21,000], but even of the EC's poorest country, Greece [$6,600].) Last by far among the fifteen republics was Tajikistan (1,151 rubles), just barely exceeded by Azerbaijan (1,221 rubles), Uzbekistan (1,258 rubles), Turkmenia (1,548 rubles), and Kyrgyzia (1,697 rubles). The Baltic states topped the list—Estonia (3,182 rubles), Latvia (2,989 rubles), and Lithuania (2,758 rubles)—followed by Russia (2,781 rubles), Belarus (2,497 rubles), and the Ukraine (2,173 rubles).

Tables prepared by the Deutsche Bank using other indicators, such as educational level of the population, market economy mentality, or infrastructure rank the Ukraine first, with 83 out of a possible 100 points, followed by the Baltic republics with 77, Russia with 72, and Georgia with 61. Belarus and Kazakhstan showed a moderate level of economic development, with 55 points each, followed by Moldova with 49 and Armenia and Azerbaijan each with 47 points. At the bottom of the list are Uzbekistan with 32 points, Turkmenia with 27 points, Kyrgyzia with 24 points, and Tajikistan with only 18 points.

Despite these substantial differences in level of economic development, altogether the republics formed a vast interdependent economic network. This was especially true of the Baltic republics, which proclaimed their secession from the Soviet Union much earlier than the others: Estonia exports 66 percent, Latvia 64 percent, and Lithuania 60.9 percent of their respective social products to the former Soviet republics. Only Belarus had a higher figure in this regard, with 69.6 percent of its total product implicated in the interrepublic division of labor. For the Asian republics, the figures were 50.7 percent for Turkmenistan, 50.2 percent for Kyrgyzia, 42.2 percent for Uzbekistan, and 41.8 percent for Tajikistan. Russia—which, with its considerable reserves of raw materials and fuels is more autarkic—the Ukraine, and Kazakhstan were the least dependent, with export percentages of 18 percent, 39.1 percent, and 30.9 percent, respectively. It would be wrong, however, to assume that Russia was the benefactor of this unequal division of labor. A study by the Kiel Institute for the World Economy, published in January 1992 based on statistics for 1987, shows that if Russia's exports to the other union republics were assessed at world market prices instead of at domestic prices, its surplus in interrepublic trade would rise from 3.6 billion to 20.5 billion rubles. These close economic dependencies, forged over an entire century, are being destroyed by the struggle for "total independence." In glaring contrast to the ever greater integration of Western Europe, with its resolute movement toward the formation of a single economic sphere with no customs duties and visions of monetary union, customs barriers are being erected between the republics of the former Soviet Union, as national currencies, delivery quotas, and other restrictions are being introduced.

The Outer Ring of the Soviet Empire: Sheer Size— An Insupportable Burden

By the signing of the Hitler–Stalin pact on August 23, 1939, socialism already perverted by Stalin into a dictatorial regime and a command economy was invested with a new, anti-human face. The pact was more than a pact of conquest, it was an ideological pact with Hitler's fascism. The world public correctly understood Stalin's toast to the führer as "the beloved of the German people." The deeds that would cement the alliance between the two dictators followed shortly thereafter. Countless German communists were delivered to the Nazi führer, and *Pravda* made nothing of it. Seventeen days after German troops marched into Poland, Foreign Minister Molotov called Poland the "bastard of the Treaty of Versailles." As the Polish army was being crushed and the cities bombed, and in the face of Warsaw's heroic but futile resistance, the Red Army moved in swiftly to occupy Poland's eastern territories. The annexation of the Baltic states, Bukovina, Bessarabia, and the trans-Carpathian Ukraine followed soon thereafter, and in winter 1940 the Soviet Union started the war against Finland. The Soviet General Staff—decimated by the Great Purges—needed four long months to bring that country down.

Until this juncture, it could be argued that the Soviet Union was merely recovering some of the territories lost by the tsarist empire at the end of World War I. But the true beginning of the Soviet Union's fateful evolution into a conquering imperial power came after the victory over Hitler's Germany: the Soviet Union promptly set about building a *cordon sanitaire* for itself in the countries of Eastern and Central Europe, in flagrant violation of the principles of the Atlantic Charter to end the war without conquests or reparations, although it had itself accepted these principles. That was the spirit of the Yalta and Potsdam treaties concluded with the Western allies.

Within a few years after the signing of the peace accords ending World War II, however, Stalin had forcibly imposed the Soviet system upon Eastern and Central Europe. This was not a system of utopian communism foretokening liberty, equality, and fraternity, but the system Stalin had forged in the Soviet Union, a system in which the state was omnipotent in all domains of social life and the economy was run by command.

In further violation of the Atlantic Charter, the Soviet Union imposed all but crippling reparations upon its "fraternal" countries. For instance, to East Germany's extreme detriment, the large industrial enterprises of the Soviet zone were dismantled, although the advantage the victorious occupying power derived from this was minimal. Nor was that the only form of reparations exacted from the future GDR. In addition, two hundred large enterprises were merged into Soviet shareholding companies (SAGs—i.e., *Sovietische Aktiengesellschaften*) and forced to deliver goods to the Soviet Union without payment. These shareholding companies were dissolved after Stalin's death, but not before they had transferred as much as 15 percent of the East German social product between 1945 and 1953 to the Soviet Union (according to estimates of the German Institute for Economic Research in West Berlin). West Germany, by contrast, had to pay no reparations and received $3,907 million in Marshall Plan aid.

It was not only East Germany that had to pay reparations. Romania was forced to form joint enterprises (*Sovroms*) without any contributions of Soviet capital. Until 1953, the Romanian *Sovroms* also delivered vast volumes of goods free of payment to the Soviet Union. Poland was forced to hand over to the Soviet Union all plants that had even the least connection with Hitler's war machine, even though it had been the prime victim of Nazi aggression, having lost 40 percent of the state's total assets in World War II.

The incorporation of the economies of Eastern and Central Europe into the Soviet Union's huge military-industrial complex had perhaps the gravest consequences of all for those states. A system of production geared to heavy industry and arms was imposed upon them all, regardless of their traditional economic structures. Costly iron and steel foundries were built, agriculture, light industry, and consumer goods manufacture were neglected, and the supply system to the population was dismantled and thrown into general disarray.

Through their forced membership in the Soviet bloc's economic community (CMEA, which was established on January 9, 1949) and in the Warsaw Pact (concluded on May 14, 1955), the countries of Eastern and Central Europe had to bear a prohibitively large share of arms expenditures, as well as to contribute considerable sums of "fraternal assistance" to the Soviet superpower in its permanent confrontation with the West.

Every attempt to improve the dwindling performance of the economy through radical reforms of the overall system were effectively obstructed, often only out of fear lest "Big Brother" might not approve.

In June 1953 Soviet troops intervened in East Germany to crush a workers' uprising. In October 1956 they marched into Hungary. In a five-nation Warsaw Pact alliance they subdued the Prague Spring in August 1968. An invasion of rebellious Poland in October 1956 was only prevented through the intercession of the Chinese and Italian Communist Parties. The Soviet Army was prepared to march into Poland a second time to smash workers' uprisings on the Baltic coast in 1980 and 1981. Only the declaration of martial law on December 13, 1981, prevented this intervention—or so, at least, claimed both General Jaruzelski, then Poland's minister of defense and head of the Polish Communist Party, and General Dubinin, until recently the commander-in-chief of Soviet troops in Poland.

Whatever the results of an exact cost–benefit analysis of Soviet hegemony in Central and Eastern Europe—the national leaderships took varying advantage of the freedom they were allowed—not only the population but also a large portion of the economic and political elite tended to blame the Soviet Union for all failures, whether or not it was actually to blame. If the 1989 revolution was accomplished effortlessly, this was not only due to an eruption of popular rage, but also to the lack of resistance from the establishment, which had, as in 1789 in France, lost its faith in its own right to exist.

From Reforms within the System to Perestroika

The first comprehensive reform was introduced by Nikita Khrushchev in May 1957. Stalin's successors wanted to remove some of the power of the cumbersome central state apparatus molded by the dictator. The way to this end was to decentralize economic powers, by limiting the omnipotence of the state planning commission (Gosplan), dissolving the branch ministries, the monopolistic fortresses of economic management, and delegating decision-making powers to regional economic administrations (*Sovnarkhozy*).

One hundred and five regional economic administrations were established with jurisdiction over the economic units in a region independent of the production profile. Instead of the branch principle, whereby all the enterprises in one branch were under the jurisdiction of one ministry, a regional principle was introduced. Regional economic authorities, the *Sovnarkhozy*, brought together the larger industrial and construction firms under one roof; smaller firms remained under the authority of the regional soviet.

The creative impulses of the new organizational structure, however, were already exhausted while Khrushchev was still in power, and new, perhaps even greater, defects emerged. Regional autarky (local self-sufficiency) caused perhaps even greater economic damage than the former economic segregation of industrial ministries. Khrushchev attempted unsuccessfully to alleviate this ill by concentrating authority (the number of *Sovnarkhozy* was reduced from 105 to 47 in March 1963), and, in the small Soviet republics, by making their area of influence congruent with the confines of administrative territories, and finally by creating central coordinating authorities. But Khrushchev's fall in October 1964 brought an end to his great experiment.

Leonid Brezhnev and Aleksei Kosygin again abolished the decentralized economic administration introduced by Khrushchev, which had already been discredited during Khrushchev's term in power. The main reason for this action was that the regional administrative authorities tended toward autarky, and did not give sufficient consideration to state interests. The plenary session of the Central Committee of the CPSU in September 1965 resolved to restore the economic ministries and to reaffirm the powers of the state planning commission (Gosplan). But henceforth central planning was to concentrate on the most important areas of the economy. Economic steering mechanisms were given greater leeway than before, and economic accounting at the microlevel was to play a greater role. Finally, thenceforth sales and profitability, and profits relative to fixed and circulating capital, were to be the criteria for evaluating economic efficiency, rather than gross output, as before.

The low efficiency, the growing disproportions between the individual areas of the economy, and above all the gap between the excessively expanded capacities of the manufacturing industries and the raw materials and fuel industries forced the leadership into a continual search for new ways of planning and administering the Soviet economy. The resolution of the CPSU Central Committee and the Council of Ministers of July 12, 1979, marked the beginning of a new stage.

The most important item in the July resolution was measures to combat the autarky of the economic ministries abolished by Khrushchev. The vertical plans of the economic ministries were to be coordinated with the horizontal development plans of the large regions, and the governments of the republics were to receive greater powers to manage and administer the economic complexes under their jurisdiction. The July 1979 resolution downgraded rather than upgraded planning at the micro-level, and stressed the imperative character of central planning even more than before.

Leonid Brezhnev's eighteen years in power have rightly gone down in the history of his country as years of stagnation and immobility. The ruling elite had never before felt so secure and so firmly ensconced in power than during the 1970s under Brezhnev's leadership. Economic growth rates, however, decreased from 7.5 percent in the five-year period from 1966 to 1970, to 5.8 percent and 3.8 percent in the next two five-year periods, and finally to 2.5 percent in the last two years of the Brezhnev era. Yet arms spending increased from 14 percent of the national income in the early 1970s to 17 percent by the end of the decade.[4] The Soviet Union's share in world defense spending ($810 billion) in 1983 reached $258 billion. U.S. spending was $187 billion. China was in a distant third place with $34 billion, followed by Great Britain with $27.4 billion, Saudi Arabia with $27.2 billion, and France and the Federal Republic of Germany with $23.8 billion and $23.6 percent, respectively.[5] One should bear in mind that the gross national product of the Soviet Union was at that time not much greater than that of Great Britain.

It is no accident that the CPSU Politburo elected Yurii Andropov, head of the KGB, as general secretary after the death of the long-ailing Leonid Brezhnev, in view of the steadily declining economic performance and the growing disproportions and the decline in labor discipline. Andropov was the man who was supposed to bring some life and discipline into the stagnating and collapsing social system. He assumed the office of general secretary in order to "overcome the 'years of neglect,'" and, as he put it even more clearly later, "to introduce some movement into the 'accumulated inertia.' " Eight months after taking office, he admitted at the June 1983 session of the Central Committee, "If we are honest, we must admit we have not yet completely learned the laws, and above all the economic laws, that govern the society in which we live and work." Two months later the Party leader was saying: "We would be poor students of our teachers if we contented ourselves with merely reiterating the truths they discovered, and if we relied merely on the magic powers of quotations learned by heart." Andropov regarded opposition forces not only as imperialist agents but as simply criminal. "There are few people of this sort in our society," he said on the occasion of the hundredth anniversary of Felix Dzherzhinskii, the first head of the secret police in that country.

Andropov could never have dreamt that the flaws in the social system would give dissident groups—still at that time small—such tremendous strength that eight years later they would be toppling the "Iron Felix" from his pedestal in front of the head offices of the secret police, and doing so, moreover, under the very eyes of the latter, who themselves no longer had the energy to prevent the dismantling of their own bronze-cast symbol. The Party head purged the state apparatus of corrupt and indolent functionaries with an iron hand: one in three of the regional Party secretaries, one in four of the ninety ministers, and nine of the twenty-three section leaders of the Central Committee fell victim to the campaign of purges. But very little was done to breathe life into the depleted forces of the economic and political system.

The Andropov era, destined to be short-lived, left only two programmatic documents behind: on "Work collectives and enhancing their role in managing firms and organizations," and the decision of July 26, 1983, on "Supplementary measures to expand the rights of firms in planning and economic activity, and to increase their responsibility for the outcomes of production." The purpose of both was to expand the economic authority of production units and their work force, as well as to improve labor discipline. In contrast to the slogans of the Bad Godesberg Program of the German Socialist Party (SPD) in 1959, "Market as far as possible, planning as far as necessary," the two Andropov documents can be summed up in the succinct proposition, priority to central planning, with a minimum of powers at the microlevel and even more stringent labor discipline.

Andropov ruled the country for eighteen months. His successor, Konstantin Chernenko, a loyal Brezhnev servant, was in office even more briefly, hardly long enough to initiate anything of importance. Then, on March 11, 1985, came Mikhail Gorbachev, with his much-heralded slogans *perestroika* and *glasnost.*

The youngest person in the Politburo was elected the number one person in the state, with the mission of finally making the social system more firmly competitive with the progressive West. Gorbachev traveled around the country for two years, spoke with factory work forces, observed, and had a few insignificant laws passed. He then painted a somber picture of the state of the nation to the programmatic meeting of the 307 Central Committee members on January 27, 1987: "A parasitic ideology has grown up, a psychology of leveling and equalizing has set in within the minds of the people." And further, "Disregard for the law, corruption, and toadying have had a fateful influence on the moral atmosphere; bureaucracy and formalism have grown poisonous blossoms. . . . Criticism is met with extreme intolerance."[6]

Gorbachev subjected the economy to a merciless critique:

> Most of the targets of the state plans have not been fulfilled since the beginning of the seventies. Economic managers were not open to innovation, and a considerable portion of manufactured goods did not meet modern quality standards. Profits had been exaggerated through manipulation of the figures. Economic growth declined by half in the last fifteen years. (*Pravda*, March 12, 1992)

The general secretary saw the causes of the crisis in a weakening of the economic mechanisms as well as in the obsolete "political and theoretical principles, which sometimes were remote from reality." He concluded his somber portrayal with words that are today quoted continually: "We must move forward because we have no other way." He tried to conjure this forward movement with two magic formulas: "perestroika" and "glasnost." But the gap between the claims and the reality became increasingly obvious. In *Perestroika: The Second Russian Revolution*, published in 1987, Gorbachev wrote that the new edition of the Russian Revolution was the "greatest transformation since 1921," when Lenin put an end to War Communism with his New Economic Policy (NEP).

Gorbachev pointed to the lawfulness of the revolution he had started. Other countries of Europe as well, he said, had required several revolutions to solve their political, economic, and social problems: the great French Revolution of 1789 was followed by smaller ones in 1830, 1848, and 1871; Oliver Cromwell's revolution in 1649 was followed by two smaller ones in 1688 and 1833, and even Germany had experienced two great upheavals in 1848 and 1918, in addition to the interim of critical reforms of the 1860s, which Bismarck called "iron and blood."

Gorbachev's great promises and conjurations, however, failed to be followed by deeds. The central planning authorities and central administration declined steadily in authority and influence under the barrage of criticism. None of the projected economic mechanisms had yet been implemented when Gorbachev left office. The few improvements, introduced in homeopathic doses, were carbon copies of the reforms of other planned economies, which were also without effect.

Perestroika, conceived as a panacea for the stagnating economy, made no discernible progress; stagnation escalated into a deep recession.

Gorbachev's popularity in the West increased unabated. *Time* magazine named him "Man of the Century": he, the peacemaker, concluded far-reaching disarmament agreements and withdrew Soviet troops from Afghanistan, and received the Nobel Peace Prize. But his popularity within the country continued to decline. Glasnost turned the mass media inside out and they turned not only against the ossified Party apparatus, but also, ever more vehemently, against the great reformer himself. Caught between on the one hand the insolent intellectuals condemned for long years to silence or to apologia for the miserable conditions, and on the other the top bureaucracy fearful for its elite status, the general secretary and later president oscillated between the two social poles, unable to achieve a balance or to bring about effective progress.

The project Gorbachev had undertaken was vast and ambitious, considering that the great Russian bureaucracy had always been omnipresent and all-powerful; Gorbachev, the Joseph II of the Soviet establishment, was just as powerless in vying with this huge bureaucratic apparatus as his predecessors on the Kremlin throne had been. "Even the Tsar is powerless before this bureaucracy," wrote John Stuart Mill in 1859. After his return from the Soviet Union in 1920, Bertrand Russell wrote, "Power is exercised by the bureaucracy composed of three classes: believers, careerists, and specialists."

"There are also people in the Soviet Union who abuse the process of democratization and defame our social order," said Gorbachev, in a discussion on September 30, 1987, with 350 scholars, politicians, clergy, and writers in France. When Roland Leroi, the editor-in-chief of *Humanité*, the French Communist Party organ, spoke of pluralism of opinion, Gorbachev corrected him: "But you must add the adjective 'socialist.' " The intellectuals who supported him, however, wanted a democratic pluralism without adjectival addenda and without ifs and buts.

Perestroika proceeded at a snail's pace, and, instead of cleaning up the economy, it deepened the crisis and caused further hitches in supply to the population. Gorbachev's comrades-in-arms were enraged. They wanted a functioning competitive market economy of a Western stripe. The republics did not want autonomy within the Soviet Union; they wanted nothing less than independence. The outer ring of the empire wanted total sovereignty, not "limited" sovereignty. Gorbachev himself realized that his solemnly proclaimed words at the grave of his predecessor Chernenko, "The countries of Eastern Europe have remained a solid cohesive and inalienable component of the Eastern community," had lost touch with reality. But these countries also knew that the Soviet Union under Gorbachev's leadership would not venture a military invasion. The developments of 1989 clearly showed how the people hated Soviet hegemony. Yet the revolution also encountered no resistance because the eruption of mass discontent was accompanied by an implosion of the national economic and political elites, who had been humiliated for decades and precluded from showing any initiative of their own.

The events unfolded almost exactly as Prince Karl Schwarzenberg, the former Prague state chancellor, described it at a symposium organized by the European journal *Transit* on the topic "The Old Continent of Europe" on April 5, 1992: "1989 was not a year of revolution in Eastern Europe. Inferior government withdrew from the scene under public applause."

Stalin had smashed all independent social mechanisms and replaced them with the commands of the Party and state apparatus, which was expanding without limits. Khrushchev failed in his attempt to crush the all-powerful central apparatus; it proved to be stronger than the reformer himself and overthrew that head of Party and government in the palace revolution of October 1964. The bureaucracy experienced an unprecedented period of prosperity under Brezhnev's rule. Gorbachev had good reason to fear this all-powerful bureaucracy. He knew the inertia and the power of resistance of the apparatus that had chosen him, an apparatchik, from its ranks to be the number one person in the state. The intellectuals demanded radical steps, but Gorbachev vacillated. The apparatus armed itself for a struggle to defend its political positions and privileges. On August 21, 1991, it instituted a putsch against the president when he was vacationing in the Crimea, even though he knew quite well that a putsch was being prepared. The putschists were his closest colleagues, whom he himself had appointed: the vice-president, Genadi Yanaev; the head of government, Valerii Pavlov; the minister of defense, Dmitrii Yazov; and the head of the KGB, Vladimir Kryuchkov.

The August 1991 putschists were unable to bring down the Party and state leader in a palace revolution, as had been done on October 14, 1964, against Khrushchev. At that time, and in 1991, the apparatus was a similar group of defenders of the military-industrial complex of the Soviet empire. But the people had changed since 1964, and that was unequivocally the merit of glasnost and Gorbachev. He returned from the Crimea, but not as victor: it was the people under the leadership of Boris Yeltsin who had triumphed. It was Gorbachev's tragedy that he based his struggle against the apparatus on the intellectuals, who were steadily moving further away from his notions of reform. Gorbachev still believed that his perestroika would be able to preserve the empire as a confederation of autonomous republics with a pluralistic but socialist democracy for its political system and a socialist market economy.

The final act of Gorbachev's tragedy came when Boris Yeltsin, freely elected president of Russia, pronounced the following fateful words at a session of the People's Congress presided over by the president of the union: "I now sign the decree suspending CP activity on the territory of Russia." The general secretary of the Communist Party mounted no resistance and thus lost the only political force on which he could rely. The now powerless leader sought in vain to stay the collapse of the disintegrating Soviet Union. At the September 1991 conference of the thirteen republics in Alma Ata, he declared to journalists that "The country is about to come apart if there is no integration. This is a fatal path which I am not disposed to follow." One republic after another declared its independence. The Soviet Union, founded on December 30, 1922, collapsed on its seventieth birthday. The president without a country was relieved of his office.

Attempts at Reform in the Midst of Deep Crisis
for the State and Economy

The difficulties experienced by the successor states of the Soviet Union are greater than those of the reform countries of Central and Eastern Europe because, in the first place, the division of labor that had evolved over the course of centuries in the Russian, and later in the Soviet, empire collapsed. The transition to a market economy is bound to be more difficult because the command economy had functioned for a longer time in the former Soviet Union, having struck deeper roots, and because the population's attitude toward a private economy was more negative there than elsewhere.

The first step in the reform—namely, liberalization of prices in early 1992—had graver consequences than in the other East European countries. Neither the economy nor the administrative apparatus was prepared. The command system, whose effectiveness had already grown much weaker in the 1970s, finally, during the six years of perestroika, lost the properties that had allowed it to function. The economic bureaucracy lost its self-confidence and authority under a barrage of criticism. Their plan directives increasingly encountered rejection from the production firms, which had learned to fulfill the plan. Work discipline and delivery discipline diminished appreciably. Stagnation, which had been inherent for some time, developed into a deep recession. Economic performance declined for four years in a row.

The most difficult year was 1991, following the bankruptcy of War Communism: the gross domestic product fell by 17 percent, and industrial production lost 7.5 percent compared with the preceding year. The grain harvest yielded 165 million tons, about 70 million tons less than in 1990. Grain deliveries decreased dramatically because farmers could not buy much with their proceeds and were waiting for a rise in prices. Supply collapsed. Goods of better quality were only available on the black market at prices many times higher than on the state market. The two biggest republics—Russia and the Ukraine—were hardest hit by the recession. The national income decreased by 11 percent compared with 1990. The decline in the Asian republics was somewhat less: by 10 percent in Kazakhstan, 9 percent in Tajikistan, 0.6 percent in Turkmenistan, and 0.9 percent in Uzbekistan.[7]

The entire financial system was caught up in the process: the state budget deficit reached 200 billion rubles, and the rate of the deficit in relation to the national product increased from 4 percent to 12 percent. The internal state debt rose from 628 billion to 1 trillion rubles, 90 percent of which was for loans to finance the state budget deficit. Seventy percent of the money brought additionally into circulation was used to finance the budget deficit, according to a report of Grigorii Matyukhin, former president of the Russian Central Bank.[8]

The foreign trade balance deteriorated dramatically: in 1990 it reached a negative balance of $16.9 billion (including $15.7 billion in relation to the former CMEA countries), the deficit in the balance of services increased to $7.2 billion, principally due to a debt of $4 billion in interest payments to Western banks. To prevent a further increase in the balance of payments deficit, imports were reduced from $120.7 billion in 1990 to $68.2 billion, including imports from the former partner states of the CMEA, which were reduced from $67.9 billion to $23.9 billion. But exports were also drastically reduced from $103.8 billion to $70.2 billion, including a reduction of $52.2 billion to $23.1 billion exports to the former CMEA countries. Russia's share in total exports was estimated at 78 percent, while its share in total imports was estimated at 67 percent.

The total debt to Western banks, over $80 billion, was divided up in accordance with the share of the individual republics in the national product of the former Soviet Union: Russia's share was 61.1 percent, the Ukraine's 16.2 percent. The terms of payment are still being negotiated.

The liberalization of prices that coincided with the total collapse of supply, resulting in a profound discrepancy between supply and demand, resembled Poland's shock therapy. Prices for food increased five-to-six-fold immediately, as happened in Poland. But, whereas in other reform states, difficulties in supply could be surmounted through, among other things, imports, thanks to internal convertibility of the currency and rapidly proceeding privatization of the trade network, in Russia the shop shelves remained empty. Privatization is still in embryo: of 73 million employed in Russia and 25 million in the Ukraine, only 7.8 percent and 3.8 percent, respectively, are working in the private economy. Out of fear that a flight of goods to Russia would result if the earlier price system were retained, the former republics followed in the steps of Yeltsin's reform, but at the same time they took measures to shield the national market by introducing coupons. The former republics responded to the cutback in the supplies of raw material and fuel from Russia with a cutback in deliveries of agrarian products and foods. The collapse of the unified monetary system necessitated barter transactions, such as crude oil for grain. The supply to the population and to industrial plants worsened still further: in the first quarter of 1992, Russia's industrial production diminished by another 13 percent.

There was a great fear of a further rise in unemployment: by early March it had reached 2.2 million in Russia.[9] The International Labour Organization (ILO) feared that the number of unemployed could increase to 11 million, which would mean an unemployment rate of 15 percent. But Russia was a country that had been programmed for full employment, and therefore no insurance network had been created. Of course, the number of people underemployed in the factories was very high. It was estimated, according to Alexander Yakovlev, former Politburo member and intimate adviser to Gorbachev, that there were at least 40 million parasitic jobs in the former USSR: "The ritual of doing nothing, i.e., simply being present at one's job, is the very essence of such a work ethic."[10] The number of unemployed should be increased as a result of converting the armaments industry, which now employs 7.5 million people, and by a reduction of at least 2 million in the armed forces. According to data from the former economic minister, Andrei Nechaev, the 1992 industrial output of steel foundries decreased by 15 percent, the production of consumer goods declined by 13 percent, and food production decreased by 18 percent. The gross domestic product decreased in 1992 by 22 percent and in 1993 by 13 percent.[11]

A Marshall Plan for Russia?

After long vacillation, the industrial countries of the West decided nonetheless to put together an aid package for Russia. The total sum of $24 billion was nominally higher than the amount earmarked by the Marshall Plan for the seventeen countries of Europe ($13 billion), but much lower than that figure would be at 1991 prices ($70 billion).[12] It is worth noting that the United States also finally decided to contribute $4.35 billion. Of course, the contemplated aid would not be provided exclusively by the industrial countries of the West. The International Monetary Fund (IMF) and the World Bank were also to commit shares of $4.5 billion. Two and a half billion dollars were intended to finance a rescheduling of the debt, and $11.2 billion were to be used as credit guarantees through bilateral agreements to finance imports, as well as for humanitarian aid. A fund to stabilize the ruble was included ($6 billion); in accordance with an agreement made with the IMF on August 1, 1992, the ruble was to become internally convertible at 80 rubles to 1 dollar (in early May 1992, the exchange rate was 120 rubles per dollar; at the end of March 1993, however, it was 650 rubles per dollar). The announcement of the aid package in early April, directly before the session of the People's Congress, was generally regarded as unequivocal backing for Yeltsin and Gaidar's reform plans.

Although Russia faced (and still faces) problems similar to those faced by Europe just after the end of World War II, its ability to solve them is much weaker. At the end of the war, Europe had experience with a market economy, as well as a management that knew the market. And while the Marshall Plan made a major contribution to the recovery of Europe's industrial potential after the war, all in all Europe had its own efforts to thank for its dynamic economic growth. The ratio of Marshall Plan aid to gross national product was no more than 2.5 percent. West German industry increased by 312 percent between 1947 and 1951, whereas Marshall Plan aid was only $4 billion.

In the context of the debate on loans in aid, the opinion of two prominent politicians who had traveled around the republics of the former Soviet Union and had talks with many authoritative people caused a mild sensation. Henry Kissinger, the former U.S. secretary of state, wrote: "We're doing no favors to the Russian leaders and are maneuvering ourselves into an extremely bad position if we create the impression that aid from without would enable the country to avoid a painful phase of economic hardship that will probably last for years."[13] And the former leader of the opposition and German Federal Minister Hans Jochen Vogel said: "Financial aid is necessary. However, it must be concentrated on concrete projects. The structural preconditions for unearmarked state credits or even a Marshall Plan are still lacking. Such aid would be dissipated and have no effect."[14]

Kissinger, however, who is generally something of a skeptic, believes that such support could help to alleviate the pain of transition to a market economy a little. But the prospects of financial aid of $4 billion to finance the import of all goods necessary to promote the course of reform are of greatest importance. This aid could benefit the oil industry, for example, which has been left in a critical state by a lack of technology.[15] In connection with the Spring 1993 conference of the International Monetary Fund and the World Bank, the president of the World Bank, Lewis Preston, commented that aid to agriculture had top priority, followed by aid to the oil industry, and then the transport and communications system. The financial need of the CIS for 1992 was estimated at about $43 billion, according to Michel Camdessus, executive director of the IMF.

Overcoming the Economic Crisis Takes Priority

The International Monetary Fund's financial aid to Russia and other successor states is contingent on a restrictive money, credit, and budget policy, as well as on the continuation of the reform plans that have been introduced. Yeltsin responded that he was not willing to submit to these impositions. The dramatic rise in prices was met by growing discontent among the population. Yeltsin experienced the effects of this dissatisfaction with the way the reform was going at the April 1992 session of the People's Congress. Enterprises were being strained under the burden of prices for raw materials and fuel that had increased by up to tenfold and under the burden of drastically increased interest and taxes, reduced or totally abolished state subsidies, and delivery commitments that were not honored. Some government members wondered whether it might not be advisable to relieve the rigorous credit and budgetary discipline. Andrei Nechaev, the former minister of the economy, had the following to say: "I think an economic collapse is more dangerous than hyper-inflation."[16] "We cannot afford an economic decline for three years running," said Yegor Gaidar, former head of government and architect of the reform. "Over the long term, the agony of the economy will create an intolerable situation; we must unconditionally find our way back to economic growth."[17]

In 1992, those government members responsible for the economy proclaimed themselves ready to accept a rate of inflation of 3 percent monthly or 40 percent for the current year (Yegor Gaidar). G. Matyukhin, former president of the Central Bank, said he would have regarded an inflation rate of 5 to 6 percent as a maximum. In March 1993 the monthly rate of inflation was already 20 percent. The bank president also resisted a fixed exchange rate for the ruble. The discrepancy between the official rate and the black market rate was always 25 to 30 percent relative to the U.S. dollar. A loan from the Central Bank to the commercial banks of 200 billion rubles was discussed in order to relieve the restrictive credit conditions. A presidential decree on bank-ruptcy procedure was being prepared. Ten to fifteen bankruptcy declarations could alter the behavior of plant managers fundamentally, said the economics minister. The minister would have liked to support the conversion of the armaments industry with 42 billion rubles. The price of oil was scheduled to be increased from 2,000 to 2,600 rubles per ton by midyear, which would bring it to the world-market level. The original idea to reduce the budget deficit to zero was abandoned, but the deficit nonetheless had to remain below 5 percent of the national product. Export quotas were to be raised and imports would be taxed at 6 to 10 percent.

Meanwhile, a consistent model for privatization was being developed: commercial firms, small industrial firms, small crafts, restaurants, and shops were to be auctioned off or sold to the plant managers and workers. Large enterprises with over 5,000 employees were to be transferred into joint stock companies with the state as the principal stockholder. The big auto factory, the VAZ, which produced 700,000 of the 1.2 million cars in the country, was denationalized in this way. The 150 managerial staff were to acquire 5 percent and the 200,000-person work force was to acquire 25 percent of the package of shares at moderate prices. The rest would remain the property of the state, which would later sell its shares to solvent firms, including foreign firms, at market prices. Only a few key branches such as the oil industry would remain in state hands.

No Prospects for a Functioning Commonwealth, but a Growing Risk of Disintegration of the Russian Federation

Few people believe that the treaty signed on December 30, 1991, by the eleven successor states in Minsk on the establishment of the CIS can survive. Leonid Kravchuk, the president of the Ukraine, describes this structure as neither a unified state nor a state community. There is no supranational executive that can pass and enforce laws. The centrifugal tendencies seem to be insurmountable. Increasing nationalism makes the possibility of finding a solution quite small. A hitherto insoluble conflict has arisen between the Ukraine and Russia—namely, the struggle for the peninsula of the Crimea, which in 1954 was awarded to the Ukraine. Inhabitants of the Crimea consist of about 60 percent Russians: the remaining 40 percent are not only Ukrainian, but also from various minorities, including a growing number of Tatars returning from exile. The Black Sea fleet is stationed in the harbors of the Crimea, and the Ukraine and Russia have been unable to agree on how to divide it up. The Crimean Parliament passed a decision on May 5, 1992, concerning the secession of the Ukraine, but the Ukraine abrogated it the very next day. A long-term and lasting solution is unlikely.

Breakaway tendencies also exist in the Asian successor states; the influence of Islamic fundamentalism is growing steadily. Iran is mediating in the conflict between Armenia and Azerbaijan over Nagorny Karabakh and Turkish President Demirel is establishing contacts with Turkish tribes and the nations of Central Asia. Kazakhstan, with 16 million inhabitants—giving it, after Uzbekistan, the second highest population among Asian republics—is, on the other hand, seeking contacts with China together with advice on matters of economic reform.[18]

Russia, which is in the federation with twenty small autonomous republics, finds itself increasingly confronted with problems similar to those that faced the former Soviet Union. The most influential of the small republics, Tatarstan, declared itself independent following a referendum held on March 2, 1992. The northern Caucasian republic inhabited by Chechens and Ingushi regards itself as independent of Russia, under the leadership of General Dudaev. These two autonomous republics did not sign the federation treaty concluded on March 31, 1992. Centrifugal tendencies are evident in some of the other autonomous republics that have been able to assert themselves economically because of their natural resources: Tiumen, Bashkiria, Dagestan, and Kalmykia have oil deposits; the Komi republic, Buriatia, and Tuva have coal; Yakutia has gold; and Karelia and Kabardino-Balkaria have iron ore.

The escalating struggle for power in Moscow has intensified these centrifugal tendencies. The eighteen autonomous republics are calling for the establishment of a federation council which could not, however, be established owing to differences of opinion between the executive and the legislative branches. Directly before the Eighth Congress of the People's Congress, the Tatars declared that they, together with the largest republic in Russia, Sakha/Yakutia, as well as Bashkortostan, would firmly resist Moscow. The Parliament of Sakha, a republic that produces 99 percent of the total of Russia's diamonds, passed a law in 1991 giving local legislation priority over the laws of the federation. When Boris Yeltsin took office as president of Russia, he promised to give the internal republics "as much power as they could handle" but, given the steadily escalating conflict with its parliament, he is unable to introduce any measures to prevent the dangerous threat of a collapse of the federation.

Chapter 2

The Collapse of Communism
and the Uncertain Future
of Post-Communism

One hundred and fifty years ago we had the specter of communism, today we have the specter of post-communism.

—Vaclav Havel

"Who killed communism?" asked American sociologist Theodore Draper,[1] thus situating the mystery of this historical event not so much in the evolution of this once powerful ideology as in the manner in which it died. No one, according to Draper, expected that such an all-embracing system would die. Many thought it ought to be killed, but in fact it collapsed like a house of cards. Jeane J. Kirkpatrick, the former U.S. ambassador to the United Nations, took a similar view: the collapse of communism was the fantastic surprise of modern history—surprise above all in response to the speed with which the communist regime in Eastern Europe and in its fatherland, the Soviet Union, collapsed, once it could no longer rely upon brute force.[2] Severyn Bialer of Columbia University pointed out that in the darkest winter of 1990–91, observers were dealing with one single question—whether the Soviet Union's search for an anchor to save itself would end with a bang or with a whimper.[3] Levon Ter-Petrossian, president of Armenia, more clearly pinpoints the cause of the empire's death: the center of power committed suicide. However, while the former

Politburo member and Russia's present president Boris Yeltsin assured the July session of the CSCE forum in 1992 that communism had left Europe forever, the former dissident and ex-president of the former Czechoslovakia, Vaclav Havel, disappointed by the somber developments in his own and other reform countries, ventured the poetic statement that opened this chapter before the same forum.

The second question of concern to Soviet experts is why the people who appeared on the scene in order to improve the Soviet system were the very same ones who earlier had been concerned to bring it down, together with its hundred-year-old empire. The experts seem to have reached the end of the line. The German newspaper *Die Welt* had this to say in a commentary on the April 1992 session of the Göttingen Working Group on the topic "Transformation of the Soviet Union": "it might appear to laymen that people were trying to look at an earthquake through a microscope." It was not the earth, but human civilization that was quaking. The fatal cracks in the seventy-year-old formation were ignored.

Innumerable scholars have pinpointed and criticized the flaws of the Soviet system and sketched out various divisions, but the only one who predicted its fall, the Russian exile Andrei Amalrik, situated the causes not in the emergent economic and political crisis, but in defeat in a war against another communist state. In *Will the Soviet Union Survive until 1984?*, published in the United States in 1976, Amalrik predicted that the Soviet superpower would lose a war against China between 1975 and 1980 and collapse. Amalrik was right about one thing: China's political regime survived the Soviet Union. Although the Soviet version of communism had failed just as completely in China as in the alma mater of scientific socialism, Chinese leaders have no intention of abandoning Marxism as a state ideology or the omnipotence of the Communist Party. But they do want to improve the regime, just as Gorbachev, the father of perestroika, wanted in his time. The Chinese, however, want to do this without glasnost—that is, without calling into question the existing manner of exercising power and without allowing political pluralism into the bargain. They would like above all to distance themselves as quickly as possible from the Soviet economic order—from the Asiatic mode of production, the most inefficient and most chaotic of all, which has been erroneously called a planned economy. However, where the architects of perestroika have even now not yet succeeded—namely, freeing the peasants from state-controlled collective farms and state farms—the Chinese accomplished that in the course of a single year. China's 800 million peasants were freed from their agrarian communes and received land on hereditary leases. The chronic difficulties in supply, the unmistakable trademark of a planned economy and command system, were brought to an end.

Permanent reforms are now being carried out in state industry. The purpose is the same as in the reform countries of Eastern Europe: namely, to remove state enterprises from state protection and to abolish state subsidies, for they are being successively subordinated to the rules of the market (i.e., competition). In this struggle, inefficient and unprofitable firms fail and workers then receive unemployment compensation, rather than wages, for no work. The economic strategies of China are superior to those in Eastern Europe; the political situation is stable and the economic reform has been accompanied by increasing buying power among the people, with growing economic activity rather than with shrinking economic activity, as in the reform countries of Eastern Europe.

The peculiar version of communism that became the reality of an omnipotent totalitarian one-party regime, against all intentions, has also met an inglorious end. "The collapse of communism," writes Kirkpatrick, "and of the communist regimes in Europe and in the Soviet Union, is more like Plato's description of the decline of an ideal state than what Karl Marx and Vladimir Ilich Lenin wrote."[4] Communism as a vision of liberty, equality, and fraternity could not die because what has never lived cannot die. Socialism has reverted from its definition as a science to its pre-Marxist utopian origin. The devastating practical realities of Marxian socialism have discredited it as a social theory once and for all. But unlike in the former Soviet Union and Eastern Europe, China's unbroken ruling elite would like to maintain communism as a state ideology.

In contrast to Ludwig Erhard, who described his social market economy as one in which the rich may not become poorer but the poor may become richer, Deng Xiaoping would like to minimize the contrast between rich and poor. Even if there is some reasonable doubt whether equality is the best way to overcome secular backwardness, the attempt to shore up a contentious ideology, this vanishing relic of the most recent past, seems to confirm the pragmatism of China's reform architects: to give nothing up, even in matters of ideology, before one has something better to offer. Or, as Konrad Adenauer used to say, don't pour out the dirty water before you have clean water to offer.

The suicide of the Soviet system is, after all, not so puzzling. It took place just as the famous historian and politician, Alexis de Toqueville, described in 1856 in *Social Order and Revolution*: "A genuine danger for a government in crisis can only arise when it begins to reform itself." But the Eastern expert Timur Kuran was right that to search for one single factor that had triggered this or that revolution was equivalent to attempting to identify the spark that caused a forest fire.[5]

The causes of the failed attempts at reform and the ensuing collapse of the Soviet Union are deeper: they lie in the character of the October Revolution and its protagonists, and are moreover just as evident in the shape of its phases of development as in the limited margin this social system allowed for reform and reformers.

The upheavals in this region of the world, for many years regarded as an island of stability, seem to confirm once more the notion that great revolutions produce no lasting solutions for social and political problems, despite their immense influence on the course of world history. Every revolution is followed by a Thermidor specific to the spirit of the times, with a retreat from all too ambitious change. And adoration for the historical deeds of revolutionaries and the heroic lack of planning in their actions are followed by a sobering phase.

The witnesses of the period, the great minds of that time, hailed the 1789 French Revolution as the greatest event in human history. When Immanuel Kant learned of the storming of the Bastille, he interrupted his walk along the city walls of Königsberg to praise this heroic act of the French. And he continued to praise them after the Revolution drowned in a sea of blood. The victory of the defenders of the Revolution over Prussia and Austria at Valmy was proclaimed by Goethe as a "new epoch in world history." Hegel spoke of a splendid sunrise.

Innumerable bards praised the October Revolution of 1917. John Reed, an American journalist and first-hand observer of those events, called his impressions of these events *Ten Days That Shook The World*. German historian Oswald Spengler spoke of the "Decline of the West." Admirers of the Revolution included great writers such as Romain Rolland, Louis Aragon, Leon Feuchtwanger, Pablo Neruda, and André Gide—the latter, true, only until he saw the consequences with his own eyes.

None of the great revolutions, however, succeeded in making man "king of the earth," as Rousseau put it. After a short-lived euphoria and a long-lasting wave of terror, the rebellious nations always return to traditional and sometimes even worse methods of rule than before. The Bastille, whose storming also shook the world, had few prisoners on that fateful day of July 14, 1789: seven people in all. Eight-hundred and sixty Parisians stormed the Bastille. At this same time, France's capital had 700,000 inhabitants. But five years after the Revolution, France had 400,000 prisoners. Historian René Tédillot estimated the number of dead victims between 1789 and 1850 as 2 million, including 1 million victims of the Napoleonic Wars. The *Great Revolution* dethroned the weakling King Louis XVI, only to crown the autocrat Napoleon Bonaparte as emperor of the French a few years later, and then to restore the hated Bourbons after Napoleon's defeat at Waterloo.

The great French Revolution promoted the third estate (the bourgeoisie) on line with the spirit of the times. "What Is This Third Estate?" asks the priest Emmanuel Joseph Sieyès to his pioneering pamphlet of that name. "Everything," he answers, and asks further: "What had it been in the previous state order?" "Nothing." But it did want to be "something." Sieyès was elected by the enthusiastic Parisian bourgeoisie to the General Assembly in which the third estate had 578 members, the nobility 285, and the clergy 241. The third estate became the most important and the most creative social stratum of the next century.

The background of the October Revolution of 1917 was more complicated and its consequences were more grave. But the 17,000 Bolsheviks who seized power in that coup d'état acted in conformity with the times only with their slogan, *"Peace at any price"*; in all other respects they acted against that spirit. The Bolsheviks overthrew a bourgeois government that after the February 1917 revolution should have accomplished a task that has not yet been accomplished, even today in the advanced, civilized West. What they did was destroy precisely that social stratum, namely, the middle class, the bourgeoisie, who, as Marx and Engels wrote in their *Communist Manifesto* of 1848, had played a highly revolutionary role in France. In Russia, by contrast, this stratum could not fulfill its imputed revolutionary role because its activities had been forcibly suppressed. Lenin, the instigator of the October Revolution, knew best of all that his country, whose middle class was still in embryo and which was itself the most backward, uncivilized country of Europe, was least suited of any, while its proletariat, which comprised no more than 5 percent of the total population, was least capable of fulfilling the historical vision of the dictatorship of the proletariat. In January 1917 Lenin declared to students in Zurich that his generation (the Bolshevik Lenin was forty-seven years old at the time) would not experience communism. However, he seized the first opportunity to return to Russia, with the help of Erich von Ludendorff, to proclaim his fateful April Theses on the transition from a bourgeois to a proletarian revolution.

General Ludendorff also made no secret of the fact in his memoirs that a revolution in Russia had always been his dream, and that in April–May 1917 it was not the victory on the Aisne or in Champagne that had saved Germany, but the Russian Revolution.[6] The supreme military command was content. On April 21, 1921, the chief of staff telegraphed to the political division of the General Staff: "Lenin's entry into Russia successful, he is working fully as we have wished."

The Bolsheviks seized power but they did not know how to exercise it. Lenin's ideas, which he had set down in his pragmatic *State and Revolution* (the postscript was written a few weeks after the Revolution, on November 30, 1917), were far removed from reality. "All citizens," wrote Lenin, "are transformed into remunerated employees of the state,"[7] and "the entire economy will become an office and a factory." The revolutionary leader's ideas about how to control and manage production units, brought together in an all-embracing state syndicate, were vaguer still: he stated that "everyone who can read and write will be capable of carrying this out. The person would need only to supervise and take notes; it will be enough that this person knows the four basic rules of arithmetic and be able to issue appropriate receipts."[8] Lenin never doubted that the Bolsheviks would be able to cope with administrative work. "After 1905," he wrote, "Russia was governed by 130,000 estate owners, so should not 240,000 members of the Bolshevik Party be able to rule Russia in the interests of the poor and against the rich?"[9] Later developments, however, showed that 240,000 Bolsheviks were *not* capable of doing so. Economic performance declined and the country descended into starvation and misery. When Lenin was also finally forced to recognize that the German proletariat would venture no uprising of the Russian kind in order to save the October Revolution, as it had apparently done earlier to save the kaiser's generals from a debacle, he called for a retreat and introduced the New Economic Policy (NEP) in March 1921.

Lenin's attempt to transcend the economy of the invisible hand of the market and to rule the state with his own iron hand failed, as did every other such attempt after him. Stalin, whom he appointed general secretary, availed himself of totalitarian power in order to nationalize the entire economy, and to transfer its administration to the swollen and all-powerful state bureaucracy. The point of no return of the ultra-totalitarian regime Stalin had forged seemed to have arrived. After the rather nonbloody revolution (there were only six deaths) and the bloody years thereafter (as of February 1922, there were 280,000 victims of the Cheka terrors), Stalin reverted to the traditional methods of rule of tsarist Russia. No other person recognized the historical continuity and character traits of this regime better than the famous French historian Alain Besançon, who wrote in his monumental work *Soviet Present Russian Past*, that the fathers of Soviet communism were linked with Russia's rich past through the uninterrupted "continuity of the concept of an everlasting state." In this notion of the state Besançon perceived the following characteristics: Byzantine ritualism, Mongolian cruelty, and the messianism of the sixteenth century. Under Stalin's rule each of these traits assumed sharper contours than ever before. Mongolian cruelty knew no bounds in Stalin's purges with their hosts of victims, and traditional messianism evolved into the mission of the "fatherland of all workers" to carry global revolution to all corners of the world: into the countries of Eastern and Central Europe on bayonets, and in the form of "fraternal aid" for all adventurers defining themselves as Marxists on all continents of this world.

But this mission proved to be more fateful for the existence of the state than for any other system. An economy oriented more toward full employment and egalitarianism than toward productivity and profits was inevitably less efficient. And when this wasteful economy had to spend a quarter of its national income on arms and subordinate its economic structures to a giant military-industrial complex in order to maintain a balance of deterrence, it bled itself dry, and reduced public consumption to a marginal level.

It was this situation—that is, a shrinking economy and steadily declining economic performance, as well as the hopeless and costly war in Afghanistan—that Mikhail Gorbachev inherited when he mounted the Kremlin throne on March 11, 1985.

Of course, Gorbachev would have earned the gratitude of the world and especially of the Soviet people if he had abandoned the hopeless arms race against the much stronger nations of the world together with a costly confrontation with the West; but Gorbachev wanted more. He wanted to strengthen the country's economy in order to restore some vigor to the country's role as a superpower. But when he assumed office, the Soviet economy was already strained to the breaking point by its excess of armaments spending, while production and social discipline were low. Even so, no one had doubted the political stability and the position of the Soviet state as a superpower. Nor did anyone doubt that it had enough substance to maintain its leading role in the world. After six years of Gorbachev's perestroika, however, the Soviet Union ceased to exist.

"What had he done wrong?" observers and analysts ask. First, his objectives were too ambitious for the means at his disposal. When the countries of Central and Eastern Europe define the restoration of a capitalist system as a revolution, one could contest the validity of the definition, but the changes introduced were indeed thoroughly revolutionary. But when Gorbachev called the perestroika, he undertook a new edition of the Russian Revolution, he aroused false hopes that revolutionary change could have a chance of success in the Soviet Union. Perestroika's man, however, did not want to alter the fundamentals of the existing system. He was definitely able to improve quite a bit within the system, but the quantity of the reforms projected, though very rarely realized, could certainly not be transformed into a new quality for the system.

The October Revolution strained human understanding when it abandoned the steering mechanisms built up over centuries from the collective wisdom of innumerable generations, when it destroyed traditional property relations and exterminated the social strata that formed the basis for that property, and, moreover, when it presumed to be able to administer a modern society via the reasoning of a ruling social elite. But Gorbachev strained his own capabilities and those of his team much more. He imagined that he could give a new impetus to the historical continuity of the social system by means of half-hearted reforms. Gorbachev's political downfall once again showed that no statesman, however great his art of governing, must succumb to the temptation of interrupting the course of history and trying to begin anew at point zero. To repeat the words of Friedrich Hayek, "Man's arrogance now threatens to withdraw its support."[10]

Gorbachev's project gave a new impetus to world history, but it put an end to the history of the Soviet Union of which he was leader.

Gorbachev's Belief in the Permanence of the Empire

Mikhail Gorbachev was the most intelligent and most dynamic states-man of his epoch—on that point all observers agree. But the task that he seemed to recognize as flowing from the crisis of the social system, and that he undertook to resolve—namely, to give a new impetus to the historical continuity of the regime—strained the capacities of the reforms as well as available potential for solving problems. There was no precedent for revolutionary change in such a social system and in such an empire, and there was no patent recipe. Comparisons with the transitional process to a democratic pluralistic regime in other totalitarian states, such as Spain, Portugal, or Argentina, are not very enlightening. The point is that the former Soviet Union was not only a totalitarian social system, but a system that was embedded in an empire that had lasted three hundred years, in which even the control of the economy lay totally in the hands of the state. The way the reform movement was organized was without precedent. The political scientist Russell Bova rightly points out that, unlike Poland, where General Jaruzelski found a negotiating partner in Solidarity and in Lech Walesa, with whom he could also conclude agreements, "Gorbachev with his self-designed reform package acted as a representative of both the established regime and of the reform team at one and the same time."[11] "If," Bova goes on, "some describe Gorbachev's role as the role of both the Pope and Luther at one and the same time, he prefers to see his role with Jaruzelski's and Walesa's roles combined in his own person."[12] The principles on which the regime operated reveal the unique continuity with the principles of the Soviet empire. What was epochal in the outcome of the undertaking, which for the West was successful but for Gorbachev a failure, was the disintegration of the great Russian empire that had been embodied over the past seventy years in the Soviet Union: first its outer ring, and later, not without some causal connection, the disintegration of the empire itself. However important the defusing of the East–West confrontation may be, it was definitely not Gorbachev's intention to bring about this historical turning point by abolishing the community of nations that he headed. The tragedy of this outstanding statesman was, first and foremost, that he did not realize where his reforms were leading and that he was convinced to the last that the empire could be held together.

To the bitter end, when disintegration of the outer ring of the empire was already visible on the horizon, Gorbachev remained true to the vow that he had given at the graveside of his predecessor Konstantin Chernenko, to keep the "world system of socialism" together. Gorbachev had articulated this determined will to defend the community of socialist states at the Tenth Congress of the United Polish Workers' Party on December 30, 1986:

> Socialism is an international fact, an alliance of nations bound together by political, economic, cultural, and defense interests. Any attempt to undermine the socialist system, to eviscerate it, or to exclude any member country from the community signifies an attack on the post-war order and ultimately on world peace.

Alluding to measures that Poland's Communist Party government had taken under martial law, which had been proclaimed on December 13, 1981, in order to crush the Solidarity movement, Gorbachev said, "History will come to recognize the true value of the UPWP leadership, all the patriots of this country, and the Party and non-Party members who are shepherding the country out of this dramatic situation using its own forces and relying on the solidarity of friends and allies" (from the memoirs of General Wojciech Jaruzelski). Gorbachev spoke these words exactly three years before the historical Round Table on June 4, 1989, when his then-host concluded the fateful compromise over the sharing of power: "Your President, our Prime Minister." Shortly after that, all power was transferred to the postcommunist government on the basis of the results of the free election.

When Gorbachev spoke these words in mid-1986 he was only just starting out on his reform odyssey. Even so, they unmistakably indicate that the architect of perestroika had no intention of retreating from the inherited empire or from socialism as an ideology of integration. And three years later, in Autumn 1989, when a postcommunist government was already in office in Poland while a wave of fleeing refugees streamed into Hungary from East Germany, and there were unmistakable signs of a historical turn in the other Eastern countries, he remained faithful to the principles of the Soviet system and it became clear that this great mover of world history had lost his overview of the progress of the reforms that he himself had introduced. Specifically, he was too late in realizing that the collapse of the outer ring of the empire was inevitable, that this would reverberate throughout the empire, and that socialism as an integrating ideology had served its time.

Gorbachev's last meeting with municipal dignitaries from the countries of Central and Eastern Europe took place in October 1989 on the occasion of the fortieth and last anniversary of the founding of the GDR in East Berlin. Mieczyslaw Rakowski, the already dismissed head of Poland's Communist Party government, who provided an eye-witness account of Gorbachev's ambivalent behavior in the last stage of Soviet history, took part in these festivities as a member of his country's delegation together with the (still) communist President Wojciech Jaruzelski and the newly appointed noncommunist foreign minister, Krzysztof Skubiszewski. In his memoirs, *The First, The Last*, Rakowski describes the festive course of events in the last days of the Eastern community, which even in its death throes still attempted to give the appearance of an unshakable fortress. Gorbachev's words were greeted with loud, appreciative applause, writes Rakowski; his country, he said, was interested in the stability and further development of the GDR. The Eastern grandees chattered even louder when Gorbachev said that the independence and the destiny of the GDR were decided in Berlin, not in Moscow. How, asked Rakowski, could the president utter such words at such a time when his foreign minister, Eduard Shevardnadze, had already outlined the prospects of German reunification in a conversation with his FRG counterpart, Dietrich Genscher? At that point, however, everything seemed just as it always had been. Erich Honecker spoke, as was usual on such occasions, on the achievements of the GDR and the approaching tasks, stressing that the GDR was the pillar of stability and security in Europe. Nor were any appreciable changes in ranking order reflected in the seating arrangements. Poland was already a lost cause for the communists, yet General Jaruzelski, still president of the Round Table compromise, was given a respectable place at the official dinner, opposite Gorbachev and Raisa and to the left of Nicolae Ceausescu. But the general was not prepared to make a show of even the smallest courtesy toward his neighbor. Only after "my three admonitions," says Rakowski, was Jaruzelski able to contribute a few words of his own:

"You, comrades, all have a nice tan, I hope you have enjoyed your holiday."

While the leaders were celebrating in the Palace of the Republic, thousands upon thousands were demonstrating in the streets of Berlin against the Communist regime. Rakowski recalls that "Gorbachev enjoyed the calls from the young people of Berlin: 'Gorby, Gorby, help us!' just as the young people of Prague had called in 1987: 'Gorby, stay with us!'" However, doubts that the architect of perestroika may have failed to recognize the signs of the times had not yet occurred to Rakowski until Gorbachev, in a private conversation with Poland's delegate about his meeting with the SED Politburo, said: "They have very interesting ideas. They are optimists!" before interrupting the conversation with a wave of the hand toward the ceiling (on your guard, listening devices!). Rakowski's comment that "the young of Berlin are expecting another liberation from you" was met by an embarrassed smile, and the president invited him, the last head of the CP government, who had lost his power in an anticommunist and procapitalist movement, to keep himself informed about how those fraternal parties, which although they had lost power, were nonetheless continuing their activity in opposition within a new environment.

That talk took place a few days later on October 11, 1989, in Moscow. The host began with the following words: "At the Round Table of June 4, 1989, a report was prepared which we are now about to enjoy; how it has been cooked and how it is swallowed is a question for which an adequate answer must be sought." Poland was a testing ground for the CPSU. The general secretary, says Rakowski, was nonetheless attempting to work out why the historical turn had occurred, and hoped that Poland could still hold on after the People's United Workers' Party (PUWP) lost power. To relinquish Poland would be a strategic loss for his country, said Gorbachev. Cooperation with Tadeusz Mazowiecki's noncommunist government was therefore necessary and even possible because every country had the right to determine its own social system. The fraternal parties, on the other hand, had to continue to work closely together, concluded the Soviet president, and gave assurance that the CPSU would extend a helping hand where needed.

Rakowski goes on to say that, after a two-hour conversation, it was still unclear whether Gorbachev had appreciated the danger of a collapse of the outer ring of the Soviet empire. Two months later there was no longer any doubt that the communist hegemony in Central Europe was finally over. At the final Congress of the Warsaw Pact on December 4, 1989, only one Communist Party leader of Eastern Europe took part, namely, Nicolae Ceausescu, just a few days before he was executed.

Gorbachev quickly realized what kind of society he was being constrained to operate in, and talked about his impressions of his meetings with the pope: in the affairs of Europe and of the entire world, the pope was as close to him as in matters of peace, Gorbachev said, and he commented on how much he enjoyed the "wonderful gift" he had received (a thirteenth-century painting of Christ). He spoke with similar enthusiasm of his meeting with the U.S. president on Malta. George Bush knew how to listen, he said, and had come up with various suggestions. However, he was not particularly happy about Bush's new policy on Europe: "Just as the Americans once reproached us for exporting revolution, they now want to export their own values, which would end in the destruction of socialism," Gorbachev complained. "Our response to this," he continued, "was to propose that every state should decide for itself what kind of social system it wants without outside pressure." These words, Rakowski writes, were, of course, directed toward the delegation leaders from the former Soviet-bloc countries, who still addressed one another as "comrade," further writes Rakowski.

But the information on the meeting with the pope and with President Bush was only a preface to the main topic of conversation—namely, the future of the GDR. This meeting took place after huge demonstrations in Berlin and Leipzig, after the fall of the Berlin Wall, and after Honecker had been deposed and Hans Modrow's reform government had been established. The dissolution of the GDR as a state already seemed to be decided. The delegates were therefore quite astonished when their host explained that the Americans recognized the inviolability of the borders as well as the existence of two German states, but, while the emotional side played a major role in Germany, the process of unification was not going to be accelerated. It was implausible, writes Rakowski, that this was said by a politician who, only a few months later, in mid-June 1990, cast aside all reservations over reunification during his meeting with Chancellor Helmut Kohl in Stavropol. Rakowski goes on to say that the delegation leaders may well have heard these words with satisfaction, as he himself did (he confesses that he had originally regarded the division of Germany as a gift from heaven). Only Hans Modrow demonstrated dissatisfaction: there was, said Modrow, some communion of interest between the two German states. To this Gorbachev rejoined: "I assume that relations between the two German states are heading for new agreements, but these agreements will neither call into question the existence of the GDR, nor lead to a confederation."

Events took a different course: Gorbachev's last hope that the states of Western Europe would oppose the unanimous desire of the people of East Germany for reunification, which he would no longer suppress now that liberalization was under way, was not fulfilled. Indeed, the governments of the West feared a reunited great Germany: Rakowski recalls Margaret Thatcher's opinion expressed in a talk with Poland's president Wojciech Jaruzelski: "This event signifies a disaster and marks the decline of Europe." Similar views could be heard in other Western countries, but bringing the ruinous East–West confrontation to an end and restoring a unified worldwide democratic and market social system took highest priority.

In mid-June 1990, Gorbachev put his seal of approval on Germany's reunification in a talk with Helmut Kohl, and on August 23, 1990, the Volkskammer decided to incorporate the GDR into the Federal Republic, marking the definitive dissolution of the outer ring of the Soviet empire. But Gorbachev was no longer able to prevent the anti-imperialist revolution from taking effect on the inner territory of the huge empire as well; nothing else was to be expected. Given the conditions for free expression of opinion created by glasnost, communism was bound to collapse as a communal ideology in order to make way for national aspirations. For the first time in Soviet history, the nations of this multiethnic state were able to speak openly of their own glorious histories, and rediscovered national pride as an antidote to the amorphous cosmopolitan Soviet patriotism.

Only a few months after the events of 1989, Lithuania issued its declaration of independence in March 1990. The Baltic countries, the last of the republics to join the Soviet Union, were the first to begin the breakup of the empire, which had lasted three hundred years. The death knell of the Soviet empire was sounded when the ideology of unity could no longer adequately bind the whole together, yet force, which every Kremlin ruler had used as a means of last resort, could no longer be applied.

The mystery of the Bolshevik success, wrote Jeane J. Kirkpatrick, was "violence and ideology." The reason for their defeat, on the other hand, was the revision of the ideology that had led the Soviet elite to hesitate over using force to maintain their sphere of influence in Eastern Europe and later in their inner empire. It is this that Kirkpatrick finds to Gorbachev's great credit, not, as she says, appearing on the cover of *Time* magazine or being awarded the Nobel Prize. Michael Mandelbaum, whom Kirkpatrick also quotes,[13] has a similar opinion: Gorbachev renounced the fundamental methods of rule of his predecessors, and was not prepared to shoot. For that alone he deserved the Nobel Prize.[14]

Although one can perhaps validly claim that Gorbachev's reforms did not change, or had not yet changed, the fundamentals of social, political, or economic relations, they nonetheless served to trigger (albeit against the will of the reformer) the greatest world political event of the late twentieth century—the collapse of the Russian and Soviet empire. For the first time in world history, a great empire collapsed without having been destroyed by a lost war, as, for example, was the fate of the Austro-Hungarian empire. Nor was the decline and fall forced by a war of independence of oppressed nations—compare the collapse of the colonial rule of Great Britain or France as a consequence of the long years of struggle for liberation in India, Algeria, or Vietnam.

The Russian and later the Soviet empire was unique in its kind regarding its geopolitical constellation. Its dominion did not comprise remote colonies on other continents but contiguous areas in Eurasia. The Soviet Union relinquished not a single one of the territories inherited from the tsarist empire. It changed much in terms of method of rule, but it did not become a melting pot of peoples, as the United States supposedly did. The patriotism demanded by the Soviet state, defined as "national in form, socialistic in content," was unable to affect cultural, religious, and social particularities. Russia remained the dominant nation in the federation of nations, if only because of its economic and cultural dominance. This territory was twice the size of all the other republics put together, and its population of 152 million comprised 60 percent of the population of the entire Soviet Union, with 25 million Russians living beyond its borders. Russia had the best universities and research institutions, where the best specialists from all the other nations studied and taught, and Russian was the second language of every other nation in the union.

But although the Russian Socialist Federation was renamed the Union of Soviet Socialist Republics on December 30, 1922, five years after the October Revolution, the status of the other republics within the state system remained unchanged. The new name was as illusory as it was meaningless: the USSR was not socialist in the utopian spirit of the term—that is, liberty, fraternity, and equality—and was even less "Soviet": the soviets (councils), which were to have embraced the whole of society and should have formed the real structures of power, were impotent from the very outset. The ruling party was the sole source of decision making at every level of the state system. The unanimously "elected" Supreme Soviet handed down unanimous resolutions that had been decided upon beforehand in the relevant Party committees.

Russia was not a *primus inter pares*. As a republic it predominated over all the others within the Soviet state, and as a nation the Russian people played a dominant role not only within the Central Party and government apparatus but, within the other republics. The 25 million Russians living outside Russia played a dominant role in the economy as well as in political and cultural organizations, even when the Party and government apparatus were run mainly by people from the indigenous nationality.

The Russian empire had always been called a prison for all the nations within it, even where their own leaders had accepted Russia's domination as the best possible option under conditions of civil war or of an external threat. This applied especially to the second largest republic in the union, the Ukraine, with its population of 52 million. In the seventeenth century, after long years of a war of liberation against Poland, the *Hetman*, the military leader Bogdan Chmielnitsky, decided to join Russia on the basis of the provisions of the *Pereiaslavskaia Rada* of 1654. Russian history tells of the voluntary union—under constraining conditions—of Armenia, Georgia, Kazakhstan, and Uzbekistan. The eastern part of Armenia joined Russia as a consequence of the war between Russia and Persia in 1828, which devastated the country. The rest of Armenia joined in 1878 in the aftermath of the war between Russia and Turkey. Georgia (Kolchida), which had already functioned as an independent state in the fifth century B.C. and experienced its golden age under the rule of Queen Tamara (1184–1213), turned most of the country into a Russian protectorate during the rule of King Heraclius II in 1783; the rest of the country was absorbed by Russia after the Persian invasion in 1801–1810. Kazakhstan, which appears in the fifteenth century as an independent state, decided to accept the protection of the Russian tsars for the first time in 1731 during the confrontation between China and Russia, and then later definitively in 1819. The Uzbeks conquered Bukhara in 1499 and 1500, and their emir agreed, for the country, to become a protectorate of Russia in 1868 and 1873.

The fate of the third Slavic country, White Russia (Belarus), has been mixed. Between the ninth and fourteenth centuries, Belarus was under Lithuanian rule, but after its union with Poland in 1569 (the Lublin Union), it became a part of the Polish kingdom. After the partition of Poland between 1772 and 1795, all of Belarus came under Russian rule.

National suppression was considerable under the tsars, and only in the late eighteenth century did subjugated Poland dare a resolute if hopeless resistance to the great Russian empire, manifested in three bloody uprisings in 1794, 1830, and 1863. The Ukraine, the Caucasus, and a few Asian republics struggled for a few years against the imposition of Soviet power, but thereafter resistance subsided. State terror was too massive to risk a struggle for independence: to serve as an example, entire nations were uprooted and resettled during and after World War II. Each of the republics has its own history of persecution to lament: millions of Ukrainians were victims in the forced collectivization of the 1930s; and the economies of the Asian republics were turned into single-crop economies, such as cotton in Uzbekistan, which only made them lag still further behind the other republics. While illiteracy was successfully defeated in the years of Soviet power, the dominance of Russian culture and the Russian language was unmistakable. The indigenous cultures of the small nations were always under the suspicion of nationalist indoctrination and were subjected to especially rigid censorship. Even though hundreds of dissidents of the small republics languished in prisons and concentration camps for many years, there was no organized mass movement for national liberation.

The collapse of the Soviet Union was brought about not by the struggle of non-Russian nations, but by Russia itself, the dominant nation in the Soviet Union. "Ironically," writes Severyn Bialer, "the most important declaration of sovereignty took place not on the periphery, but in Russia itself, the very heart of the Soviet Union. The Russian parliament's declaration of sovereignty was a revolutionary watershed. It destroyed the Soviet Union."[15] Dimitri K. Simes makes a similar point: "After all, if it had not been for action taken by Russia, the Soviet communist empire would still be in place. . . . In turn, Russia was the central force in the destruction of the Soviet totalitarian state."[16]

It is interesting, however, that it was not only the death of the ideology that had bound the nations of the Soviet Union together, coupled with the renunciation of violence as a means to rule, that decided the collapse of the Soviet Union, but also, to no less a degree, the power struggle between two powerful rivals: between the president of the disintegrating Soviet Union who was struggling to hold it together, and the freely elected president of Russia, who had placed his bet on Russia's card and on the most powerful nation in the union. The question Simes asks—namely, whether on June 12, 1990, when Russia's parliament proclaimed Russia's sovereignty, Yeltsin and his men realized that they had begun thereby the irreversible dissolution of the Soviet Union—is quite valid. His answer appears correct: "Yeltsin and his associates hardly anticipated the consequences of the Soviet state's demise. In this sense they were similar to Gorbachev, who, while systematically undermining the foundations of the Soviet regime, honestly believed that he was laboring to improve it."[17]

Professor Iurii Afanasev, the respected Russian historian, describes how the president of the Soviet Union was cast out in the coup d'état: "The way the Slavic *troika*, which included Boris Yeltsin, treated Mikhail Gorbachev, marked a reversion to the Eurasian-Russian tradition."[18]

The Ukraine waited for a year and a half to declare itself sovereign after it became evident that the collapse of the Soviet Union could no longer be prevented. Independence became a fact in the referendum of December 1, 1991, with a vote of 84 percent in favor, including 96 to 98 percent yes votes in the western Ukraine, but only 76.8 percent in the industrial regions of the Donbas and 56 percent of the inhabitants of the Crimean peninsula. Kazakhstan, the most influential republic in Asia, declared independence on December 16, 1991, only a few days before the eleven successor republics gathered in the Kazakh capital Alma Ata on December 21 to declare their full independence and sovereignty.

The Commonwealth of Independent States (CIS)—
Neither a Political nor an Economic Community

When the founders of the community of states that was supposed to succeed the collapsing Soviet Union gathered in Bialovieskaia Pushcha in Belarus on December 8, 1991, to sketch out a model for the Commonwealth, Mikhail Gorbachev was still president of the still-existing Soviet Union. However, he was not invited to take part. Not all of the fifteen republics were to be members. Four of them, the Baltic Republics and Georgia, were already lost causes. But the Asian successor states were also not to be included in the original model for the Commonwealth. The draft treaty concluded by the representatives of Russia, the Ukraine, and Belarus was given the unofficial title *Slavic Federation*. Professor Iurii Afanasev lamented that even the Kazakh president Narsultan Nazarbaev was not invited, though he had worked harder than any other head of state for the establishment of the new formation. Afanasev goes on to say that Kazakhstan's participation would have spared them many second thoughts: not only was it a country that had nuclear weapons, but half its people were Slavs and half were of Turkic origin. However, he also regretted that the official representatives of the Russian Republic did not consider such a federation necessary (a view they hold to this day), and pointed out that Russia was not a Slavic but a Eurasian state. This view is all too reminiscent of the Russian Prince Trubetskoi, who said: "We are not the back yard of Europe, we are the front door to Asia."

It was Russia's president, Boris Yeltsin, however, who originally wanted to extend the community to other states, although it was originally restricted to Slavic states. And the five Asian republics were, most of all, interested in economic cooperation with all the former republics. At a conference held in Ashkhabad, the capital of Turkmenistan, they decided to join the Commonwealth, and on December 21, 1991, the Eurasian CIS was born in Alma Ata in Kazakhstan. The successor states, however, now freed from the imperial power, did not wish to create a new superpower with a supranational parliament and executive that could pass laws and force compliance with them. There is a CIS army, but the republics have each already created their own national armies.

Opinions differ on the cohesion of the new Commonwealth. Whereas Leonid Kravchuk, the then president of the Ukraine, stated that the CIS was neither a unified state nor a community of nations, Boris Yeltsin expressed the hope that this would be more than a jointly devised formula for a "civilized divorce"; however, the respective political and economic strengths of the members vary so greatly that what unifies them cannot be easily reduced to a common denominator, especially since there is no longer any imperial coercion. Russia, super powerful with its 152 million inhabitants (out of a total of 288 million), produced 61.1 percent of the net output of the former Soviet Union: 90 percent of crude oil, 80 percent of natural gas, 70 percent of gold, and 62 percent of electrical energy. The second largest successor state, the Ukraine, with its 52 million inhabitants, accounted for 16.2 percent of the total output, and produced 25 percent of fish products, 55 percent of vegetable oil, 46 percent of canned vegetables, 23 percent of coal, 35 percent of iron, 43 percent of steel, and 50 percent of the iron ore. The three Slavic republics, including Belarus which with its 10.3 million inhabitants accounted for 4.2 percent of the net output, produced 81.5 percent of Soviet output. The economic performance of the Asian republics was much lower. The per-capita income of that region's economically strongest republic, Kazakhstan (also rich in raw materials and fuels), was 25 percent lower than the union average. The other Asian republics were even further behind: Turkmenistan 30 percent and Tajikistan as much as 50 percent lower than the average.

All of these territories of the empire had established intimate economic ties over the years through their common energy systems, oil and gas conduits, and transportation lines, or through their gigantic monopoly enterprises, which not infrequently supplied the entire vast empire. For example, Belarus supplied 69.6 percent, Estonia 66.5 percent, Moldova 62.1 percent, and the Ukraine 39.1 percent, but Russia only 18 percent of manufactured goods and raw materials to other regions of the country.

Maintaining a common market therefore seemed to be the most meaningful task of the new CIS. Its members, however, were moving in a different direction from the countries of Western Europe. They preferred to abandon the ruble as a common currency and introduce their own national currencies. This has been the path chosen by the Ukraine, for example, which has already taken measures to replace the ruble by the *grivna*, printed in Canada. Some of the other successor states have taken similar steps.

There is, however, little reason to believe that the CIS could develop into a commonwealth of the British type. For example, it is scarcely conceivable that the president of Russia, who had served as metropole both in the tsarist and the Soviet empire, could be elected head of the community. The least suspicion that Russia was intent on regaining its imperial power would mean the ineluctable downfall of the Commonwealth. Although the smaller republics had regarded Russia in the preceding two years as their ally in the struggle against Soviet imperialism—Russia was one of the first republics to declare itself independent and its president had vehemently opposed the use of force in the Baltic—the fear soon spread that this largest of nations would once again resume its claim to hegemony in the new Commonwealth of states.

At a research meeting at Goettingen University, held in late April 1992, Cologne historian Gerhard Simon and Boris Meisner, a specialist on Eastern Europe, pointed out that the Russians could encounter their greatest problems in their search for a new identity, since Russia's "historical self-conception" had always been related to its dominant role within the empire. Dimitri Simes was of a similar view: "Russia has paid an enormous price, not just in terms of loss of its superpower status and its essential economic ties with the other republics, but also in its sense of identity and purpose. Since the time of Peter the Great, Russia has had no experience of living as anything other than empire."[19]

Several Western countries were in the forefront of negotiations with Russia on economic aid. All too often, Western nations tend to regard Russia not as one of the fifteen successor countries but as the only successor country of the dissolved Soviet Union. That Russia has been assigned a special role is reinforced by the fact that it was automatically granted a seat in the Security Council of the United Nations. While Boris Yeltsin was able with great skill to defuse the recurrent conflicts peacefully, other politicians acted as though they were representatives of the traditional Russian empire. For example, Russia's parliament, elected after the collapse of the Soviet Union, refused to accept the end of the USSR at its April 1992 session.

Russia is encountering insurmountable problems not only in relation to the independent countries of the new, if vacuous, Commonwealth, but also in respect of the centrifugal tendencies within the Russian Federation. The thirty-one autonomous republics and regions, which account for 20 percent of the total population of Russia and 40 percent of its territory, would like to go their own way. Tatarstan, the most influential of them, declared itself independent after the March 2, 1992, referendum, while the North Caucasus autonomous republics, inhabited by Chechens and Ingushi, under the leadership of the militant General Dudaev, regard themselves as independent of Russia. And in fact these two groups did not sign the Federation Treaty concluded on March 31, 1992. Indeed, the conflict with Chechnya has since turned into war. Centrifugal tendencies are also discernible in other national regions that have been able to assert themselves thanks to their natural resources: Tiumen, Bashkiria, Dagestan, and Kalmykia have oil; Buriatia and Tuva have coal; Iakutia has gold; and Karelia and Kabardina-Balkaria have iron ore.

Unlike the members of the CIS, the autonomous republics and regions do not have borders beyond the territory of Russia, and Russians account for half of their population. In some, Russians are even in the majority. Russia's president has been attempting to dampen the recurrent conflicts through concessions and by granting greater freedom in the management of their internal affairs. The conflict between Russia and its inner ring of autonomous republics and the other ring of independent republics is, however, a growing menace to peace within the CIS: at the end of August 1992 Russia's general prosecutor's office initiated legal procedures against the Confederation of Caucasian Peoples, founded by the fourteen natural groups of nations on the Federation territory, on charges of nationalist feuding and acts of terrorism.

The Confederation has called for military support to Abkhazia in its struggle against Georgia. It is becoming increasingly difficult for Russia's government to remain neutral in Georgia's war against Abkhazia and Southern Osetia, or in the war between Armenia and Azerbaijan over Nagorny Karabakh. But relations between the two largest CIS members, Russia and the Ukraine, will prove decisive for the situation within the CIS. No solution satisfactory to both sides has yet been found for the Crimea and for the Black Sea Fleet stationed there. The Ukraine, which finally achieved its independence after being part of the Russian and Soviet empires for centuries, still regards Moscow as the greatest threat to its existence as a state. Dmitri Pavlichko, chairman of the Parliamentary Committee of the Ukraine for Foreign Affairs, averred at a political and cultural round table discussion in Arpbach on August 27, 1992, that "The greatest threat for an independent Ukraine still comes from Moscow." Pavlichko sees the CIS as an unstable labored alliance that has an intrinsic tendency toward self-destruction. At the same forum, Viacheslav Chernovil, chairman of the strong Rukh movement, demanded the Ukraine's immediate withdrawal from the CIS.

The case of the Ukraine, however, involves more than just the issue of the Crimea, which Khrushchev annexed to the Ukraine in 1954, or of the Black Sea fleet. The Ukraine is marked by the wounded pride of a great nation that looks back to its leading role in founding the state of *Rus*, but was later subject to much suffering under the hegemony of Russia in the tsarist and Soviet empires. Rus, which comprised the territory of what is now Russia, White Russia, and the Ukraine, was founded in the ninth century. Kiev was the capital of the Grand Principality of Kievan Rus. The capital was transferred to Vladimir on the Klyazma river, and subsequently to Moscow much later in 1169, following the breaking up of feudal lands. For two hundred and fifty years, between 1230 and 1480, when the entire land languished under Mongolian rule, there were no conflicts between north and south. They flared up again, however, in the sixteenth century when the Ukraine had to fight for its independence against Russia and Poland. The union formed between Poland and Lithuania in 1569 placed the Western Ukraine under the dominion of the United Realm. After a bloody uprising against Poland, its leader and instigator Bogdan Chmielnitsky merged the Eastern Ukraine with Russia on the basis of the agreements of the *Pereiaslavskaia Rada* of 1654. Western Ukraine also came under Russia in 1772 after the partition of Poland among the three great powers. It was returned to Poland after World War I, and, having been reclaimed by Russia on the basis of the September 1939 Hitler–Stalin pact, remained so after the victory in World War II. The Western Ukraine was always a part of West European culture. The liberation movement Rukh began in the Western Ukraine, where it had a decisive influence on the Ukraine's struggle for independence. From 96 to 98 percent of the inhabitants of the western regions of Lviv, Ivano-Frankivsk, and Ternopil voted for the country's independence in the December 1991 referendum.

The emancipation movement was stronger in the Ukraine than elsewhere, because the Ukraine had suffered more than the other republics under Soviet rule. Forced collectivization claimed millions of victims while the Ukrainian intelligentsia suffered gravely under the domination of the Russian language and culture. One reason Khrushchev handed the Crimea over to the Ukraine on the occasion of the three-hundredth anniversary of the Ukraine's incorporation into the tsarist kingdom was that he wanted to make at least partial reparation for the damage the Ukraine had suffered.

The Ukraine also attaches great value to the rapid establishment of the institutions of an independent state. After the referendum, the parliament passed a resolution in December 1991 on the establishment of a national army, and on December 12 Leonid Kravchuk was appointed commander-in-chief of all the nonstrategic armed forces stationed on Ukraine territory. Officers who refused to swear an oath to the newly established national army were replaced and 40,000 soldiers were sent to other republics. By early April 1992, 483,000 officers and soldiers had sworn an oath of allegiance to the Ukraine Army. Fifty-five percent of the soldiers were native Ukrainians, and Leonid Kravchuk declared his willingness to take on all 400,000 Ukrainian citizens who were doing their military service outside the state borders. At the same time, however, in April 1992 the parliament passed a resolution striving for the status of a neutral and nonnuclear state, and to send 4,000 nuclear warheads back to Russia to be destroyed.

The Ukraine has no desire for the CIS to form a cohesive community of states and has resisted every attempt to build a prominent coordinating body or a central authority. To prevent the country from being drawn into a congeries of Russian-dominated states, the president's advisory committee, the Duma, recommended at its session of March 24, 1992, to reduce imports from the ruble zone and to divert exports to other regions, as well as to introduce customs tariffs along state borders.

The opposition mounted by the Ukraine was instrumental in preventing the CIS from developing into a potent federation of states. At the March 1992 meeting Leonid Kravchuk accepted only four of the eighteen resolutions presented, and he declined to participate in the meeting of May 15, issuing the following statement: "I would be happy if history were one day to report that Kravchuk had been one of those who had done much to bring the empire down and that the Ukraine had played a crucial role in this."[20]

While Russia has been struggling to reassert its lost greatness and the Ukraine has defended itself vehemently against any dominance within the CIS, the third Slavic successor state, Belarus, has been trying to extract the best terms for itself in the newly created constellation of states. Belarus is a reluctant player in the reform game. The government, under the leadership of Viacheslav Kebich, is still made up of the old Communist Party cadres: the influence of the oppositional people's front movement *Adrashenne* (Rebirth) and the newly established autonomous labor organization are still too slight to put pressure on the government. The people are still suffering the effects of the Chernobyl disaster. Seventy percent of the radioactive precipitation contaminated up to 3 million people in Belarus. Belarus, which sells almost 70 percent of its overall output to other republics of the former Soviet Union, is still dependent on Russia and wants to keep the ruble as its common currency. Relations with the countries of Western Europe are slight. Only a few joint ventures have been formed with Western firms, and Austria and Poland are the two most important partners in foreign trade. A veritable return to the old communist apparat took place on January 26, 1994, as a former communist functionary replaced Stanislaw Shushkevich in the position of the parliament chairman.

Although Belarus, together with the Ukraine, has been a member of the United Nations since the UN's founding, it has so far played no political role on the international stage.

The Successor States of Central Asia in Search of a New Identity

On the basis of a resolution adopted on December 16, 1992, in Ashkabad, Turkmenistan, the five successor states of Central Asia joined the Confederation of States that had been initiated by the three Slavic countries. They had good reasons for doing this since collectively they were economically the weakest region of the former Soviet Union, they were more tied to the common Soviet market, and they were more dependent than other areas on subsidies from the central authorities. Their 50 million inhabitants, 17 percent of the total Soviet population, produced less than 10 percent of the total product.

Only one of the five republics, Kazakhstan, is rated "moderately strong" by experts of the Deutsche Bank (55 of 100 possible rating points). The other four are characterized as "economically weak":

Uzbekistan (32 points), Turkmenistan (27 points), Kyrgyzia (24 points), with Tajikistan the weakest of these weak republics (only 18 of 100 possible points). Turkmenistan and Kyrgyzia sell 50.7 percent and 50.2 percent, respectively, of their net material product to other republics of the former Soviet Union, while this figure is 43.2 percent for Uzbekistan, 41.8 percent for Tajikistan, and 30.9 percent for Kazakhstan.

Exports abroad showed rather low figures: Uzbekistan exported 7.4 percent, thanks to cotton, Tajikistan 6.9 percent, mainly uranium, while the share of exports in total product was 4.2 percent for Turkmenistan, 3.0 percent for Kazakhstan, and only 1.2 percent for Kyrgyzia.[21]

But the mutual dependence was above all the consequence of the huge monopoly enterprises, which were geared to a closed, unified market, the vast network of oil and gas pipelines, or the single-crop cultures planted in Central Asia (80 percent of Uzbek cultivated area was used for cotton) that were transferred to other parts of the huge empire.

Martha Brill Olcott rightly notes that the industrial enterprises of northern Kazakhstan were more dependent on the south Siberian economy than on the agricultural territories in the south of Kazakhstan.[22] Kazakhstan delivered coal for the power network of Siberia, but got electric current itself from Kyrgyzia. Turkmenistan delivered oil to Russia, but processed Siberian oil in its own refineries.[23]

Once these countries were freed from imperial oppression, democratization of the political regime and the transition from an administrative to a market economy began in Central Asia as well. Free elections were held, the mass media enjoyed freedom of opinion without the censor watching over them, and the stage was being set for a plurality of parties. The free elections, however, usually elected the general secretaries of the dissolved Communist Parties, now renamed socialist parties. Olcott explained the reason for the popularity of the politicians of the discredited regime: "The princes of these republics became sponsors of national arts, benefactors, who helped to reorganize state buildings in mosques and in other religious institutions as well as to pass over from the Russian to the national language."[24]

Severyn Bialer suggests the following reasons for the merger of the Central Asian governing elites with the people: "These elites paid lip service to Moscow and enormous bribes to central inspectors, they amassed fortunes and engaged in an intricate network of private businesses and contacts."[25] Bialer's favorite example comes from Uzbekistan, where a harvest of one million tons of cotton was sold for private profit. This wealth trickled down to segments of the population.

The former communists who were elected presidents of their respective republics now identified with the renascent Islamic religion and expressed their fidelity to democracy and a market economy. Islam Karimov, the former communist who was elected president of Uzbekistan, declared, "If the fraternal Turkish nation recognizes us, Allah will be at our side." During a visit to Ankara, Sapanmurad Niazov, former communist leader and later president of Turkmenistan, had some cordial words for the Turkish head of state, Turgut Oezal, and requested that he build a pipeline that could supply Turkey with natural gas for six years. Niazov, however, was also attacked by his Central Asian colleagues at the CIS summit on October 9, 1992, because of Turkmenistan's open borders and lively weapons trade with Iran. Narsultan Nazarbaev, an old communist and former member of the Politburo of the CPSU Central Committee, was elected president of Kazakhstan; he, however, was more intent on cooperating with the CIS, and along with Boris Yeltsin played an important role at the Bishkek session of heads of state in October 1992.

The presidential elections in Kyrgyzia and Tajikistan had differing outcomes. At its October 1990 session, the Kyrgyzia Supreme Soviet decided in favor of Askar Akaev, president of the Academy of Sciences, instead of Absamat Masaliev, First Communist Party Secretary, whose incompetence had disqualified him from governing. Akaev, who represented the still modest democratic movement, was able to forge an accord with the old communist cadres.

But no such calm was established in Tajikistan. After the October Revolution, the "Bashmat Movement" mounted stubborn resistance to Soviet power. Tajikistan had been promoted to the status of Union Republic much later than the other national territories of Central Asia—on October 10, 1929. It is now the republic of Central Asia where the ruling Communist Party elite, with their hands still on the levers of power, are conducting a permanent war against the Islamic-nationalist government.

Former CP leader Rakhman Nabiev, dismissed by Gorbachev in 1985 in the drive against corruption and incompetence, had been able to win by forming an alliance with the Islamic and democratic movements in a campaign against the chairman of the Supreme Soviet, Makhar Makharisov. Shortly afterwards, however, the newly elected president legalized the Communist Party, which had been dissolved in 1989, and returned its confiscated assets. His former allies rebelled and in a May 1992 uprising forced him into a coalition government. But the Islamic movement grew. At the end of September it dared to mount a mass uprising against the unpopular old communists. Nabiev had to resign. But the change in power brought no peace to restless Tajikistan. A conference held on October 9, 1992, by the heads of states and governments of the ten successor states therefore decided to send peace troops consisting of 450 soldiers (the recently elected president Iskanderov had requested 10,000) from Kyrgyzia to Tajikistan. Nabiev is no longer alive, but the civil war in Tajikistan continues.

The Islamic Countries: Building Pipelines and Mosques in the Successor States of Central Asia

Highly placed politicians from Iran, Turkey, and other Islamic countries often travel to Alma Ata, Ashkhabad, Bishkek, Dushanbe, and Tashkent. Politicians from Kazakhstan, Kyrgyzstan, Tajikistan, Turkmenistan, and Uzbekistan visit Ankara and Teheran. They are received with Islamic greetings, they pray together to Allah in the innumerable newly built mosques (whose number has increased from 150 to 5,000 in the last two years), and the politicians of the former Soviet republics, converted to Islam, make pilgrimages to tap the giant market of 50 million inhabitants in Central Asia, which have to find a replacement for the tottering Soviet market to which they had been bound for centuries.

Iran leads the pack. It can look back on ancient economic, political, and cultural ties with this region, and it seeks to take advantage of them: Shiite Azerbaijan was a part of Persia until the early nineteenth century. It was therefore reasonable for Iran to step in to mediate the conflict over Nagorny Karabakh. A lively border commerce has meanwhile sprung up along the River Araxes where Russian vodka and caviar are traded against the Koran. Turkmenistan, which shares an 800-kilometer border with Iran, envisions regaining its former role as a transfer point in trade between the orient and the territories of the former tsarist kingdom. In its relations with Uzbekistan, Iran is reviving its ancient common cultural traditions: the big cities of Uzbekistan, Bukhara and Samarkand, have always been regarded as the cradle of the Persian language and literature. Iran not only has a common language with Tajikistan, it also has a common ethnic origin. The Tajik prime minister, Izabullah Khaiaev, expressed the affinity between these two nations in his first meeting with the Iranian foreign minister with the following florid words of greeting: "We are two nations of the same blood, belief and culture, two separated brothers, who seek to find afresh the path towards each other."

Iran's Foreign Minister Velayati was the first Islamic statesman to visit all five capital cities of Central Asia and Azerbaijan. He returned to Iran with a multitude of agreements concluded on commerce and culture. Kazakhstan was promised aid to prospect for new oil deposits and to tap new wells. Kazakh ports on the Caspian Sea were to be expanded in order to transport Tengiz oil to Iran. Economic relations with Turkmenistan were to be expanded, and there would be joint ventures to tap more oil and gas and to build a gas pipeline to bring gas to Turkey, Pakistan, and Iran. In addition to the nine bilateral economic agreements concluded in 1990, a number of new capital investment projects were planned.

The construction of oil pipelines to supply the Ukraine with Iranian oil was agreed with Azerbaijan. An agreement was also reached on the exchange of television programs.

But other Islamic countries, especially Turkey, would like to have their share of the ruins of the bankrupt Soviet Union. This secular republic appeals to many of the Turkish people of Central Asia more than the Iranian theocracy, while pan-Turkism holds still greater appeal than pan-Slavism. But Turkey does not have the material resources to set up attractive capital investment projects. It is therefore trying to be active culturally. Turkey was the first country to recognize Azerbaijan, and was successful with its suggestion to replace the Cyrillic script there with Latin script. It was similarly successful in Kyrgyzstan. Uzbekistan, however, decided to switch to Arabic script and has asked Iran to supply appropriate material.

The arms trade in Central Asia, already well established, could pose a threat to world peace. Kazakhstan has a tremendous nuclear potential, although President Nazarbaev has declared his willingness to send nuclear weapons to Russia, and has repeatedly declared his country a nuclear-free zone. However, no suitable solution has yet been found. Kazakhstan, Tajikistan, and Uzbekistan have considerable uranium deposits, and Tajikistan has a factory producing uranium 238.[26]

Kazakhstan has converted its arms enterprises into private firms with the consent of the competent military commanders in order to continue with business as usual. Iran and Libya have already announced their interest in the nuclear potential of the Central Asian successor states. Iran, Pakistan, and Turkey have taken measures to bring this region into the Islamic community. All the countries of Central Asia with the exception of Kazakhstan are represented in the Coordinating Committee formed by these countries. Kazakhstan, whose interests lie in good relations with Russia, has so far been satisfied with the status of observer.

In mid-December 1991, Azerbaijan joined the Islamic World Conference as its forty-sixth member, and on October 7, 1992, its national council voted, forty-three to one, to leave the CIS. President Elcibey criticized the CIS for serving as an anchor for the survival of the postcommunist regimes in Central Asia, and called these regimes the most zealous participants in the CIS.[27] But the president also reported at the same time that Azerbaijan did not wish to break all contacts with the CIS community, and that it would be willing to remain as an observer or as an associate member. Bilateral agreements, he said, should be made with Russia and the Ukraine.

Prospects

After Azerbaijan left the CIS, only ten of the fifteen former Soviet republics remained: the three Slavic states, the five Central Asian nations, Armenia, and Moldova. Their future remained vague. The seventh summit conference prepared by the Russian and Kazakh presidents in the Kyrgyzian capital of Bishkek showed unequivocally that ideas about what the CIS should be doing, and what its organizational structure should be, differed so widely that even finding the lowest common denominators was unlikely.

Although an agreement was reached to form a ruble currency union and to establish a CIS bank that would control issuance and the amount of money in circulation, the extent to which the ten members would join this union remained unclear. Russia's former Prime Minister

Yegor Gaidar spoke of serious differences of opinion. Kazakhstan's proposal to form a council to coordinate economic policy was not supported by a majority. Instead, the participants decided to found an economic advisory committee with no clearly defined powers and responsibilities. One thing, however, was clear: the Ukraine had no interest in a currency union; it had already announced that it was going to leave the ruble zone, and would quite soon produce its own currency, the *grivna*.

The Ukraine was in the process of forming a national state, with its own army and currency. The idea of maintaining close ties with a successor community was not very popular. The opposition *Rukh* called for resignation from the CIS, which they regarded as inevitably dominated by Russia. But a community with no clearly defined area of influence and no effective executive, or without the Ukraine as a member, would be meaningless. The opinion expressed by Yurii Afanasev, that "it is possible that the European part of the Community would develop toward the Christian West, the Asiatic part would develop toward the Moslem south and toward the polyconfessional Far East,"[28] seemed, however, to lack foundation from the present-day perspective.

Sooner or later the successor states of Central Asia would be bound to conclude that the Islamic countries were more prepared and capable for Islamization than for effective economic cooperation, and would support the CIS, inasmuch as they were economically independent on it. The Ukraine, on the other hand, was bound to go its own way. Under these conditions, the CIS had no chances of development. It was virtually inevitable that mutual relations among the successor states of the disintegrating Soviet Union would be settled multilaterally.

From Gorbachev's Failed Perestroika to Yeltsin's Big Crash

Boris Yeltsin's victory over the gang of eight, who had failed in their bold but ill-fated attempt to turn back the wheel of Soviet and world history on those fateful days in August 1991, marked the beginning of a real "perestroika" of the seventy-year-old political and economic system that defined itself as socialist.

By September 1991 Russia's president had dissolved the Communist Party, guardian of the state ideology and the country's guiding hand, and dealt a final blow to the Soviet empire in December of that year. The fifteen successor states were abandoned to their own fates as they set out on the preordained path to a market economy and a pluralist democracy. In Russia price liberalization began on January 2, 1992, marking the presumed first step in the transition from a command economy to a market economy. Other republics followed, not always voluntarily, but compelled because of the common currency.

The question now being raised among the world public was whether Yeltsin in Russia, Kravchuk in the Ukraine, and the other new leaders would be more successful in transforming the existing system than Gorbachev had been with perestroika and glasnost. The answer seemed unequivocal. The independent successor states would find it more difficult because their production and distribution systems were geared to a unified state: large enterprises that produced up to 70 percent of the total needs of the vast empire were no exception. Almost all of the republics were dependent on Russia's crude oil and natural gas, Uzbek cotton, Ukrainian sugar, and other agrarian products. The entire economic and communications infrastructure was tailored to a unified state. Customs barriers now divided separate economies that had once formed a single cohesive system, and this tendency toward isolation persists in the aspirations to establish national currencies.

Reorganization was complicated most of all by the fact that it was not just a transition to a diametrically opposed system, but from a *politically* determined economic structure, remote from human needs and subordinate to the military-industrial complex of a military superpower, to a structure geared to human needs. Moreover, the efficiency and strength of the production potential of this system were greatly overestimated by official statistics as well as by Eastern specialists in the West. It was absolutely wrong to use traditional standards for measuring the efficiency of an economy organized by sector and fashioned arbitrarily in accordance with the political priorities of the central authorities—an economy producing goods of inferior quality; it was wrong moreover to compare that system with a qualitatively different production system determined by the rules of the market. Meaningful comparison was further hindered by the fact that the overall efficiency of a planned economy was aggregated on the basis of "imaginary statistics," produced to embellish a sparse reality in order to conform to the wishes of the central authorities.

It was just such statistics that produced the misleading indicators such as gross output, favoring the "ton ideology," which maximized input, and not effective performance geared to the satisfaction of human needs. In addition, there was the tightrope act on fictitious prices and exchange rates which made any reasonable cost–benefit analysis impossible, and gave no consideration to the relation between supply and demand. Ludwig von Mises, the Austrian economist, had recognized early on the unviability of economic mechanisms reduced to technical accounting instruments: "It might come about that some categories of the capitalist market will be maintained, but they will express quite different things from what they do in an authentic market economy."[29]

These fictitious statistics reduced the ratio of the gross national product of the purported superpower to that of the real superpower to 60 percent in optimistic estimates, to 50 percent in less optimistic estimates. Now, however, the ratio of the respective economic performances of the former Soviet Union and the United States is estimated at between 28 percent and 33 percent.

If official statistics and CIA estimates could have been trusted, the slogan of the Soviet leaders—"catch up and overtake the West"—might have been realistic. As the world economy underwent its worst crisis ever and threatened to collapse into misery and chaos, the Soviet Union amazed the world public with its dynamic growth and full employment: Abram Bergson, the pioneer of U.S. sovietologists, calculated that between 1928 and 1940, when the U.S. national product declined by 33 percent, the Soviet national GNP increased by 60 percent. Perhaps this 60 percent growth rate for the Soviet Union was correct. The years from 1928 to 1940 were the period of forced industrialization at any price, when all available resources, and the nation's total energy, were geared to achieving that goal. The above-average growth rates in the postwar reconstruction period were also believable (the resources of defeated Germany had indeed also contributed to that growth).

But this Asiatic mode of production—which called itself socialist, however—progressively drained its inner resources in an attempt to move from the stage of early industrialization to the technological age of the modern world. The mighty state industry, administered by a sterile bureaucracy, was better suited to extracting fuels and raw materials from deposits located in the vicinity of industrial centers, and to building gigantic foundries, and producing enormous quantities of iron and steel through the use of twice as much material and labor as in the West, than to producing and frugally employing the hi-tech of the modern age, such as chips and computers. The resources of forced growth dwindled progressively when the time came to replace the predatory methods of plundering deposits in the western part of the country with sources situated in the permafrost territories of Siberia and the Far East, and to transport crude oil and gas over thousands of kilometers of pipelines. Economic disparities grew. The five-year plans were filled and exceeded, yet there was an insurmountable, chronic shortage of consumer goods and means of production, while the stockpiles of mostly unsalable goods were by far the highest compared to the national product. The goods structure of Soviet foreign trade was similar to that of Third World nations. Three-quarters of exports were raw materials and fuels, as well as durables, while the main import item was machinery and equipment.

This wasteful mode of production became financially unworkable; the preposterous idea of financing industrialization by "primitive accumulation" from agriculture boomeranged. The state was forced to subsidize the loss-burdened *kolkhozy* and *sovkhozy* with about 100 billion rubles per year, and to import up to 30 million tons of grain annually to supply the population and livestock.

Growth rates decreased even according to official statistics: from 7.4 percent annually for 1966–70, to 6.5 percent, 6.3 percent, 4.2 percent, and 3.5 percent in the following five-year periods. The indicators calculated by economist G. Chanin were even lower: 4.1 percent, 3.2 percent, 1.6 percent, and 0.6 percent.[30] The real economic growth indicators, however, do not necessarily suggest an approaching economic disaster. Growth was not much greater and in some cases it was even lower in the Western industrial countries, but no one in the West spoke of disaster.

The correct interpretation was that the fall of the Soviet command economy was due primarily to the shaky economic structures, further distorted by the steadily growing arms complex, rather than by falling growth rates. The arms race against the economically much stronger United States to maintain a balance of deterrence made it necessary to place so much emphasis on the arms industry in the 1970s that the consumer industry was reduced to a vestige. A. J. Katzenellenbogen, a Russian economist exiled in the United States, rightly pointed out that

Soviet arms expenditure was equal to all other state expenditure minus production costs for consumer goods and services, which would have to be curtailed even further in case of war.[31]

The Soviet Union was able to keep pace with the United States in the arms race; it was even able to overtake it in some areas, but according to Soviet research data it was in seventy-seventh place in individual consumption.[32] Helmut Schmidt, former chancellor of the Federal Republic of Germany, had an apt definition for this military super-power with the living standard of a developing country: "Upper Volta with missiles."

This appellation seems especially apt for the Brezhnev era when the Asiatic mode of production began to exhibit ever-clearer symptoms of fatigue, while the race to maintain an equilibrium in armaments demanded ever-greater expenditure that was increasingly difficult to bear. The unexpected rise in the prices of crude oil and gold were enough to finance the rising armaments costs, but the economic sectors that produced for human needs were increasingly neglected. The economic crisis came out into the open when these sources of financing began to fail owing to falling oil prices and cutbacks in production. Gorbachev recognized the potential danger of economic collapse and therefore embarked upon his policy of detente and disarmament, in addition to economic and political restructuring. But, while his plans for disarmament found a corresponding resonance in government circles in the West, perestroika encountered the stubborn resistance of Soviet state functionaries, who feared for their privileges and power. The failure of perestroika was inevitable. Traditional steering mechanisms were progressively dismantled without being replaced by more effective market-oriented mechanisms. Labor discipline declined steadily, and economic performance fell to a level that imperiled fulfillment of the needs of the population. In 1990, for the first time in Soviet history, official statistics recorded a 5 percent decline in the national product.

It would be wrong, however, to conclude that the failure of perestroika was due to the inactivity of the reformers. One reform model followed another, and countless measures were taken to put the economy in order again. The lack of self-adjusting mechanisms—which had always been the weakest point in the command system—became fatefully evident just at a time when the country found itself in a crisis situation that demanded action. The solutions sent down from above produced new contradictions before the old ones could be surmounted. The system was incapable of averting an economic crisis, and that crisis would ultimately lead to the collapse of the social system. The system's traditional mechanisms proved to be more obstinate, and the capacity of the state bureaucracy to resist movement proved stronger than was generally assumed. The far-ranging disarmament agreement created conditions for reconverting the arms industry to civilian purposes, but this was countered by the stubborn resistance of pressure groups from the military-industrial complex. One other reason for the difficulty in changing the traditional priorities of industrial branches—which would have modified the cumbersome economic structures—lay in the fact that Gorbachev's reform team had assumed the burden of 350,000 uncompleted capital investment projects with an average construction term of ten years, and putting a freeze on them would have produced tremendous losses. In addition, Gorbachev harbored the same illusion as his predecessors, namely, that the economy could be saved from collapse by replacing some of the components of the ailing system, after which the dynamic growth rates of yesteryear could be restored. His first innovation slogan was: "Acceleration through modernization." Between 1986 and 1990, 45 percent of plant equipment was to be replaced by modern equipment of the latest world standards. Not only was there not enough money for this, however, but it also proved extremely difficult to overcome the deeply rooted (at both macro- and microlevels) behavior and intricate structural networks that preferred new construction projects to modernization. It was not until Gorbachev realized that, given the elaborate system of security the state had created for itself no further progress was possible, that the second stage of perestroika began. But once again proposals were confined to changes within the system. Gorbachev's perceived objective had never been to create a competition-oriented market economy in the normal sense of the term, but rather a "socialist" market economy, that is, an economy steered mainly by the state.

The first measures to alter the system were taken in 1987: the *diktat* of the central economic plan was to be abolished. Goods vital to the state, their quality, and their volume, would be defined by state orders (*Goszakaz*) and the rest of production was to be agreed upon contractually with business partners. Direct planning was to be replaced by indicator planning, and regulated by market mechanisms. At the same time measures were taken to restore an economic meaning to economic parameters that had been reduced to purely technical accounting instruments. No longer would credits be automatically given to every needy enterprise, but only to those that could prove their solvency. The state bank, which in the traditional command system had a monopoly on all credit and clearing operations through its various branches, was transformed into the bank of banks; henceforth its function would be to supply funds to the newly established network of commercial banks. The interest rate would no longer be determined as a component of banking costs, but would be a parameter for the creditor's calculations and would function as the market price of money. The price of goods and services would become sensitive to supply and demand, and would help to reduce the ever larger state subsidies. The decision-making powers of industrial firms were expanded. The economically harmful practice of using the profits of successful enterprises to help finance the losses of economically inefficient ones was abolished. Henceforth an enterprise could use a large portion of industrial profits for its own purposes and on its own accountability. The official statistics indicate that the proportion of profits left in the hands of enterprises rose from 46 percent in 1986 to 51 percent in 1990. The proportion of capital investments financed from enterprises' own resources in the total volume increased from 3.1 percent (5.3 billion rubles) in 1986 and to 51 percent (102.4 billion rubles) in 1989.

The precipitous developments in the first two years of perestroika, however, confirmed the experiences accumulated earlier in Poland and Hungary, that even a far-reaching reform of the infrastructure could neither create a new system nor improve economic performance if the existing system were maintained. The steering mechanisms of a fundamentally different economic system were reduced to impotence when transplanted to a state-controlled economy. A bankruptcy procedure for insolvent firms was introduced, but unviable firms were allowed to continue operating out of fear of mass unemployment and concern for maintaining social peace. Their losses were then further financed by state subsidies.

For state firms, the state and its all-embracing domination continued to be the ultimate point of reference; firms now worked for state orders just as they had previously worked for the state plan. There was even less concern for profitable activity than before perestroika, since everyone knew that the state would cover the costs. Official statistics show that between 1985 and 1990, state subsidies increased from 66.4 billion to 97.6 billion rubles. The rights granted to industrial enterprises to use industrial earnings for capital investment purposes at their own discretion were unable to alter traditional production structures, given the acute supply difficulties, the intricate network of traditional ties, and the meager allocation parameters. The development funds of industrial enterprises increased eightfold in the three years between 1985 and 1988, but capital investments declined from year to year. In 1991 industrial firms used 14 percent less resources for developmental purposes, but twice as much as in the preceding year for social services.[33]

But perestroika raised the self-awareness of the work force. To gain worker support for the reforms, Gorbachev found himself compelled to present a market economy in a more democratic light than prefigured in the industrial countries of the West. Plant managers were henceforth to be elected by the work force. Managers appointed in this way therefore felt themselves bound more to the work force than to the economic authorities above them. The work force had learned to use strikes to drive home their demands. Wages increased even more—by 8 percent in 1988, 9 percent in 1989, and by 10 percent even in 1990—whereas the national product only increased by 4.4 percent in 1988 and by 2.5 percent in 1989, and in 1990 even decreased by 5 percent. The central state budget deficit increased owing to expanding subsidies and shrinking transfers from the republics and had to be financed by printing money and by credits from the state bank. As of the end of 1990, the share of state-granted credits in the total volume was 58 percent.[34]

The view had finally come to prevail that half measures could not halt the decline in the economy, and thoroughgoing reforms were contemplated. However, the Soviet Union came to an end without the implementation of one single reform model. Some particular aspects of reform, however, were discussed in the successor republics as a foundation for the transition to a market economy, and hence warrant discussion. In October 1989, the Reform Commission of the Council of Ministers, under the direction of Leonid Abalkin, presented its project "Radical Economic Reforms," as well as a number of ideas on "short-term and long-term measures" that would have to be implemented over the next five years to put the economy in order again.

The proposed model was divided into three stages. In 1990 legislative documents to alter property relations and the tax and banking system would be adopted and measures would be taken to reduce the budget deficit and to put the brakes on the expansion of credit. Firms that were operating at a loss would be leased out. In the second stage, the entire package of market mechanisms would be implemented by 1991–92: prices for most areas of commerce would be liberalized, all wage controls would be abolished, and unviable industrial enterprises and farms would be closed. In the third and last stage (1993–95), 25 to 30 percent of state enterprises would be converted to leaseholds and 30 to 40 percent would be converted to shareholding companies. Economic equilibrium would be restored. Abalkin's reform model—the first to propose thoroughgoing changes in existing property relations since Lenin's NEP of 1921—was not accepted. The government at that time, headed by Ryzhkov, presented its own reform model in December 1989. Its primary focus was on strengthening labor and contractual discipline.[35] State orders would account for 90 percent of the total output in the first reform years, and harsh sanctions were provided for nonfulfillment. The People's Congress accepted the government's model. But the economic situation deteriorated dramatically over the next months so that no one dared to implement this model. In Spring 1990, a structural crisis struck many areas of the country and forced considerable concessions.

On May 24, 1990, a new reform model was proposed that was similar to the Abalkin plan. The emphasis of the new model was on equilibrium prices: in early 1991 there would be a 55 percent increase in prices for farm products, a 46 percent increase in wholesale prices for industrial goods, and a 43 percent increase in retail prices for consumer goods. News of the imminent price rises resulted in hoarding, which cleared the shelves of the state commercial shop network. The people had to turn to the black market, which was progressively replacing the state shops.

In Summer 1990, according to the data of a work team established by Gorbachev and Yeltsin, 42 percent of meat and meat products, 55 percent of vegetables, and 75 percent of potatoes reached consumers from outside the state network.

But this second government model remained on paper as well, since it was feared that any thoroughgoing measure would cause the economic situation to deteriorate even further. A new reform model, the

Shatalin-Iavlinskii Five Hundred Day Plan, was presented to the public. This plan differed from all others, and indeed from Central European plans as well, in that its first purpose was to restore economic stability, in the first instance by reducing state defense spending by 10 percent, spending on security by 20 percent, spending on state subsidies for unprofitable enterprises by 30 to 40 percent, and state-financed capital investment projects by 20 to 30 percent. All long-term projects with a construction time of three to five years were to be canceled, and no project with a cost estimate of over 100 billion rubles would be started. But above all foreign aid would be reduced by 70 to 80 percent. The Shatalin-Iavlinskii Plan was intended to end the state budget deficit by March 1991. A far-ranging privatization program would begin: 70 percent of the commercial shop network and 80 percent of restaurants and coffeehouses would be transferred to private proprietors by the end of 1991. This privatization model differed in two respects from all others: 40 percent of the means of production would remain state property for five years after the start of privatization, and, what seems even more important in the context of other privatization plans, the relinquishment of state property without payment was out of the question. A voucher procedure, such as in the former Czechoslovakia and later in Russia, was not contemplated under this plan.

The demonopolization of large state enterprises was critical. Consider that 96 percent of all diesel locomotives, 100 percent of all air conditioners, and two-thirds of all batteries were produced by one single monopoly enterprise. There were firms that concentrated on the manufacture of up to two thousand products, as stated in the "Five Hundred Day" model. Their demonopolization therefore was an important step. Effecting the transition from a command system to a market economy in five hundred days was much too ambitious an objective. The task posed by the authors of the reform model and above all the wide-ranging privatization plans were much too complicated to be accomplished in such a time frame, if they could even be accomplished at all.

The experiences of the countries of Central Europe during the previous three years offered the ultimate proof of how difficult it is to privatize a totally nationalized economy. Moreover, the authors of the plan did not intend to effect the transition to an extremely different economic system in one great leap. In the first, if very short, stage of one hundred to two hundred days, emphasis would continue to be placed on discipline in centrally defined duties. The institution of state orders, introduced in 1987 as an alternative to the imperatives of the state plan, would be maintained. However, they were not to be imposed on industrial firms. Failure to fulfill orders would not be penalized, as in Ryzhkov's model; rather, they would be based upon mutual consent, and prompt fulfillment would be promoted through special, favorable facilities such as credits at reduced interest rates.

What is most significant about the Five Hundred Day Plan, however, is that it proposed realistic foundations for maintaining traditional economic relations between the republics joined in a looser union, as envisioned. The plan recommends: "To allow no quotas, restrictions, or customs barriers for any commerce agreed upon within the framework of the inter-republic treaty." The republics, as stated in the reform model, would gain full sovereignty over national assets. Land and capital would, with few exceptions, become the national property of the republics. The republics would coordinate economic matters with the central government within an economic union. The banking system was given an important role. It would be built along the lines of the U.S. Federal Reserve, and coordinated by a central bank council headed by a president. The decisions of the central council on monetary and credit policy would serve as a guideline for all republics.

At the last moment, however, Gorbachev withdrew his support from this visionary model as well, perhaps because its implementation would have cost 12 million persons (9 percent of the work force) their jobs. He ordered his adviser Abel Aganbegian to prepare a new model. In September 1990, that model was ready, but the Supreme Soviet rejected both models, and adopted a compromise model, developed by Shatalin, Aganbegian, and Iasin, entitled "Basic guidelines for stabilizing the economy and for making the transition to a market economy." There was no indication, however, that the new model, which allowed for many alternatives, would ever be implemented. After the August 1991 putsch, there were no more possibilities for reform within the Soviet empire. Gorbachev announced that he was open to any kind of reform, but he was extremely reticent when it came to putting reforms into practice. He had come upon the scene in order to bring about a historical turn in East–West relations as well as in his country's social system. When he had to abandon his office of president of the former huge empire in late 1991, he could look back at the work he had completed—namely, putting an end to the confrontation between East and West—but the Soviet Union no longer existed as the world's second superpower. The dismantling of the traditional economic system before a more effective one could be brought to bear plunged his country's economy into disaster. The last year in the history of the Soviet empire, 1991, was the most difficult in its seventy years of existence.

The Wrong Prelude to Reform: Liberalization of Prices

Gorbachev wanted to establish a market economy with the restrictive adjective "socialist," bringing openness into the formation of opinions and democratic relations, transforming the Union of Soviet Republics into a commonwealth, and putting an end to confrontation with the West. Yeltsin, who like Gorbachev had also enjoyed a meteoric career in the Communist Party apparatus, no longer wanted communism, a socialist market, or the Soviet Union. As he said, he wanted to return Russia to the "civilized world." He dissolved the Communist Party and accelerated the disintegration of the Soviet Union by declaring Russia's independence. As soon as the foundation of the *ancien régime* had been destroyed, Russia's president set about forging new methods of economic management and relations to the successor states. A socialist market was henceforth out of the question and Yeltsin instead embarked upon the path to a capitalist market system with the freeing of prices on January 2, 1992.

Clear difficulties arose. In an interview in *Pravda*, Yeltsin said that mistakes were inevitable on the path traveled so far, and that another government would have smashed even more china in this undertaking.[36]

But it became ever more evident that the problem lay not in unavoidable mistakes within a fundamentally correct, broader strategy of change, but in an utterly false start. The liberalization of prices, while other spheres of the economic infrastructure and property relations remained fundamentally unchanged, plunged the economy into an even deeper abyss and the people into indescribable misery. The false start in the reform, with its serious consequences, not only made the course of reform difficult in Russia, it also totally destroyed the monetary system of the other former Soviet republics by triggering the unreined devaluation of the ruble, and made it impossible for a common economic zone, the core of the newly founded Commonwealth of Independent States, to function.

The way into the "civilized world" which Boris Yeltsin wanted to initiate, or a return to normality, as others put it, was by no means necessarily in the cards. "What is normality?" asked Karol Modzelewski, the Polish historian and a long-time prisoner of the communist regime, and went on to state that he was against a unified model of civilization for mankind in accordance with the one single paradigm of neoclassical economics and neoliberal social philosophy. This historian was not in the least disposed to viewing historical development as mankind's long journey along one single trajectory.

The civilized world is certainly not uniform in its composition or in the level of development achieved. One cannot assume that Russia or some other successor state will be able to reach the level of a modern industrial society in the near future. The level that seems realistic in the short term is one on a par with relatively developed countries of the Third World. But the outcome of the competition between Asia's giant, a reformed communist China, emerging from its backwardness, and India, lingering in the early stage of capitalist development, is by no means decided. A state-planned economy still seems to be a viable alternative for developing countries that have no hope of success in competition with the powerful industrial countries of the West. Yeltsin has complained that the Civic Union organized by Arkadii Volskii would like to establish a Chinese model in Russia, that is, a strong authoritarian government with gradual economic reforms and state subsidies for state enterprises.[37]

Had the Civic Union striven against "reform utopias and neo-Bolsheviks" in order to find the Russian model of the future, and had Yeltsin striven for a return to the real civilized world, the way ahead for both would have been as difficult as it was uncertain. One thing that was certain was that Yeltsin's starting off with inordinately high prices and a stifling poverty as a way of returning to the fold of the world he praised was neither the right way nor the right direction. Even if prices had to be increased under the given conditions, this should only have taken place together with the reconstitution of a stratum leading to a civilized society—that is, with the creation of a "third estate." The bourgeoisie was a social stratum that was able, after acquiring wealth and respect over the course of centuries, to stake its claim on power and moreover to gain that power through the revolutions of 1789 and 1848 in Western Europe and 1905 and February 1917 in Russia. Bourgeois society in Western Europe and North America was unable to achieve prosperity in a pluralist democracy without a devastating economic crisis and without going politically astray. But Lenin had utterly precluded the civilized way to social progress with his absurd idea that the bourgeois revolution had played out its role in Russia in only six months. The October Revolution destroyed the third estate of property owners and entrepreneurs and declared the proletariat (which at that time made up 5 percent of the population) the demiurge of the great Russian empire, heralding its dictatorship as a legitimate successor to tsarist rule. What followed was a crude dictatorship of the Party bureaucracy and the secret service.

Russia's president may want to return to the traces of the bourgeois revolution of February 1917, but such a revolutionary retreat in order to advance cannot be accomplished with a brigade of hussars or shock therapy in six months, or in five hundred days as Gorbachev's radical reformers wanted. It was easier to confiscate the means of production from their legitimate owners than to find anyone who could afford to buy them. The expropriated are no longer alive and the production potential that has been created meanwhile exceeds by many times that of the originally confiscated means of production. There is no private capital in Russia. The transformation of all legally competent citizens into private owners through vouchers or other kinds of privatization gimmicks seems to be no less utopian than bringing happiness to the people through the "victorious proletarian revolution" with the property of legitimate owners transformed into state property. People's capitalism—that is, transforming all legally competent citizens into shareholders—seems just as unrealistic as once was the transformation of people into the owners of collective property nationalized by the state and administered by the state bureaucracy.

When Modzelewski states that great social upheavals have always begun with utopian slogans, which, however, usually could not be realized, the difference between revolutions of the past and the transformation now taking place is unmistakable. The force of attraction of the humanist adjurations, "Liberty, fraternity, equality," which continued the message of the world religions, was irresistible. The ideology of revolution became a religion in which millions believed, and for which millions were ready to endure every sacrifice. But the transformation now taking place on the East European continent was not introduced in the name of an unrealizable utopia. The call was for a return to "normality"—to a social system that actually existed, whose advantages and disadvantages are well known. The only aspect that might prove utopian is the hope that the living standard of the First World will be achieved in the foreseeable future, and that these newly emergent market economies will be able to avoid the calamities of such an economy (such as unemployment), for which even the developed welfare market economies—with their perfect economic infrastructure and highly skilled management—still have not found an effective cure.

But the attempt to move from an authoritarian state to the laissez-faire state of classical capitalism and the hope of instituting far-ranging reforms that alter the very basis of the system and lead the economy out of its worst crisis of the postwar period have proved counterproductive. After a brief reform period, it rapidly became clear that the way to the civilized world of the present would be far more difficult for Russia and the other reform states than it was for those states that accomplished the development from early to mature capitalism without a "socialist" intermediary stage. The Russians and the other nations freed from communist rule, with their highly trained and highly educated cadres, who had to endure unbearable privations but who also enjoyed the protection of the state, will assuredly not accept the exploitative methods of early capitalism. They will willingly do without a "socialist" economy but not a "social" market economy. Yet the competitive market economy only became social—that is, a welfare state— after it had reached the mature stage of the industrial countries of the West. The successor states of the former Soviet Union, as well as the countries of Eastern and Central Europe, are a long way from this stage. In the interim, what can be seen on the horizon, is, as Czech Prime Minister Vaclav Klaus put it, a market economy without adjectives—that is, still more privations for the vast majority but possibilities for advancement and enrichment for a small minority of clever and enterprising spirits who are better able than most to take advantage of the equality of opportunity that has now been given to them.

People obviously place a high value on their recently acquired rights in a pluralist democracy: free parliamentary elections, freedom to travel, and so on. A growing section of the population, however, is failing to take advantage of the right to choose among the innumerable political parties, since only a few of these offer a clear, defensible political platform; so many are more concerned with condemning a shady past than with working toward a viable future. Very often only half of those entitled to vote make use of this dearly won privilege; Landsbergis in Lithuania and Gamsakhurdia in Georgia, both of whom fought for their country's independence, have lost their power to reform communists such as Brazauskas or Shevardnadze, while parliamentary majorities change their composition at breathtaking speed. What this means in a nutshell is that the newly established democratic regimes need to bring forth cogent arguments if they are to win people's trust.

Narsultan Nazarbaev, former CPSU Politburo member, elected president of Kazakhstan in free elections, when asked his opinion of the newly emergent democracy, said: "Democratic societies should not lead to the impoverishment of the people. We make no secret of the fact that here in Kazakhstan many people prefer to have enough to eat under an authoritarian regime than to be hungry under a democratic one." In a rejoinder to the comment that many people put "freedom above hunger," he went on to say that "the hungry do not live long, and freedom dies with them."[38]

It was originally thought, or hoped, that the destroyed structures and infrastructures that had evolved within society over the centuries could be revived by a new regime's act of creation within, if not six days, then surely within five hundred, that a modern democratic system could be established after many years of totalitarian dictatorship, and that the command economy could be easily replaced by a competitive market system. Such thoughts proved to be delusions. Moreover, attempting to introduce a new beginning without considering the effects of the past proved to have fateful consequences: in Russia and the other successor states the CPSU dictatorship and the Asiatic mode of production, defined as socialist, lingered on for much longer, having struck deeper roots in the life of society in Russia and the other successor states than in the outer ring of the Soviet empire.

No less a person than Leszek Kolakowski, professor of philosophy at Oxford University, an unimpeachable critic of Poland's regime, described the abrupt turn taken at the crossroads between the tragic past and an uncertain future in trenchant terms. In an article with the provocative title, "The Never-Ending Beginning of History," he wrote: "If one shares Hegel's view that times of happiness should be seen as a carte blanche for world history, then the seventy years of Soviet power will provide the best evidence to support this tendency."[39] Kolakowski warns, however, against regarding this past as lost years.

The freeing of prices on January 2, 1992, at a time when there was an unbridgeable gap between supply and demand, a supply network in total disarray, a profound crisis in agriculture, and a food industry in desperate straits, marked the new beginning, attempted in disregard of the previous economic system. Far from paving the way for a market economy, this measure effectively blocked it. Prices for basic foods increased fivefold immediately, and more than tenfold over the course of a year, decimating the people's savings.

Parliamentary deputies of the Civic Union, critical of the reforms, said that the strategy of paving the way to a free market by liberalizing prices was wrong, and called on the leadership to "resign if Russia is dear to you."[40] The deputies reminded Yeltsin of his statement at the meeting of the First Congress of People's Deputies prior to his election as president of the Supreme Soviet of Russia:

> Proposals to raise prices at the cost of the people in order to introduce the market are wrong and Russia should reject this policy, which is against the nation's interest. The most important thing is to effect the transition to a market economy without violence, and without reducing the living standard.

But, said the Civic Union deputies, once elected president of independent Russia, Yeltsin did precisely what he had hitherto for quite sound reasons vehemently rejected. What is more, the fateful decision to free prices while retaining a single currency, without allowing for any possibility of effecting significant changes in other parts of the economic and social system, had reduced the people of both Russia and the other former republics to poverty. The sacrifices that the long-suffering people of the disintegrated Soviet Union have had to bear have been far greater than the president's domestic and foreign advisers could have suspected. The much-coveted market is not yet even on the horizon. Yurii Maltsev, professor of economics at Carthage College, criticized Yeltsin's price reforms as combining exploitation, price inflation, and the printing of billions of rubles into a single package. The freeing of prices on January 2, 1992, was an absurd, economically counterproductive measure, and will in no way lead to the market.[41]

Martin Malia, professor of history at the University of California, Berkeley, compares Russia's present catastrophic social and economic situation with the somber period of 1604–13, when tsarist rule had totally collapsed and the country's hierarchical structures were in a state of advanced dissolution: historians refer to this period as *Smuta*— a time of chaos and confusion.

The years 1648 to 1660 in Poland were equally somber, according to Professor Malia. The Cossack rebellions and the Swedish invasion totally devastated the country. That period has gone down in history as a fall from grace, immortalized by the Nobel-Prize-winning Polish writer Henryk Sienkiewicz. The Thirty Years War from 1618 to 1646 in Germany, the Hundred Years War of 1380–1453 in France, or the Wars of the Roses of 1455–85 in England are analogous to Russia's present situation, according to Malia.[42]

Nikolai Ryzhkov, prime minister of the Soviet Union between 1986 and 1990, did not paint a much more optimistic picture of Russia's situation when he addressed the Constitutional Court:

> There were only two economic crises in the history of the former Soviet Union that bear comparison with the present one. The crisis of the last year of World War I and the civil war following the October Revolution in 1917, when national income was cut by 50 percent and industrial production by 80 percent. The second crisis was in the first two years of World War II, 1941–1942, when the occupation of a large segment of Soviet territory resulted in a 34 percent decrease in national income and a 23 percent decrease in industrial production.[43]

Given the total collapse of supply and the expanding black market, a monetary and price reform similar to that carried out in Western Europe or in the Soviet Union in the first years after World War II would have been much more suitable for restoring equilibrium to the consumer market than the massive reduction in solvent public demand produced by price liberalization. A thorough analysis of the debate and of later developments strongly suggests that the architects of this shock measure did not intend it as a therapy for the overall economy, but rather were proposing to create favorable ground for future reform by a drastic reduction in the volume of money. It is not impossible that this was a miscalculation on the part of the originators. William Nordhaus of Yale University, in an extensive analysis carried out before the reform, estimated that the proposed liberalization would result in a price increase of between 30 percent and 150 percent.[44] One should remember that the Soviet Union had already begun gradually to dismantle price controls. Retail prices for luxury goods and consumer durables, and wholesale prices and prices for commercial transactions between enterprises were freed from all administrative controls on November 15, 1990, and January 1, 1991, respectively. But, according to official statistics, retail prices increased more slowly (by 1.3 percent in 1987, 0.6 percent in 1988, 2 percent in 1989, and 4.8 percent in 1990) than the volume of money in circulation over the same period: 15.7 percent, 15.4 percent, 14.5 percent, and 13.4 percent, respectively.

Of course, there was a monetary surplus or, as Nordhaus puts it more precisely, a surplus of the monetary assets that would be necessary to bring output to buyers at official prices.[45] But this was the consequence of the steadily rising budget deficit, which reached 10 percent of the gross national product in the last years of the Soviet era. This deficit was a result of growing subsidies, including those on foods and other mass consumer goods, which made up 24 percent of the total sales volume in 1990. However, incomes also diminished, since some of the republics refused to continue their payments to the central budget on the same scale as before; tax revenues also decreased as a result of, among other things, the antialcohol campaign, and export earnings were halved owing to the decline in prices for petroleum and petroleum products. It is important to understand that an equilibrium could be established only if the growing budget deficit could have been brought under control. So long as property relations remained unchanged, the requisite basis for an incisive decrease in state subsidies continued to be lacking, and declining production and investments offered no possibilities for building up budget proceeds. There would consequently be still less chance that price liberalization would restore economic stability. Given the deep discrepancy between meager supply and growing demand even as prices soared unchecked, it was highly likely that the price rises resulting from liberalization would remain within the 30 to 150 percent limit. By early July 1990, prices had risen by 1024 percent.

But the very worst was that inflation of this order, which otherwise occurs only in wartime, depressed the incomes of a large segment of the population to below the subsistence level, and the gap between supply and demand persisted. Unlike Poland and the other countries of Central Europe, where the rise in prices brought a large range of goods onto the market following privatization of trade and internal currency convertibility—thus meeting the demand of the newly rich—the shelves in Russia and the other successor states remained half empty, and trade shifted gradually to a black economy.

Yet Russia's government would not be deterred from price liberalization, insisted V. Vailukov, vice-president of the Central Bank, even after it was pointed out to him that the population was being plunged into poverty without, however, restoration of the urgently necessary economic and financial stability.[46] Yegor Gaidar's prognosis that the U.S. dollar would be worth eighty rubles in autumn 1990 was monumentally wide of the mark: at the end of November the dollar fetched no less than four hundred rubles. Nor did Boris Yeltsin see his wish fulfilled—namely, that by July 1, 1992, the U.S. dollar would have been driven out of circulation as a secondary currency. On October 16, 1992, *Pravda* commented that because of the unabated devaluation of the ruble, industrial enterprises preferred to convert their savings into foreign currency and to transfer them abroad through commercial banks. Illegal assets accumulated in this way in foreign banks were estimated at $8 billion. Some estimates even placed the figure at $20 to $30 billion. At the same time, negotiations were going on with creditor banks to postpone loan payments of $70 billion for one year.

Runaway Inflation

Several of the successor states of the Soviet Union have been disengaging from the steadily devaluing ruble. The Baltic republics were the first to introduce their own national currencies: the ruble was abolished in Lithuania on October 1, 1992, and business was thenceforth conducted with coupons. Lithuania created the Lithuanian *rublis* in July 1992, at a 1 : 0.75 parity with the Russian ruble. Estonia introduced the crown at a parity of 8 : 2 deutsche marks, though it is not convertible into rubles. The money and credit system, however, was plunged almost immediately into crisis after the monetary reform. In mid-November 1992, the Estonian Central Bank's difficulties in meeting payments forced the bank temporarily to close the three largest commercial banks, the Union Baltic Bank, the North Estonian Bank, and the Tallinn Commercial Bank. Teams of experts were appointed to investigate the causes of the payments crisis. Sun Kalls, head of the Central Bank, avoided the ominous word *bankrupt*, but even so the three banks are still unable to cover customer claims of 300 billion crowns.

The payments situation in Azerbaijan is in a similar crisis. When the liquidity deficit reached four billion rubles in mid-1992, the national currency *manat* was introduced in August of that year at a parity of 1 : 10.

The Ukraine introduced money coupons immediately after the freeing of prices on January 2, 1992, to protect the national market from the depreciating ruble. At the same time, measures were undertaken to introduce the *grivna*, printed in Canada at a cost of $30 million. The Ukraine had strongly resisted a ruble-based currency union at a meeting of CIS heads of state in Bishkek, Kyrgyzia, in mid-October 1994, and withdrew the ruble from circulation as a parallel currency immediately after this meeting.

President Nazarbaev of Kazakhstan, the principal architect of the Bishkek meeting, rightfully attributes the collapse of the ruble zone to the failed price reform. In 1992 he said that price liberalization extended the shock therapy to the entire ruble zone. Instead of accelerating the transition to a functioning market, it destroyed the entire economy. The decline in production reached 15 to 20 percent, the standard of living fell dramatically, and many social strata were vegetating below the minimal subsistence level. Nazarbaev proposed putting an end to the anarchy in the currency and financial systems and in collaboration with other heads of state presented a draft proposal for an "agreement on a unified monetary system and a coordinated money and credit policy for the successor states with the ruble as the unit of payment."

The project proposed establishing monetary relations on two levels: first, for those successor states that accepted the ruble as a clearing unit and a payment unit, and second, for those that had begun to issue their own currencies in addition to the ruble.

The experience of the European Payments Union in the 1950s was taken into account in implementing this measure. According to Nazarbaev, this was a useful practice that was on the verge of being wrecked. The Kazakh *tanga* was put into circulation in Kazakhstan alongside the ruble at a 1 : 100 parity. However, Nazerbaev's proposals have found less and less support. He has been able to count only on the support of Belarus and the new nations of Central Asia. Belarus's former president, Stanislaw Shushkevich, commented that a currency union was an indispensable condition for reviving his country's economic relations with the other successor states.

At a meeting with the board of directors of the Amkodor Corporation, Shushkevich said that his republic was especially interested in strengthening cooperative ventures, because Belarus exported about 80 percent of its total product to the successor states of the former Soviet Union and used the earnings to purchase raw materials and fuels. His country had no foreign exchange holdings, and could only pay with rubles. The partner states, Shushkevich continued, were not fulfilling the terms of the trade and clearing treaties concluded with them, hence his government was considering whether it might not be more expedient to withdraw from the ruble zone. Bogdankevich, head of the Belarusan Central Bank, said that the ruble was no longer used in trade with Lithuania or Ukraine, and that clearing was done in coupons. Referring to this, *Pravda* commented that by pursuing an incorrect economic and financial policy, the Russian government was responsible for the collapse of the ruble zone.[47]

The situation worsened dramatically after the CIS's Bishkek Summit, with the successor states gradually leaving the ruble zone and creating their own national currencies. These currencies, however, were not being used as a clearing unit in commerce between the republics. The Russian government found itself compelled to set up customs barriers on the borders to the former Soviet Republics on November 15, 1992, out of fear that it would be inundated by the rubles that had been withdrawn from circulation in those new states. On November 16, 1992, Vice-President Aleksandr Rutskoi declared that his country had to introduce a new currency because, after the Ukraine and the Baltic countries abolished the ruble, it was useless to try and maintain the ruble zone.

Another imperative of the centrally steered economy was prices that covered costs through the device of adding on a profit, differentiated by the industrial sector. The slackening of labor discipline and the declining productivity of the 1980s upset this alignment; a steadily growing budget deficit was the result.

Of course, price liberalization was an indispensable condition for the transition from a command economy to a free market economy, and from controlled distribution to normal commodity and money relations. But the failure of the price liberalization initiated in January 1992 was predictable from the outset because the premises did not yet exist for a free competitive market in which the rules governing price formation in a market economy could come into play. Not only were the foodstuffs and consumer goods industries in the hands of the state, but almost the entire commercial network was state controlled. By retaining its monopoly, the state prevented competition. There was therefore was no basis for stabilizing prices after an unavoidably drastic rise. The measure was also inhumane because the unbridgeable gap between supply and demand was inevitably a heavy blow to the majority of the population, as could easily have been foreseen. "The liberalization of prices will be tantamount to robbing the population so long as there is no private property," said Aleksandr Rutskoi, Russia's vice-president, in *Pravda* of February 8, 1992. Ten months later Rutskoi declared to the deputies of the People's Congress that the government was in large measure responsible for the miserable economic situation in that it had chosen to adopt Western models and Western aid. Gaidar, the architect of the reforms, reassured the deputies of the People's Congress that the worst was now behind them, that a winter of hunger was not in sight, and that the feared social unrest had not occurred. The prime minister also told the deputies, however, that the amount of money in circulation had increased by 250 percent since that July, and that inflation had spun out of control. The vote of confidence called for at the beginning of the sessions on December 1, 1992, failed to achieve the requisite majority of 522 votes: only 423 voted in favor. But the devastating consequences of the drastic devaluation of the ruble caused by the failed price reform remained. The ruble was disqualified as a common unit of currency in the CIS, thus impairing economic cooperation, and chances for a currency union are minimal.

The Path from Private to State Property and Back

The inferiority of state ownership of the means of production compared with the mixed ownership in Western industrial countries has been demonstrated with tangible statistical indicators over the seventy-four years of Soviet practice. Almost one and a half centuries after the writing of the *Communist Manifesto*, and about seventy years after the Russian Bolsheviks attempted to translate the message of the *Manifesto* into practice, the last leader and the last president of the Soviet Union declared the Soviet system, including its property relations, to be in need of restructuring (perestroika). But perestroika was not to be a success. The principal architect and chief ideologue of perestroika, Aleksandr Yakovlev, former adviser to Gorbachev, wrote, "Private property, the market and democracy are the genetic code of a normal civilization."[48] With this idea, the ex-communist Yakovlev comes rather close to the ideas of Nobel laureate Friedrich von Hayek, who is regarded in the West as an arch-conservative. Hayek wrote that the continued survival of our civilization depends on what is generally called capitalism, or a market economy, but he himself refers to it simply as the extended order of human cooperation.[49] Because it is based upon irrefutable facts, Yakovlev's argument is more convincing than Hayek's. "Private property is unassailable because it is absolutely effective," he writes, and further, "Only private property, which by virtue of its genetic program is oriented toward scarcity on the grounds of scientific and technical progress, can withstand devastation by land, water, and the forests, and all of life." Drawing on the somber indicators of collective farm activities, Yakovlev gives a clear answer to the question raised by Friedrich Engels in the second Russian edition of the *Communist Manifesto* in 1882—namely, whether the Russian *obshchina* (peasant commune), which at the time Engels was writing retained a major portion of the land in the common possession of the peasants, could "make a direct transition into the higher level of communist common property." Yakovlev's answer was: "Will and wisdom are needed in order gradually to abolish the *kolkhozy*, the Bolshevik peasant communes which, though they might still give milk, are nonetheless the hopelessly sick cows of the system." Further, "The collective farms and state farms will die out by themselves, as they are gradually replaced by individual peasants, rationally organized cooperatives, and agrobusinesses."

The Wrong Sequence: First Price Stabilization and the Rest to Follow

Privatization had not even truly begun when, on December 4, 1992, Russia's People's Congress called upon the government on December 4, 1992, to dampen the zeal of privatization. The liberalization of prices early in the year destabilized the economy so much that the deputies gave majority approval to this proposal. Mikhail Gorbachev had put forth a similar proposal in a talk in Buenos Aires on December 2. The director of the Institute for New Economic Structures and Privatization, V. Kulikov, also called attention to the incorrect reform strategy: "The economic reform should have been begun before privatization; instead, liberalization of prices came first."[50]

According to official statistics, 96 percent of the national patrimony of the USSR was in the hands of the state or in its various subdivisions, such as the state trade unions, the collective farms, the production associations, and other public organizations. Russia's property system was similarly structured. Quite a number of far-reaching models of reform were discussed in the last years of the Soviet Union, and even accepted (the Shatalin-Iavlinskii Five Hundred Day Plan, or the two reform models presented by Ryzhkov, head of the government), but not one of them was put into practice. Russia's government, on the other hand, drove through its privatization proposal on June 11, 1992, in Parliament, and the presidential decree on "Organizational measures to transform state enterprises and their associations into shareholding companies" was presented to the public on July 1: state assets totaling 92 billion rubles in value were to be denationalized in 1992, followed by 350 billion rubles in 1993, and assets totaling 500 billion rubles in 1994.

Data on privatizations completed in the first nine months of 1992 showed that as of the end of September 1992, 24,000 firms had been privatized, including 82 percent of communal property, 13 percent of property in the autonomous republics within the Russian Federation, and 5 percent of federal property.[51] Four-fifths of the privatized firms were part of the commercial network, restaurants, coffeehouses, and service firms. The share of private enterprises in total industrial production was no more than 4 percent in early October 1992. The report states that privatization is moving more slowly than envisioned in the government program: only 1,180 enterprises had taken the decision to privatize, and only 535 had carried out this decision. In addition, Yegor Gaidar told the People's Congress in its early December session that the government intended to transform 40,000 enterprises into shareholding companies. However, the capacities to do so are limited.

Privatization is proceeding a bit more intensively in the construction sector: the share of private firms in construction increased from 5 percent to 12 percent in the first nine months of 1992. Denationalization is moving more slowly in transportation: on October 1, 1992, there were 147 private enterprises in the sector, or only 3 percent of the total number. Privatization of commerce has not been proceeding satisfactorily: the government program scheduled the transfer of 50 to 60 percent of commercial shops to private hands, but as of October 1, there were only 10,800 private shops, or 6 percent of the total number, 3,200 private restaurants and coffeehouses (5 percent of the total number), and 6,800 private service firms (5 percent). Decollectivization of agriculture is also proceeding very slowly. As of October 1, there were only 148,700 private firms on an agrarian area of 6.3 million hectares, which amounts to only 4 percent of total agricultural output. The share of privatized housing is also low: 1.2 million, or 4 percent of the total number.

The slow process of denationalization, which has gone hand in hand with a dramatic decline in economic performance and living standards, has given rise to a lively debate on the efficiency of the privatization methods employed (as well as on the possibilities for improving past practices) which differ only slightly from those employed in the reform countries of Central Europe: large firms are being transformed into corporations. To prevent the frequent practice of transferring state assets into the hands of the former ruling nomenklatura, shares in assets are sold at public auctions to interested parties. The idea was to enable employees to obtain a large quantity of shares in privatized assets: employees are allowed to acquire one-fourth of the fixed capital without cost. These are preferred stocks without right of vote; 10 percent of the shares can be obtained at market prices. Employees of firms in need of modernization may obtain 20 percent of the capital shares at nominal prices if a proposal for a feasible modernization project is submitted. If the privatization commission rejects a denationalization proposal of this kind, the firm's assets (but not more than 51 percent of the working capital) can be sold in a free auction.

In early October 1992 a privatization procedure similar to the one employed in former Czechoslovakia was introduced—so-called voucher privatization. A hundred and fifty million coupons each worth 10,000 rubles were offered to every citizen. The total value was to be as high as 45 trillion rubles. As of October 10, 1992, 3.5 million checks for 3.5 billion rubles were given to citizens.

This mode of privatization is also a contentious issue in Czechoslovakia, which Yegor Gaidar visited in April 1992. Ota Sik, the principal architect of the economic reform in the Prague Spring in 1968, called it a "populist maneuver."[52] Ivan Svitak, another prominent politician of the 1968 reform movement and later a professor at the University of California, even calls it the "swindle of the century" because, he argues, public shareholders are unable to influence production.

Hungarian economist Janos Kornai, now a Harvard professor, has voiced his opposition to "giving away" state property, and Stanislav

Shatalin, the author of the Five Hundred Day Plan, called for the acquisition of shares at appropriate prices. Aleksandr Ivanenko, deputy chairman of the Committee for State Property (Goskomimushchestvo), published a vehement defense of voucher privatization.[53] The government's intention is thus to involve every citizen in the privatization process. Anyone holding vouchers has the right to acquire a share in the firm in which he or she works at reduced prices, or in some other firm at market prices. The voucher also gives the holder the right to acquire, sell, or keep a share in an investment fund.

Ivanenko rejects the objection that a ten-thousand-ruble voucher (or fifty dollars, given galloping inflation) has no appreciable value. He argues that it represents a worker's right to acquire a share in his firm at a basic price established many years earlier when the firm was founded. The true value of the privatization checks is ten times greater than the nominal value, he concludes. However, he admits, the infrastructure needed for the circulation of shares—that is, stockmarkets or brokers—is still in an embryonic state; he therefore advises waiting to sell the check, and then to sell not it, but the share acquired with it. The people, however, met this and similar arguments with skepticism. In a survey recently conducted by the University of Chelyabinsk, a highly industrialized region, 55 percent of respondents had no definable opinion, and 50 percent had no idea what to do with the check they had received. A. Shidov, director of the research center Manager (Cheliabinsk), when asked for his opinion, commented: "For the worker, joint stock companies mean capitalism, and he associates capitalism with unemployment." Shidov went on to say that one plant manager refused to attend a school of international management because he "had no time for it," but that he also did not want to delegate his deputy to attend the course because he feared the deputy would fail to return to the firm. Neither firms nor their management are able to adapt to these new conditions. Formerly, 80 percent of the enterprises in the Cheliabinsk industrial region worked for the Ministry of Defense, but now they have been forced to convert to producing pots and pans.[54]

Although the introduction of privatization has proceeded at an extremely moderate pace, it has unsettled state enterprises and aggravated the crisis both in the economy and in supply, yet it has also prompted fundamental debate over the emergent conflicts and the various ways of resolving them. Sergei Glashev has drawn attention to the

risks of undermining the relations that presently exist among cooperative ventures as well as to the danger of deindustrialization, which
would ensue if inappropriate methods of privatization were used.[55] The
majority of state firms function not as individual firms but as components of large, complex units that had developed unified systems of
production and cooperation over the course of decades, says Glashev.
Because these large, complex units are capable of providing for themselves, and because of their very special organizational structure, they
have become pillars of their industrial sectors. If the individual units in
these vast complexes should opt out, this would not only reduce the
economic efficiency of individual firms, but also destabilize whole
industrial complexes.

Russia's Young Democracy and the Conflict
between President and Parliament

The compromise between the legislature and the president during the
seventh session of the People's Congress, where the former forced the
removal of the head of government, Yegor Gaidar, and the president
was allowed to choose his government members as he saw fit, was
preceded by a hard power struggle, which promised no good outcome.
On the last day of the People's Congress, the executive of the police
and special units of the Ministry of Internal Affairs sent troops to
Manezhnyi Square and the Kremlin. The priest Gleb Yakunin, a former dissident imprisoned by the government and later congress deputy,
led two thousand demonstrators in support of the president. The parliamentary president, R. Khasbulatov, attempted to quell the discontent,
but also to no avail. On December 9, he called the president of the
Republic and assured him that Congress was prepared to make far-
reaching concessions, and would even confirm the unpopular Gaidar in
office. Yeltsin assured him in turn that he wanted to work with Congress. Khasbulatov therefore received quite a surprise the next day, on
December 10, when Yeltsin made a declaration castigating the
People's Congress as a hotbed of reaction and enemies of reform. The
following is from the report in *Pravda*[56]:

> What failed in August 1991 [i.e., the putsch of the Band of Eight led by
> Vice-President Genadii Yanaev], people now intend to achieve by un-
> derhanded means. This session of the People's Congress is trying to

make things unbearable for the government and the president, to demor-
alize them. The Supreme Soviet, which has become a stronghold of
conservative and reactionary forces, intended to make amendments to
the constitution that would invest it with powers without having to bear
any responsibility. It intended to hold a session of the Eighth Congress
of People's Deputies in April 1993 in order to put an end to the government, the president, the reforms, and democracy.

He could not forgive himself, Yeltsin continued, that for the sake of
political unity he had entered into unwarranted compromises that had
not been upheld. His hope for consensus was not fulfilled. The response of the people's deputies was dumb silence or aggressive anger.
We, said Yeltsin, are being driven into dangerous waters in which
destabilization and economic chaos could lead to civil war. Cooperation with this Congress was impossible and it was to be regretted that
the president of Parliament, Khasbulatov, had chosen just this course.
Yeltsin then offered the following opinion: "The course of this Congress showed how dangerous dictatorship not only of the executive but
also of the legislative can be."

After this declaration the president left the Assembly of People's
Deputies and called on them to accompany him to the Hall of Facets.
No more than 100 of the 1,041 deputies followed him. He repeated his
reproaches against the "Partiocrats" in this adjacent chamber and then
declared that he was going to form his own party.

Vice-President Aleksandr Rutskoi made it clear immediately which
side he was on: "A small political group that had the president in its
clutches" had maneuvered the president, the parliament, and the government as well, in a false direction, he said. These people, said
Rutskoi, should in future have no influence on the president and must
be called to account for their criminal doings. After the president's
declaration, the country, he said, had plunged from an economic crisis
into a political dead-end. Only reforms were able to bring the country
out of crisis, but not the ones we are implementing now. The vice-president concluded his speech with a dramatic appeal: "If we do not find a
compromise between the Congress and the popularly elected president
today, and I repeat, today, we will be leading Russia to disaster."

Pravda of December 11, 1991, made it clear which political group
Rutskoi meant without naming them. The president's declaration had
been prepared by Congress deputy V. Vavarov together with the head

of the advisory staff, G. Burbulis. The text had been simply thrust under Yeltsin's nose and he had "swallowed it," as he had already done on previous occasions.

Yegor Gaidar distanced himself from the president's declaration: "This was unexpected of the government," he said. The parliamentary president Khasbulatov announced his resignation and said: "For centuries the Kremlin has emanated nothing but evil. The organs of power should abandon it and the Kremlin should be turned into a national museum."

On the same day, the seventh session of the People's Congress launched an appeal to the Russian people in which the president's declaration was described as an attempt to suspend the constitutionally established balance between the legislative and executive powers, and to obstruct the work of the People's Congress. This declaration, inspired by those close to the president, aimed at destabilizing the social, economic, and political situation and concentrating all power in the executive. The deputies appealed to the political parties, social movements, functionaries of the economy, and politicians, as well as all Russian citizens, "not to let themselves be provoked into confrontation and not to respond to the call to take to the streets, but to distance themselves from declarations and activities that discriminated against constitutional bodies of government, and to work for constructive cooperation between the president and the Congress, and between the legislative and the executive branches." "The Congress of People's Deputies," the declaration went on, "would do everything to ensure a normal and healthy functioning of the state and society." Seven hundred and forty deputies approved this document, with only fifty-one opposing.

Confrontation with an uncertain outcome now seemed unavoidable. At the last moment, however, the Constitutional Court succeeded in putting together a compromise. Its chairman, Valerii Zorkin, put out an appeal that stated: "In the present crisis situation, and in view of the risk of Russia's disintegrating as a state, the Constitutional Court calls on the two pillars of power, the legislative and the executive branches, and, in the first instance, the people heading them, to conclude an immediate compromise." The appeal was heeded. Yeltsin accepted the proposal to draw up a list of several candidates for the post of head of government, and to allow a vote on it to be taken. Prime Minister Gaidar received only 400 of the 1,041 possible votes, 237 less than

Iurii Skokov, and 221 votes less than his deputy, Viktor Chernomyrdin. The president accepted the vote of the People's deputies. But he did not appoint Iurii Skokov, whose name appeared at the top of the list, as prime minister because, he said, Skokov could be more useful in the Security Council. Instead, Chernomyrdin was appointed. Laurie Hays, a commentator for the *Wall Street Journal*, conjectured, however, that Yeltsin preferred Chernomyrdin because Skokov was politically more influential and had hitherto been more negative about the reforms than was the designated prime minister.[57]

So ended the seventh session of the People's Congress. Yeltsin traveled to China. Two days later, however, he indicated his readiness for concessions but not for capitulation. When he learned that the list of candidates for the future Council of Ministers might be drawn up without him, he interrupted his state visit and flew back to Moscow—not before signing twenty-four economic agreements, but too soon to take his planned trip into the interior of the country and to confirm the suspicion that, as he declared in his message on arrival, he had wished to learn from China's experience with reform—in creating a "socialist" but not a "capitalist" market, and not allowing political liberalization. Yeltsin also failed, contrary to expectations, to meet with Deng Xiaoping, the architect of China's reform. The president returned ill with a cold, so he was able to retire to his dacha to discuss the team he desired to place under the disliked Viktor Chernomyrdin rather than remain under public scrutiny in the Kremlin. There was no question of the constitution being violated, because the constitution allowed the president to appoint ministers. However, there was a certain contradiction with the clause stipulating that the choice of candidate came under the jurisdiction of the head of government.

But there was no longer any trace of the optimism that had emanated from the president at the beginning of 1992. "You won't believe me," he said in his New Year's address in 1993, "if I say that the situation will be better in three, six, or nine months. A hard year is ahead of us." His minister of labor was more specific: "By the end of 1993 the number of unemployed will be between five and seven million or, in other words, one tenth of the total number of employed."

The president attempted to sweeten this bitter prognosis with a foreign policy surprise. On January 3, 1993, he signed the agreement on the greatest disarmament pact of all time, which had been settled within a record period of only five months: this was the START II agreement, which provided for the destruction of two-thirds of the nuclear arsenal of both sides by the year 2003. This agreement came as a surprise to most of the world, but not so much to the long-suffering Russian people. The experts knew quite well that even one-third of the total nuclear potential was enough to destroy the world several times over. Most people had other concerns. People had once been proud that Russia was, after the United States, the second greatest world power, or so at least it fancied itself. But this agreement between Russia, now degraded to the poorhouse of Eurasia, and the one world superpower left, made no one happy. People who are struggling for their bare existence have little interest in politics. The CPSU, now dissolved, and the country's one single leading political party, used to have 18 million members. The nine hundred-odd parties and groups now in existence could count up altogether no more than 100,000 members.

The Political Landscape

Russia's parliamentary democracy is young, inexperienced, and burdened by a heavy mortgage to a totalitarian past. The People's Congress and the Supreme Soviet were indeed elected freely, but at a time when the multitude of organized political parties was not yet able to exercise much influence. Glasnost had secured pluralism of opinion, and had freed the mass media from the state censor, but the only organized and cohesive political party at that time remained the CPSU, which was still able to secure itself a comfortable majority in parliament. Only 15 percent of parliamentarians had not been members of the Communist Party. In the interim, several new parties were founded. Their representation in parliament is wider than in other parliamentary democracies. The large majority of deputies were members of these new parties and only a few of them openly professed their support of communism of the old stamp, but there were considerable numbers of neo-Bolsheviks. The mass support of the newly founded parties, on the other hand, was very small. The parliamentarians bore responsibility to their faction leaders, although the esprit de corps was rather weak. They bore no responsibility, however, to their still extremely small party membership, nor did they draw any inspiration from that membership in their parliamentary activities.

There was no profiled government party and no cohesive majority from which the government might call for support. As the president of the seventh session of the People's Congress proclaimed, such a party would first have to be created. As before, the president and his government drew support from the so-called "reform coalition" in which the Democratic Party of Russia had played a dominant role. The executive branch could only occasionally call on the support of other parties as well, and above all on the Civic Union. But this did not occur without concessions, and special consideration had to be given to their functionaries when state positions were assigned. The deep economic crisis and the impoverishment of the population, for which the Gaidar government and its shock therapy had been made to bear responsibility, reduced the reform coalition to a size that threatened the government's very existence. The demand for Gaidar's dismissal became increasingly vehement. At one critical moment in the growing confrontation, the president was able to count on no more than one hundred deputies. These followed his call to accompany him to the Hall of Facets after he had declared open battle against the People's Congress. However, 740 deputies voted in favor of the declaration of the People's Congress, passed that same day.

The compromise was reached the next day, with Yegor Gaidar's dismissal and approval of Viktor Chernomyrdin, representing the economic lobby, as the new head of government, and above all with the adjustments in the reform policy he contemplated. All these actions produced a broader coalition for a new version of reform—though of course everything was conditional on approval of the composition of the government together with its modified reform model by several parliamentary factions. The party structure within the parliament, however, was extremely varied. Three political blocs and fourteen factions were represented in the People's Congress and the Supreme Soviet, which it elects. The numerically strongest and politically most defined of them was the Civic Union, which formed the center bloc. Its most influential faction was the Association of Industrialists and Entrepreneurs of Russia, founded by former Communist Party functionary Arkadii Volskii. Volskii draws the mass of his support from the work forces in the state industries, and especially the armaments industry, with an electoral potential of 25 million.

The Civic Union, and above all Arkadii Volskii, played a decisive role in re-forming the government. The union's political council condemned the militant presidential declaration of December 10 in sharp terms: "It destroyed the balance between the legislative and the executive, and made constructive cooperation impossible." Pressure from the Civic Union had been a factor in Chernomyrdin's appointment as Gaidar's vice-deputy earlier in May; it also had a hand in his appointment as prime minister on December 11, 1992. His ideas of how the reform should proceed, which he adumbrated in his first address, were almost identical with those of the Civic Union.

The government's decision to restore price controls on a number of goods, especially on basic foods, was unanimously interpreted as a clear abandonment of Gaidar's reform course. Chernomyrdin's first declaration as prime minister indicated that he was in favor of reforms, but not those his predecessor had begun in early 1992. Chernomyrdin clearly intended to institute only those reforms that would lead quickly to a revival rather than a further decline of the economy. His principal target was heavy industry, which he proposed to reorganize without fostering illusions that property relations in that sphere can be altered in any substantial way. His long-term goal, most commentators assume, was to establish state capitalism with a state-regulated market and social guarantees. His most immediate objective, as he made clear at his press conference of December 15, was to stop the economic decline. For Chernomyrdin the prerequisite for this was the reorganization of large state industries, which he intended to achieve with credits and state subsidies. Chernomyrdin was aware that such an undertaking would inevitably lead to a rise in inflation, which had already reached 2000 percent. Chernomyrdin wished to institute a well-organized wage and insurance system as he gradually restored the deteriorated standard of living, but he did not seek to institute wage controls. He assured journalists that he would do everything to eliminate the U.S. dollar as a second currency by stabilizing the monetary system. There could be no mistaking that Chernomyrdin intended to modify his predecessor's model of privatization. He was in favor of a private sector in the economy, because, he said, without it no economy can function normally. However, he did not want to give it a leading role. Is there a country, he asked rhetorically, where petty buying and selling plays a determining role in production? Certainly not in the developed industrial countries, he said. Commentators agreed that the new head of government intended to abandon the monetarist course of his predecessor, that he would base his future economic policy more on Keynes than on Hayek, and that the main thrust of his policy would not be a restoration of capital or of private enterprise, but rather a mixed system in which the private economy would have a respectable but not a vast space in which to operate.

Chernomyrdin, coming from the state economy lobby, also aimed to represent its interests. His reform model differed little from the one approved by the mid-November Congress of the Association of Industrialists and Entrepreneurs, which rejected the laissez-faire market. The transformation of the economic and political system should, in their opinion, be steered by the state. State intervention should be neither by decree nor by a general vote, however: transition through administrative shock therapy was counterproductive, they said, because it stood in gross contradiction to the laws of a functioning market. In a country as large as Russia, stressed the association's managers, the envisioned social system had to take "national traditions and peculiarities" into account. The market was not an end in itself but a means to rescuing a great and rich country from poverty. The ideas of the association and of the new prime minister on the scope of privatization, as well as on the future of state-owned enterprises, were also identical. State industry had to be protected from the threat of disintegration and needed a thoroughgoing modernization. But developing private enterprise was also one of the priorities of state policy, stated the Congress's declaration. However, in that case stress had to be laid on production, and war had to be declared on speculation with taxpayers' money. The association and Chernomyrdin also agreed that the "social costs of reform" had to be minimized.

The Democratic Party of Russia, led by labor leader Nikolai Travkin, also plays an important role in this center bloc alongside the Association of Industrialists. The third strongest union group in the parliament was Aleksandr Rutskoi's party, Free Russia. Yeltsin charged Rutskoi, vice-president of the republic and an officer in the Afghan war, with the task of dealing with agriculture, but the militant vice-president opposed Yeltsin's reform policy from the very start, claiming it was doing more harm than good to the country, without bringing them any closer to the desired goal.

The center bloc Civic Union was also supported by smaller groups such as the Union of Russia's Workers, the Industrial Union, Sovereignty and Equality, Non-Party Deputies, as well as by the somewhat more influential group *Smena* ("Change"). The latter joined the five factions which, after Yeltsin's confrontational declaration on December 10, 1992, had demanded that the People's Congress charge the state prosecutor with discovering which politicians were giving the president false information in order to undermine the deliberations of the Congress.

The elections of December 12, 1993, changed the political landscape radically. The ultranationalist party of Vladimir Zhirinovskii and neo-Bolsheviks gained majority in the second freely elected parliament.

Aggravating Economic Crisis and the Conflict between the Legislature and the Executive

Although the December about-face came as a surprise, there had been clear signs of a change several months earlier. The president and his government had not expected such devastating consequences from the reform initiated in early 1992. The freeing of prices while there was still a deep discrepancy between supply and demand had exacted higher social costs than in the other reform countries, without giving any signs of the creation of a functioning market in the foreseeable future. Unlike other reform countries, almost the entire trade network remained in state hands. With no competition and declining production, including production of foods, prices had to rise further. Inflation escalated from a creeping to a galloping pace. The rigorous credit policy, with its steadily rising interest rates, and the cutbacks or even complete withdrawal of state subsidies destroyed even fully functioning factories, without reorganizing the inefficient ones or reducing the budget deficit. Profits and state budget revenues declined along with production.

In early June 1992 the economic lobby forced through the first government reshuffle. The Gaidar team, in which, as writer Anatolii Zalutskii commented, "modest economists, elevated to the rank of the prime minister's deputies, were more inclined to enjoy the life of an elite than to carry out reforms,"[58] was enlarged by another three captains of industry, including the experienced economist Viktor Chernomyrdin, Gaidar's successor. A change of leadership at the Central Bank soon followed: Viktor Gerashchenko, the former president of the Soviet Gosbank (state bank), replaced the ineffectual Georgii Matiuchin. It came as no surprise that the new members of the government were former members of the old economic nomenklatura: before his appointment to the Moscow Politburo, Boris Yeltsin had been the feared Party boss of Sverdlovsk, Russia's largest industrial region, while his prime minister, Yegor Gaidar, had made a name for himself as the economics editor of the Communist Party organ *Kommunist*.

The abandonment of a monetarist economic policy began not with the new prime minister's declaration of intent, nor with the state controls introduced in early 1993 on prices for basic foods, but with the controls brought in much earlier on the price of fuels. However, a definitive break in the rigorous finance policy was made in mid-1992 when the newly appointed head of the Central Bank arranged to halve the mutual debt among large factories.

It was not Chernomyrdin who first announced the change of course on December 15, 1992, but the president of the Republic, two weeks before the seventh session of the People's Congress on November 17, 1992, when for the first time Yeltsin described the country's sorry predicament in straightforward terms: "The path that lies behind us could not have been traversed without mistakes," said Yeltsin in his address to the Russian people.[59] "Contrary to the forecasts," he continued, "the decline in production has hit all branches of the economy, even those that produce consumer goods for the population, and not only the strategically important ones." His criticism was therefore directed mainly against the Ministry for the Economy which, he said, shied away from using command methods. The president concluded that "amendments to the reform had become an absolute necessity." This, he emphasized, is being demanded by the president of the Republic who, empowered by parliament, had sensed and understood the limits and the risks. Yeltsin, of course, spoke of the need to come to grips with inflation and to push ahead with privatization. But his main emphasis was less on continuing monetarist reform practices than on using Keynesian instruments to stimulate a waning economy. Enterprises that expanded their production capacities should receive tax benefits. In his opinion, the most important measure was to restore the ruble to its function as the country's sole means of payment, and so to undermine the circulation of the U.S. dollar as a secondary currency. The president therefore demanded that exporting enterprises sell all of their export earnings to the exchange markets. Foreigners would also be permitted to buy foreign exchange. Yeltsin wanted to focus economic policy on providing social security for those who would suffer most. Finally, he was determined to put an end to the omnipresent Mafia, a murky collaboration between some officials and the underground "business people."

Western advisers to the Russian government feared that the December 1992 cabinet reshuffle would slow down reform and push it in a different direction than the former government had pursued. They perhaps did not see that, even without this about-face, under the momentum of economic decline, the reform had already taken a different course from what was originally projected. The powerful economic lobby had concluded that the cure would kill the patient before any of the expected signs of recovery appeared.

Anders Aslund, the Swedish adviser to the Russian government, complained that Gaidar had entered into many compromises of a political and personal nature, and that the changes in the system were going too slowly rather than too fast. Aslund feared that attempts to revive the economy by Keynesian methods would drive up inflation, which was already high.[60] Jeffrey Sachs, Harvard professor and adviser to many governments of the Third World and reform countries in the East, judged Chernomyrdin's appointment as prime minister as "a first-order and potentially catastrophic setback for reforms."[61] His conclusion was that the turnabout was a victory for the military-industrial complex. Russia needed more shops and more kiosks, not more MIGs, submarines, or steel, commented Sachs, and rightly so.

The government's advisers had perhaps not recognized early enough that not only the powerful economic lobby, but also the president had reached the conclusion that such a dramatic and unprecedented transformation of the social system should be entrusted to pragmatists and people with practical economic experience rather than to intellectuals and romantics. But Yeltsin quite certainly knew how Georgii Arbatov, the director of the Institute for the United States and Canada, felt about Gaidar:

> Gaidar is a competent scholar and an honest man. However, I see much that is sectarian in him, a character trait of a fanatic neophyte, who had once been totally immersed in Marxism, but is now sailing in quite contrary waters, namely, extremely conservative Western economic theory, without having the least experience of economic practice.[62]

Yeltsin had also probably come to the conclusion that a change in direction also required a new team in government, or at least some new faces.

But in the West as well, assessments of the most recent developments covered a wide range and included perhaps even more skeptical opinions on the possibilities of reform. David Kotz, professor of economics at the University of Massachusetts, commented that the West should not shed tears over the end of shock therapy. When the radical reforms were started in January 1992, they had many supporters in Russia as well as in the West. A policy, however, must be evaluated in terms of its results, which in this case were dismal. The decline in industrial output in 1992 was three times that of the preceding years. Gaidar's dismissal did not mean the end of democratic reforms, said Kotz, but another six months of shock therapy might have presented a genuine threat to democracy. The inevitable unrest could bring a fascistic group of *National Salvation* to power, destroying any hope of a lasting democracy. However, Kotz thought that Gaidar's replacement would slow the pace of reform, with the government intensifying its interventions, taking greater consideration of the standard of living, and saving what still could be saved of the existing production potential.[63] But increasing numbers of experts had begun to doubt whether the reforms would chalk up any substantial progress, especially in regard to privatization. Ardy Stoutesdijk, director of the Moscow World Bank Mission, commented that privatization is worrisome, and went on to say: "I fear that we will not be able to move very far from the structures that now exist, i.e., from the cumbersome conglomerates, managed by their former directors who will make it difficult for anyone else to gain a foothold in their sphere of operations."[64]

The main problem of the transformation in Russia was that the freeing of prices remained the only serious reform measure. Efforts to remove the commercial network from state hands regularly failed, and privatization of state firms remained at a rudimentary level. The nomenklatura privatization, as it was called, made some progress, but was unlikely to succeed essentially in altering the prevailing property relations or methods of management. But, unlike in the reform countries of Central Europe where private firms joined forces to form influential groups, in Russia a powerful lobby was organized within the Association of Industrialists and Entrepreneurs, and this worked to maintain rather than destroy existing property relations while steadily gaining influence on political developments.

Finally, shock therapy failed even in the country where it was first tried: Poland. Leszek Balcerowicz, its architect and ex-vice-premier, returned to his scholarly pursuits of teaching, writing books, and giving lectures, but the prime ministers who were appointed subsequently had no intention of recalling him to their cabinet. Adam Michnik, once Poland's foremost dissident and now editor-in-chief of *Gazeta Wyborcza*, wrote in his newspaper:

> Under Leszek Balcerowicz, empty shops filled up with goods, the zloty became a convertible currency, and opportunity began to knock for entrepreneurs. But the other side of the coin was price rises, a fall in real income, unemployment, or fear for one's job, and speculation.[65]

In Russia, on the other hand, shock therapy caused a tremendous shock indeed, without creating conditions for a cure within the foreseeable future. Gaidar himself proclaimed that Russia's gravest crisis lay ahead, not behind it. How far could an economy decline, he asked, without creating the fear that what lay ahead was not recovery at all but total collapse?

In the first year of reform, 1992, the gross social product decreased by 20.2 percent. The most important industrial branch, oil production, declined the most, to 394 million tons (in 1991 it was 462 million tons). Technically obsolete equipment and growing problems with extraction, compounded by a lack of money to modernize, indicate that Russia might very well lose its position as the number-one oil producer in the world next to Saudi Arabia.

Food supplies are becoming a torment for a large portion of the population, whereas "Japanese audio and video technology, American jeans, French cosmetics, and German kitchen appliances" can be bought on every street corner in Moscow.[66] Australian butter, Finnish salami, or meat from Denmark are once again to be found in food shops, but for the normal consumer the high price of these goods from the "market economy paradise" puts them well out of reach.

The Soviet Union left a debt of $66 billion, comprising $50 billion owed to Western governments and $16 billion owed to commercial banks. Russia showed some indications that it might be willing to assume the Ukraine's share of the debt, amounting to 16 percent, on condition that the Ukraine would be willing to give up Soviet assets. In the meantime, Russia contracted new debts of $18 billion in 1992. Payment of the debt service on this loan was made even more difficult by the fact that Russian firms prefer to deposit their export earnings in foreign bank accounts rather than invest them at home. The illegal flight of capital from Russia was estimated in Washington financial circles at over $10 billion in 1992 alone.

The West has a great interest in pursuing reform in Russia both as a precondition for restoring the dwindling economy as well as because a further decline will have unforeseeable consequences for social peace and political developments. But this does not mean that the change in direction should be rejected totally. Jeffrey Sachs's pessimistic view that reform in Russia "is like jumping out of an airplane before the parachute has been sewn. But they have no choice, the plane is already crashing,"[67] need not prove true. The view of David Kotz, quoted earlier, seems more plausible; his advice to Bill Clinton that he should make unambiguously clear his determination to support any democratic alternative to shock therapy also seems well taken.

Renewed Conflict between the President and the
Parliament at the Eighth Meeting of the People's Congress

The Seventh Congress ended in compromise. The president was forced to dismiss Yegor Gaidar, but in return he was able to form a government of his choice. The compromise did not last long. No remedy could be found for the deepening economic crisis, for the runaway inflation and the huge budget deficit. Yeltsin insisted on maintaining his own authority in order to be able to continue transforming the system, but the deputies who supported him (about 20 percent of the total) were unable to prevent the People's Congress from nullifying one presidential power after another. Yeltsin responded on March 20, 1993, by announcing a presidential decree that was to last until the referendum set for April 25. The People's Congress reacted by placing Yeltsin's removal from power on the agenda: 617 deputies voted in favor of this measure—70 votes short of the two-thirds majority needed to pass this proposal.

The West unambiguously supported the president in this bitter and steadily escalating power struggle. His toughest opponent, the chairman of the parliament, Ruslan Khasbulatov, claimed that without this support Yeltsin would never have dared to make the bold television appeal of March 20, 1993.

The support the West deigned to offer the crisis-ridden country (aid of $1.6 billion promised in Vancouver, British Columbia, on April 4) was, however, a negligible amount compared with Russia's debt of about $70 billion. It is much too little to bring the country out of the deepest crisis in its history. This opinion was even shared within Russia's government: as Vice-Premier Boris Fedorov was appealing for further aid at the G–7 preliminary talks in Hong Kong, his colleague in the government, Vladimir Shumeiko, was saying that Russia did not need aid, but rather a form of mutually advantageous cooperation. To get out of this political and economic crisis, however, Russia needs clear power relations and a clear and feasible model for reform.

Presidential Dissolution of the Parliament

Boris Yeltsin describes the dramatic developments of September and October 1993 in his book, *The Struggle for Russia*.[68] He came to the conclusion that cooperation with the parliament elected under the *ancien régime* would not be possible. He therefore decided to dissolve parliament and to order new elections. His main problem was the resistance of the deputies, led by the parliament chairman Ruslan Khasbulatov and the vice-president, Aleksandr Rutskoi. The White House, a riverbank site of the Russian Parliament, surrounded by the police and the parapolice (OMON) "seemed to be a terrible threat to the stability of Moscow," according to Yeltsin.[69]

Yeltsin assured himself of the support of the elite military divisions. On September 12, he invited the ministers of defense, security, and foreign affairs to a government dacha and informed them of his decision to dissolve the parliament. The ministers supported his decision, as did Prime Minister Chernomyrdin upon his return from the visit to the United States.

The decree disbanding the parliament went into effect on September 22. All the leaders of the CIS countries, assembled in Moscow on September 24, supported Yeltsin's decision. But the situation became more complex as the embattled parliament sought and received support from the Constitutional Court. A blockade of the White House was drawn up. On a black day in Russia's new history, Sunday, October 3, 1993, Yeltsin realized that the "country was truly hanging by a thread, . . . that storming of the White House could not be avoided."[70] After the White House was stormed, Rutskoi and Khasbulatov landed in Lefortovo prison. But it was no victory for Yeltsin.

The elections of December 12, 1993, have not alleviated Russia's political situation. The ultranationalist party of Vladimir Zhirinovski received a plurality of votes (23 percent of the total), followed by the neo-Bolshevist party. The Russian Choice Party, formed by Yegor Gaidar to support the president, received no more than 9 percent of the votes. In February 1994, the newly elected parliament released Rutskoi, Khasbulatov, and at least a dozen other prominent deputies of the dissolved legislature from prison. The president denounced the amnesty, but conceded the need for "social peace." This peace, however, will depend on the prospects of increasing the standard of living. Otherwise, Yeltsin recognizes, the country will live "from one coup to another."[71]

The prospects of improving the economic situation, however, are very limited. In the reorganized government of Victor Chernomyrdin, the radical reformers such as Yegor Gaidar and Boris Fedorov are no longer present. But the former chief of the Soviet National Bank, Viktor Gerashchenko, strongly criticized for his antireform monetary and credit practices, remains in office as the head of Russia's central bank. Like so many others, Chernomyrdin knows the problem, but has no solutions. This situation will persist.

Chapter 3

Developments in the Non-Russian Republics

The Ukraine after the Declaration of Independence

The dissolution of the Soviet Union was brought about not by the hard-won independence of the Baltic republics, nor by Russia's declaration of sovereignty June 12, 1990. Rather, it was the referendum of December 1, 1991, in the Ukraine, in which 90.3 percent of the population voted for independence, that dealt the death blow to an empire that had lasted for three hundred years. The Ukraine, with its 51.7 million inhabitants and a share of 16 percent in the Soviet gross national product, was the second largest union republic. Three weeks after this fateful vote, the Soviet Union ceased to exist. The sovereign Ukraine, Europe's second largest state, with its tremendous sources of raw materials, a highly skilled population, an army of 700,000 soldiers and officers, larger than both the French and British armies combined, and the third largest nuclear potential in the world, now ranks among the most powerful states of Europe.

The euphoria experienced by the Ukrainian people when their dream of independence was realized knew no bounds. Kievan Rus had existed at the origins of the great Russian empire, but the Ukraine had been independent for only very short periods in its thousand years of history, and dependent on its neighbors, Russia and Poland, for hundreds of years. Euphoria, however, was followed by an abrupt sober-

102

ing. The legacy an independent Ukraine inherited from the disintegrating Soviet empire was too great to bear. The difficulties attendant on the transition to a pluralistic democracy and competitive market economy were far greater than in the other successor states. The Ukrainian economy was an organic and important part of the military-industrial complex of the collapsed Soviet Union. The Ukraine produced one-quarter of the coal and almost half of the iron ore, 35 percent of ferrous metals and 41 percent of rolled steel, and one-quarter of the electronic calculators and automation equipment produced in the Soviet Union. Providing 46 percent of agricultural output, it was the USSR's bread basket. It was, however, just as dependent on the other fourteen union republics, especially on the oil and gas delivered from Russia. Even if the economic crisis had reduced its annual need for oil from 60 million tons to 45 million tons, it was still able to cover only 4.5 million tons of this reduced need with its own production. Furthermore, its need for natural gas was 115 million cubic meters overall, yet it produced only 23 million cubic meters itself. At the end of February 1993, Russia totally stopped deliveries of natural gas to the Ukraine because the Ukraine had not paid for one single cubic meter of gas since January 1. It owed a debt of 165 billion rubles to the Russian concern Gasprom.

Because Russia's own production had declined, it could not have satisfied the Ukraine's demand in any case. At the summit meeting of January 15, 1993, the Ukrainian delegation negotiated some additional deliveries but even these covered only half the country's need. An agreement with Iran to supply one-fifth of the Ukraine's gas and one-tenth of its oil requirements was predicated on the construction of the requisite pipelines.

In its study published in August 1991 on the capacities of the fifteen former union republics, the Deutsche Bank ranked the Ukraine in first place with 83 out of 100 possible points, while Russia fell into third place with 72 points. But the economic effectiveness of this country, rich in natural resources and fertile soil, is less than modest. The U.S. Census Bureau's *World Almanac* estimates the per-capita gross social product for 1989 at 2,173 rubles. If the Soviet ruble had been pegged at parity with the U.S. dollar at that time, this performance would be roughly at one-fourth the level of a moderately developed industrial country. In the subsequent three years, this efficiency declined at least one-third further. The assumption by politicians in the free Ukraine that if the country were extricated from its former economic ties it could make the leap into Europe on its own was wrong. The Ukraine was fully immersed in the chaos resulting from the reform process initiated by Russia in early 1992.

The skyrocketing of prices after they were freed on January 2, 1992, had devastating consequences on the Ukraine's economy and the population's quality of life. Volodymir Lanovoi, the deputy prime minister, warned in his momentous speech on Ukrainian radio on March 27, 1992, that the Ukraine was unprepared for processing its own resources independently because it was only a part of the economy of another state, and that state was controlled by Moscow. The parliament approved the report of the president's council, the Duma—abolished in a governmental about-face in October 1992—which was prepared to isolate itself from the other successor states, reduce imports from the ruble zone, reorganize foreign trade in the other geographic directions, and call for customs and taxes to be levied on "all activities along the Republic's borders." The other successor states responded to these isolationist measures with similar devices. Revenues into the state budget did not increase, however, and the economic situation deteriorated even further.

Ukraine's opposition to the Commonwealth (CIS), created with the cooperation of its president, brought more disadvantages than advantages; initially the Commonwealth had been considered a tripartite alliance of the Slavic states; only later did it become a community of all the former successor states (with the exception of the Baltic region, Georgia, and later also Azerbaijan). The proposal by Russia and Kazakhstan to establish a currency union with a common central bank as the key pillar of an economic community foundered on Ukraine's resistance. Leonid Kravchuk knew that with its tremendous resources and human potential, the Ukraine was the only successor state that could act as a counterweight to Russia, and also that Russia needed the Ukraine if the community of successor states were ever to function. But he feared that Russia might also restore its traditional dominance over the territory of the disintegrated Soviet Union. The Ukraine was one of the three community members, of a total of ten, that did not sign the CIS statutes adopted at the summit meeting in Minsk on January 22, 1993. All attempts to find a replacement for the collapsed Soviet Union foundered. Poland was the first country to recognize the independence of the Ukraine after the historical referendum of

December 1, 1991. The former chief ideologue of the Communist Party, Leonid Kravchuk, who was elected president of the Republic with an impressive vote of 61 percent, hoped to make an official visit to Poland one month after the election. But the visit did not come about because a governmental crisis erupted in Poland. However, a delegation of the Foreign Ministry and the Office for National Security of Poland traveled to Kiev, but the Ukraine was not prepared for such talks, reported Poland's expert Arkadiusz Prusinowski.[1] Although Vice-Minister Milewski announced that Poland was interested in a close alliance with the Ukraine, an interest which the Ukraine reciprocated, the only result was a vacuous agreement that committed neither of the negotiating parties to anything at all. The short-lived government under Jan Olszewski, wrote Prusinowski, dreamed of an anti-Russian bloc that would include the contiguous states from the Baltic to the Black Sea. Lithuania's president, Vitaustas Landsbergis, later deposed, also dreamed of a regional anti-Russian alliance to include Lithuania, Belarus, and the Ukraine.[2]

The Ukrainian defense minister, Konstantin Morozov, a former major-general in the Soviet Army, traveled several times to Poland in the first half of 1992 on this mission. This was at a time when the conflict over the Crimea and the Black Sea fleet was coming to a head. President Leonid Kravchuk ultimately also visited Warsaw. But in the meantime Poland began to have other ideas: good relations with Russia had priority (negotiations on the withdrawal of Russian troops were in progress). Other than an empty agreement on good relations between the two neighboring countries and a few supplementary documents, nothing came about. Polish president Lech Walesa's trip to Moscow scheduled for the same time was certainly not a pure coincidence. The former prime minister, Hanna Suchocka, was scheduled to travel to Kiev: first in October, then in November, and then later still in December 1992. But she did not come until mid-January 1993. The newspaper *Vecherny Kiev* dubbed her "Lady Shock." The Polish newspaper *Polityka* commented that she lectured politicians like a schoolteacher and that the Madame Premier appeared to enjoy this role.[3] Kravchuk's visit to Washington in May 1992 was not a spectacular success. George Bush received his official counterpart with due honors, and the Ukraine was granted most favored nation status (the Ukrainian diaspora of about one million people would be playing a certain role in the upcoming elections), but there was no talk of the urgently needed economic aid. While the Ukrainian president's visit was classed as a "working visit" in diplomatic protocol, the visit of Russia's president in June 1992 was given the status of "a state visit." Yet President Clinton promised special aid five days after taking office: $170 million to finance the scrapping of the nuclear potential.

A Change of Course

The Ukraine's economy was in free fall. Russia had been waging undeclared war against the Ukraine for a year, declared the prime minister. The economy had to pay for this battle between politicians. The withdrawal from the ruble zone was effected through the introduction of coupons. The coupons were scheduled to be replaced in early 1993 by the *grivna*, to be printed in Canada and conceived as a convertible currency. The growing economic difficulties, however, prevented the grivna's establishment, and runaway inflation, for the most part home-made, continued unchecked. The rate of inflation reached the perilous level of 2,200 percent, average for the year 1992, as in Russia, though the budget deficit (44 percent of the gross national product) was four times as great as Russia's. By the end of 1993, inflation reached 4,400 percent. Finally, the internal debt rose to 1.5 trillion rubles. Freed from rigorous state control, enterprises began to forge their relations with CIS clients to their own benefit, rather than to the benefit of the independent Ukraine, and without the smallest consideration for the unwritten code of fairness among businessmen. Since prices in Russia were lower and interest rates in the Ukraine were higher, businesses deposited billions of rubles in Russian banks. And they were doing this at the same time as Russian banks were leaving their export earnings from foreign trade in Western banks. Russia's Central bank uncovered a total of 530 billion rubles accumulated in this way. But, instead of returning this money to the Ukraine, the bank appropriated it as part of the Ukraine's debt service. Through great effort, and negotiating skills, a delegation sent to Moscow was able to agree on the return of 240 billion rubles and another 40 billion rubles in the form of a stabilization fund to enable the exchange of coupons for rubles. Vice-Premier Yulii Ioffe, responsible for the fuel and energy sector, also returned to Kiev from Moscow with results. He had managed to negotiate additional oil deliveries that enabled resumption of public transportation and reactivation of ambulance services in the large cities. But the conflict about the oil supplies has not yet been resolved.

President Kravchuk stressed more than once that the Ukraine could not afford shock therapy and that a national Ukrainian reform model had to be worked out that would be in harmony with the country's traditions and its people's mentality. During the first year of independence, however, the Ukraine did nothing different than was done in Russia, or, put more emphatically, did nothing to keep itself out of the vortex of Gaidar's reforms. Prices rose and the economy shrank to a level that made supplies to the population impossible. In late September 1992, the president, the former chief ideologue of the Communist Party, decided to dismiss Vitalii Fokin, the former chief planner of the Soviet Ukraine, from his position as head of government. Leonid Danilovich Kuchma, general director of "Iushmash," one of the largest machinery concerns, specializing in the manufacture of nuclear missiles, was named the new prime minister. Kuchma had good contacts with Russia's captains of industry and the industrial managers of the other successor republics. Three and a half months earlier than Russia, Kuchma got rid of the dilettante romantics in his government and replaced them with experienced specialists in economics and culture.

Kravchuk, whose mentality had been shaped more by ideology than by economics, and who had never concealed his dislike of the corporate directors in parliament and in government, was forced to dismiss all the deputies of former Prime Minister Fokin. But he did so on condition that the democratic opposition would also accept responsibility for future government policy. Ihor Yukhnovski was appointed the First Deputy of the new government team. Yukhnovski was an opposition politician and professor of physics with great political ambitions who had made a name for himself with far-reaching economic analyses. Viktor Pynzenyk, a theoretical economist from Lviv, was also from the opposition. He had been the first person to present an alternative program to Fokin's economic policy, but in the meantime had been transformed from a passionate proponent of a free-market economy to an advocate of a state-regulated economy. The deputy prime minister, Vasilii Evtukhov, responsible for the economy, became the gray eminence in Kuchma's government, so it was claimed in informed circles. Like Arkadii Volskii in Russia, Evtukhov serves simultaneously as chairman of the Ukrainian Association of Industrialists and Entrepreneurs. Evtukhov and Volskii have also maintained good contacts with one another. Evtukhov belonged to the group New Ukraine, comprised of liberals from the former Communist Party, just as Arkadii Volskii belonged to the Civic Union, a kind of partnership organization of employers and workers established by top functionaries of the former Soviet economic apparatus.

These affinities are worth noting insofar as they indicate unambiguously the common basis shared by the Kuchma government's economic program and the modified reform model proclaimed three and a half months later by Chernomyrdin in Russia. Kuchma described his program with the slogan "How to throw off our chains without shock therapy."[4]

The head of the government of "national unity" was given special powers to bring the economy, now in a "state of emergency," out of the gravest crisis of the postwar period. By May 1, 1993, the most important measures to breathe life into the economy were put into force with a government decree. The president's request to attach his signature to government decrees was refused. The parliament accepted the proposal of its chairman, Ivan Plyushch, who had once been imprisoned by the regime, that economic decrees should be solely the affair of the government and the parliament: the government approved economic decrees, which the parliament could veto within ten days. The president thus lost his influence over the economy and henceforth concentrated mainly on foreign policy, in which the problems of the atomic arsenal were to play a chief role.

The new head of government mentioned three critical points to which his cabinet was to devote its attention. The first was stopping economic decline, primarily by reviving economic relations with Russia; in important matters the government would in the first instance rely on the counsels of enterprise work collectives. An effort would also be made to establish a balance between state intervention and market forces at all levels of economic management. In an interview with *Pravda* on November 17, 1992, the prime minister went into greater detail about his future economic policy. Early on, he said, we went to the food shops with money in our purses, and returned with a basket of food. Now we take a basket of money and return home with the food in our purses. Actually, however, Kuchma continued, people neither have a basket of money nor return home with empty or half-empty purses. We have gone to the dogs, said the prime minister, for we have destroyed economic relations that took decades or even centuries to build with Russia and other republics of the former Soviet Union. We have robbed millions of people of their vested interest in the results of their own labors, and we have totally stifled the initiative of the worker, the peasant, the engineer, and even the plant manager. We must pull ourselves out of this vicious circle as quickly as possible, but without shock therapy. That is not our way, stressed the former economic manager Leonid Kuchma, and on this point, he added, there was unanimous agreement in the government. The idea of being a special victim, or being in a hopeless position, was alien to every minister in his cabinet. Each and every one was aware of the responsibility he had taken upon himself. Above all, the peace that prevailed in the Ukraine had to be maintained. The shadow economy, whose devastating proportions and destabilizing effect he had only now properly understood, had to be brought to an end. The government's powers and the means at its disposal, however, were extremely limited. He considered it his achievement that the Duma, the consultative body that had stood between the president and the prime minister, had definitely been set aside. The executive could henceforth speak in one language, no longer forced to beg for approval from the Supreme Soviet on every trivial detail.

The head of government attached great worth to support from the work force for his policies. He recalled the words of the prime minister of the short-lived Ukrainian National Republic (1918–20), V. Vinnichenko, to explain his own fall and the fall of the republic: it failed, he said, because its policies went against the interests of millions of workers and peasants, because this policy was geared to "those who were chosen, but not to those who had been called." To disregard this maxim, said Kuchma, was not only dangerous, it was a crime against the Ukrainian people.

But Kuchma's view of how property relations should develop was most important because, as the new president since 1994, it was he who would decide on economic policy. He said that one must not disregard prevailing realities: the predominant forms of property in the Ukraine were state property and cooperative property. The advantages of this must be used rationally and should not be destroyed. Most especially, in a period in which the economy had to be stabilized, state controls had to be used, shareholding companies had to be created, small and medium-sized enterprises had to be successively privatized, and state benefits had to be offered to farmers. The whole of past experience should be constructively applied. It was at the very least unfair if the state, which had no means of providing farmers with fertilizer or equipment or of purchasing or storing their farm products, nonetheless encouraged them to establish private farms. In his opinion, the planning principle should not only be maintained throughout a transitional period while the preconditions for a sustainable economy were being created, but they should be maintained permanently. But the prime minister now had a different understanding of what was meant by planning: not directives handed down from above on what everyone had to do, but forecasts and corrective state interventions. Other developed countries did the same thing, said Kuchma, but instead of modernizing the economic mechanism, we destroyed it. The Ukraine had a tremendous scientific and technical potential, and, if it had been used intelligently, and if we had availed ourselves of the experience of Germany, the United States, China, or Hungary (Kuchma named these countries in this order), the Ukraine would now be able to take its place in the world economy as a partner among equals, rather than as a third-rate country that has to wait humbly for alms in the antechambers of the mighty.

Kuchma attached no special value to economic aid, for who wants to be saddled with this sort of competition? He also failed to understand those who complained that Western aid was too modest. The world protected only those who were worthy, strong, showed ingenuity, and were cooperative. The Ukraine had resources enough, he said, to make its way into the world community on its own strength. The sooner the broken bridges to Russia, the other successor states, and the former CMEA members could be repaired, the quicker this leap into the world community would come about.

A detailed description of the working program of the former Ukrainian prime minister is warranted here because it coincided almost point for point with the program of Viktor Chernomyrdin, the representative of the economic lobby in Russia, as well as with the projects of other republics of the former Soviet Union. Although it is still too early to discuss possible developments in specific areas, it may reasonably be assumed that after the turnabout in both the Ukraine and Russia, the contours of future economic reform policy for the successor states of the dissolved Soviet empire assumed a definitive shape, at least for the period immediately ensuing. Emphasis would be placed on breathing life into the economy, not so much through radical reform of existing property relations as through wide-ranging support of the state economy. Small and medium-sized enterprises, more in the trade and service sector than in heavy industry, would be privatized, but very slowly. Value would be attached to modernization of the existing economic infrastructure rather than to establishing a market infrastructure.

Power Relations in the Independent Ukraine

Although there was a multitude of small groups, the political life in the independent republic was dominated by two major groups, Rukh and the New Ukraine. Unlike in the other successor states, where the newly established parties had no mass basis for support and where many splinter groups of the communist movement still set the pace, Rukh, founded in September 1989 as an umbrella organization for various opposition groups and originally called the Ukrainian People's Movement for Perestroika, experienced a steady growth in its membership. By early 1993 it had 700,000 registered members and no fewer sympathizers. It was particularly influential in the Western Ukraine. In Lvov the Rukh leader Viacheslav Chernovil, who spent twelve years in exile and prisons because of "bourgeois nationalist activities," was elected mayor. The Rukh movement had a substantial influence on the results of the referendum of December 1, 1991. In the large cities of the Western Ukraine, Lviv, Ternopil, or Ivano-Frankivsk, 96 to 98 percent voted for independence; votes for independence reached 85 percent in the port city of Odessa, 76.8 percent in the industrial region of the Don basin, but only 54 percent on the Crimean peninsula. Before the referendum it had called for came about, Rukh had struggled for the republic's complete independence, and for a restoration of national symbols. After its principal objective was achieved, it began to fight to create a "bourgeois society," for comprehensive democratization, and for a functioning market economy. Chernovil certainly appreciated that the Ukraine was one of the most stable countries to have come out of the former USSR. "But in reality," he stressed at the Ukraine Dialogue Congress on August 27, 1992, in Alpach, Austria, "we still have no state. The Ukraine still has no borders, no customs activities, especially in the east and the north. But above all we still have no real internal or economic policy. At every level of government administration the members of the former communist nomenklatura are still at work." As for the objectives of the movement, he said, efforts must be made to counter both "the establishment of an authoritarian regime, and rule by presidential representatives in the various regions of the republic . . . by building and strengthening a multiparty system."

Certain things have changed in the independent Ukraine: a pragmatic and purposeful government took over the reins of government in order to revitalize the declining economy. The president's powers were curbed, state borders were drawn, and customs tariffs were introduced. The amended reform model, "caution with regard to any privatization which does not bring any immediate benefit to the economy, and more state intervention in economic matters," certainly did not concur with the wide-ranging objectives of the Rukh movement, which was probably even less happy about closer economic ties with Russia. It seemed certain, however, that the part of the Rukh movement that has always supported any government measures that would contribute toward consolidating the young state would also support some of the constructive measures of Kuchma's government.

Rukh also changed many of its ideas after state independence was achieved. Ultranationalist slogans no longer dominated its activities. Adrian Karatnycky, who is currently assistant to the president of the AFL-CIO and well acquainted with all aspects of the party scenario in the Ukraine, points out the notion of Ukrainian patriotism that this movement developed, and which, because it is not clearly defined in ethnic terms, could also be acceptable to the minorities in the republic. It was his belief that the democratic movements in the Western Ukraine had shed their original nationalist colors, putting pragmatism in the forefront, and had thus prevented the republic from being divided up into hostile camps doing battle with one another.[5]

The nationalist movement, however, was still strong enough, especially in the Western Ukraine. The Ultras coalesced around the Ukrainian National Assembly (UNA), a coalition of several nationalist movements, as well as in the Ukrainian National Self Defense (UNSO), which created a storm-trooper-like Nazi SA. Their membership was very small, only 15,000, but very militant. They had no deputies in parliament since they boycotted the elections. The nationalists had no consistent political program, and their short-term goal was to have the Ukraine secede from the CIS. This objective was partially reached on January 22, 1993, when the president refused to sign the CIS statutes. Their long-term objective was to come to power in order to ensure "strength, order, and prosperity." They struggled against Russia and Romania, against the "Americanization of the Ukraine through Coca-Cola culture," and for a greater Ukraine including Moldova, the Crimea, and the southeastern part of Poland. The ultranationalist slogans were broadly supported by the self-appointed patriarch of the Ukrainian Autokephalic Orthodox Church, Filaret. The Ultras were strongest in Lviv, Kharkiv, and Kiev. In Crimea they organized a paramilitary "demonstration of strength" with the slogan "Crimea for the Ukraine." Their newspapers, *Voice of the People* and *Nationalist*, were obtainable at any kiosk. The New Ukraine movement began to play a growing role in the political life of the Ukraine: after October 1992 it was also partly responsible for government policy. Its leading functionaries held important ministerial posts in Kuchma's cabinet. Unlike Rukh, whose main base was in the anticommunist movement active in the Western Ukraine, the New Ukraine was based on activists of the "Democratic Platform" which split off from the now dissolved Communist Party in mid-1990. New Ukraine was mainly active in the southeast of the republic, in the industrial centers, which have a large Russian population. The Russian minority—11 million citizens—play an important role in the Eastern Ukraine, especially because the Ukrainians living there had moved closer to the Russian culture and language over the course of centuries. In the most recent survey, 90 percent of the population declared itself bilingual, but only 40 percent said that they had a perfect mastery of Ukrainian. The Russians have their own newspapers, with a large and steadily growing readership, and they are often more informative and more critical than other newspapers in the Ukraine. The country's sad situation is depicted in extremely somber tones. One of the January editions of the newspaper *Kievskie vedomosti* carried the following:

> Citizens nowadays consume less meat than prisoners in Tsarist exile did. The consumption by families of the lowest income level, 91.7 grams daily, is less and that of families of middle incomes only 21.4 grams greater than a prisoner's ration in 1913.

The New Ukraine considered itself as representing the interests of the economy. Its declared objective was to build a powerful middle class in order to establish a Western style bourgeois society. Two principal divergent currents were brought under one organizational hat: advocates of a totally free market economy of the classic laissez-faire type, and social democrats in favor of regulatory state interventions into economic affairs. Volodymir Filenko, the leader of the New Ukraine, did not consider this dichotomy an obstacle to normal cooperation between the two groupings. No essential contradictions would emerge, he said, until privatization had progressed far enough to produce a clear social differentiation among the population. Volodymir Pilipchuk, chairman of the Parliamentary Committee for Economic Reforms, called the decisions of Russia's then-government to liberalize foreign trade and to liberalize prices a catastrophic mistake. The one, he said, led to uncontrolled and excessive exports of raw materials, and the other produced hyperinflation. The Ukraine did not wish to continue down this path. First, conditions must be created for a functioning market and then, before state industries could be sold off, they must be made viable. Finally, wages and salaries must be brought under state control. There was also no good reason, said Pilipchuk, to force the breakup of healthy collective farms and state farms; those that were operating at a loss should be split up and leased out on trial for five years; privatization should concentrate on commerce and housing, while privatization of heavy industry should wait. Above all, however, the Ukraine should leave the ruble zone. The rather modest reform program of Kuchma and Pilipchuk was rejected with a vote of 267 to 6 and prices for milk and sugar were brought under state control by the decision of January 25, 1993. The parliament had unequivocally yielded to the wishes of the old economic nomenklatura to slow down the course of economic reform and to strengthen state intervention.

The Ukraine's reform policy seemed to coincide with that of Russia's economic lobby. But one controversy remained, namely, the attitude toward the CIS. Russia wanted to step up its activities. But the Ukraine did not sign the statutes presented at the summit meeting in Minsk on January 22, 1993. This was in deference to Rukh, which held the view that the CIS was the "first step to a restoration of the Russian empire." Ivan Plyushch, the parliamentary chairman, did not think that the Ukraine was condemning itself to isolation by refusing to sign the CIS statutes. Plyushch, the second most important person in the Ukrainian political hierarchy, said that what the Ukraine wanted was not membership in a community but "privileged relations" with Russia. Ukrainian politicians saw no contradiction between remaining outside CIS institutions and the desire for more intensive economic relations with Russia and the other successor states. They wanted to repair damaged economic relations, but did not seek a replacement for the dissolved Soviet Union with Russia as the dominant power.

The deepening economic crisis destabilized the political landscape in Ukraine. In 1992, the gross domestic product declined by 16 percent, in 1993 by 20 percent. The industrial production fell from January to April 1994 by 39 percent compared with the same period in 1993. The money supply rose in 1992 by 2,500 percent, in 1993 by 9,000 percent. The national currency, once equal to the ruble, is now worth 5 percent of the ruble.

For the radical reformers, the economic policy of Prime Minister Kuchma, who was elected on July 10, 1994, as president of the Republic, was too conservative; for the apparat it was too radical.

The April 1994 elections brought a majority for the ex-communists. Leonid Kravchuk brought in the former chief of government of the Soviet Ukraine, Vitaly Masol, as prime minister, as the only candidate who would be approved by the parliament. The radical reformers and the nationalists abstained from this "lurch back to the communist system," as articulated by their spokesman.

As the result of the elections in July 1994, Leonid Kuchma replaced Kravchuk as the president of Ukraine. The support of the West, the $4 billion dollars in aid approved a day before the elections in the Naples G–7 meeting, came too late for Kravchuk. In particular, the eastern part of Ukraine, with its 11 million Russians, endorsed Kuchma, the advocate of rapprochement to Russia. Throughout the election campaign, Kuchma stressed that the free trade agreement with Russia is a prerequisite for Ukraine's well-being.

Problems of Transition in the Other Successor States

The first years after the collapse of the Soviet Union presented the world public with a graphic panorama of the general and specific problems attendant on the transition to a system of independent states, pluralist democracy, and a competitive market economy in each of the successor republics. With the exception of the Baltic states, none or almost none of them had any experience of independence or of democratic traditions. This was as true of Belarus as of the Central Asian republics. The independence of other republics such as Georgia or Armenia went back to a distant past, a time when Russia's original state, Kievan Rus, was still in nascent form. Almost all were forced from the tsarist autocracy into the Soviet CP dictatorship. The Soviet years, above all, had a permanent influence on the economy, culture, and life-style that would be hard to eradicate.

For the newly freed republics, the steps toward emancipation were made all the more difficult because their own economies, totally under state control, had been an integral part of the overall Soviet system, steered by the same administrative methods of a planned economy, and part of the overall Soviet division of labor. None of these republics had experience with foreign trade or credit transactions. The whole of foreign trade had been governed by the laws of the Soviet Union's foreign trade and currency monopoly. Nuclear arsenals existed in Kazakhstan and the Ukraine, in addition to Russia, yet the entire military command had been concentrated in Moscow. While the Ukraine and Belarus were cofounders of the United Nations, neither ever had its own foreign policy. The first experiences showed that the foreign policy and foreign trade of the individual successor countries could quickly assume forms of their own. The economies, on the other hand, would continue to be interdependent for a long time, especially the economies of those republics that had been most deeply integrated into the Soviet Union's division of labor—in the first instance, Belarus and the Central Asian republics.

Belarus's economic ties were mostly with Russia. Its per-capita income in 1989 of $2,497 for its 10.2 million inhabitants was 6 percent above the Soviet average. Lacking raw materials and fuels, though with developed yet technologically backward food, clothing, and machinery industries, Belarus was totally dependent on imports from the other republics. To be able to cover these imports, 69.6 percent of the social product was exported to the other republics (these figures are for 1989), but only 6 percent was exported abroad. The Deutsche Bank AG rated Belarus's economic strength at 55 out of 100 possible points, industrial strength at 8 points, but for degree of self-sufficiency rated it with only 5 of a possible 10 points.

Even after its declaration of independence Belarus continued to rely heavily on Russia. It signed the CIS statutes. There are no trade restrictions between Russia and Belarus, and the independent republic was drawn into price liberalization because it maintained a common currency with Russia. But no progress was made in denationalizing the economy. Democratic parties were allowed, but the country's leadership remained in the hands of the old nomenklatura. The Popular Front Movement "Adradshene" (Renaissance) was permitted to resume its activities, as were the autonomous labor organizations and independent trade unions. Stanislau Shushkevich as then-president, and Vecheslav Kevich as prime minister, set the pace. Both belonged to the ruling establishment of the former Soviet republic. The parliament is more conservative than the government. On January 25, 1993, a decision was taken with a majority of 177 to 8 to tighten state price controls. Fifty-three percent of retail prices were to be brought under state control. Belarus was unlikely to develop a reform model substantially different from Russia's.

Popular discontent brought victory to an outsider in the Belarus presidential elections on July 10, 1994. Aleksander Lukashenko, a former state farm manager, largely unknown before the election, garnered more than 80 percent of the vote. He promised to dismiss everyone connected with the former government and to launch a ruthless anticorruption campaign. He also stressed his desire to link Belarus more closely with Russia in matters both economic and political.

The Central Asian Republics

The five Central Asian republics have common borders, a common religion in Islam, similar cultures, and intimately intertwined economies. Their leading strata display common features as well. However, since their liberation from Soviet hegemony, the points wherein they differ have become more conspicuous. Formerly there had been no particular conflicts between these republics; now armed clashes are no rare occurrence. Nevertheless they have acted together in certain situations, particularly over the joint decision taken on December 16, 1991, in Ashabad, Turkmenistan, to join the post-Soviet community, initially conceived as a federation of the three Slavic states (i.e., without the Central Asian republics). But when their leaders met in April 1992 in Bishkek, Kyrgyzia, to agree on a unified approach within the CIS, they discovered little basis for common decision-making, according to Martha Brill Olcott. Under the Soviet regime they vied only for the favor of the center. Now they are competing over a much larger geographical area in which each republic strives to assert its distinctiveness as a state.[6]

They endeavored to establish contacts with their neighboring Islamic states, who were in turn eager to fill the vacuum left after the demise of the Soviet Union. Iran had tried to gain a foothold even before that. Iranian Foreign Minister Velaiyati, together with other officials and parliamentarians, visited these countries, established economic contacts, gave copies of the Koran as gifts, donated money for building new mosques, and were not in the least deterred by the fact that only Azerbaijan shared Iran's Shiite faith. The Uzbeks as well as the Tadzhiks and Turkmen regard themselves as Sunnites, and Kazakhstan, with 48 percent Kazakhs and 38 percent Russians, is more atheistic than Islamic.

In 1990, when Turkmenistan was still a part of the Soviet Union, it concluded nine bilateral agreements with Iran in order to tap its vast oil and gas deposits and to build a pipeline. Sapamurad Niasov, a former Communist Party official elected president of the Republic, was the first of the Central Asian leaders to attempt to extricate his republic from under the protective shield of the central power. The resourceful president arranged to have the revenues from oil and gas imports (10 percent of total Soviet exports of fuels were from Turkmenistan) deposited in New York banks.

Turkmenistan was indeed one of the richest republics in energy resources, although in overall economic efficiency it was one of the poorest of the former Soviet republics, with a per-capita income of $1,548—35 percent lower than the Soviet average. Yet Turkmenistan was reluctant to sign the CIS charter on January 22, 1993 (unlike Kazakhstan, which had been the first of the Central Asian republics to embark upon the path to independence). The president perhaps thought there would be better opportunities outside the community rather than inside it.

The principal architect of the post-Soviet community was Kazakhstan's president Narsultan Nazarbaev (whose name translated means the "Happy Sultan"). Nazarbaev, former member of the CPSU Politburo, was one of the coauthors of all the CIS founding documents, including its charter, which he signed together with the six other successor states at the last summit meeting in Minsk, capital of Belarus. Kazakhstan was territorially the second largest republic of the Soviet Union after Russia, with an area of 2,717,300 square kilometers. Yet, despite its vast natural resources, its per-capita income was $2,138, which was 10 percent lower than the Soviet average. Its population is 16.5 million, but only 8.1 million are Kazakhs. Its enormous oil and gas deposits have hardly been explored, much less tapped. Oil production is currently at 27 million tons; 17 million are consumed within the country. None of the agreements concluded with foreign firms has yet been implemented, however. Greatest hopes were placed in the joint venture, established with Chevron during the Soviet period, to tap and exploit jointly the rich Tengiz oil fields. The agreement was finally signed in early April 1993 and the establishment of the Tengiz–Chevron Oil Corporation was publicized as the project of the century. In ten years this joint venture would, it was said, make Kazakhstan one of the world's leading oil exporters. The yearly output of the Tengiz and Korovlev oil fields was projected to increase from a current 3.25 million tons to 35 million tons in the year 2010. To achieve this goal, investments of about $20 billion are necessary, of which $1.5 billion would be activated in the first three years. The joint venture was contracted for forty years. Kazakhstan receives 80.4 percent of the proceeds, Chevron the remaining 19.6 percent. The first production figures were expected in October 1993. The republic itself does not have the necessary funds. The disintegration of cooperative ties with the former Soviet republics caused enormous damage. Skilled workers left the construction sites because of salary delays of four months or more. Given such conditions, it was of no help at all, wrote the press, that the Tengiz project benefited from the highest priority, that it received requisite materials from other projects, or that the company Tengizneftegas had been given tax exemptions in order to finance the project.

The centralized economy is still alive in Kazakhstan. Privatization of the economy, and indeed of everyday life, is still in embryo. "Nomenklatura privatization" was granted some latitude in the form of joint stock companies in which the management, unchanged, not only retained its decision-making powers, but also was able to acquire a portion of a company's assets. Democratization of political and social life is making little progress. The parliament is made up of representatives of the trade unions and other public organizations. "An overhasty transition from a totalitarian to a democratic regime would be dangerous," commented Nazarbaev during his official visit to Austria in early February 1993, invoking as a reminder the bitter experiences of the great French Revolution of 1789. A gradual transition ensures not only social peace but also "smooth economic growth" in Kazakhstan, added the president, stressing the importance of cooperation within the CIS: "We need a common economic area just as much as we need common defense and the ruble zone."

Uzbekistan, the republic with the third largest population after Russia and the Ukraine, signed the CIS statutes on January 22, 1993. More densely populated but also poorer than the other successor states, Uzbekistan has 20 million people living on a territory of 447,400 square kilometers, including 69 percent Uzbeks, 11 percent Russians, 12 percent Tadzhiks and Kazakhs, and other minor nationalities. One million people live on a territory of 165,000 square kilometers in the Autonomous Republic of Karakalpakia, which is a part of the Uzbek state. The greatest resource of this republic, the Aral Sea, with its huge fishing industry and its lucrative caviar production, turned into the republic's greatest headache. The sea level has fallen by thirteen meters and the entire sea has been polluted with pesticides. The fishing industry collapsed. Cotton, covering 80 percent of the country's arable land as a single crop, was an economic disaster, dubbed the "white death." The per-capita income of $1,253 in 1989 was no more than 53 percent of the Soviet average.

Formerly, this republic was portrayed as a model for a direct transition from feudalism to socialism, bypassing capitalism. It has become the model for the insurmountable difficulties attending the transition to a functioning market economy under persistent feudal conditions. Democracy may have been a popular concept among the upper strata, but among the masses it was an alien term. Islam Karimov, former president of the Supreme Soviet and elected president of the Republic in 1990, proclaimed himself an adherent of the Turkish model, which in his opinion combined economic liberalism with paternal severity in the administration of the state. The opposition is represented in parliament and also participates in the government, but the Birlik (Unity) group, once powerful, was systematically decimated.

The Poorest of the Asian Successor States

Kyrgyzia and Tajikistan are the poorest of the Soviet republics, with per-capita incomes of $1,697 and $1,151, respectively. The study by the Deutsche Bank puts Kyrgizia and Tajikistan in the last two places, with 24 and 18 of a possible 100 points, respectively. But the degree of industrialization was given a rating of 2 out of a possible 10 points, while market economy mentality, fitness for Europe, and homogeneity of the population were rated at only 1 out of a possible 10 points. These two republics provide good examples of a dragging process of transformation, lingering conflicts between the defeated but still strong communists and an expanding Islam supported by neighboring states, an authoritarian style of government by those in power who are now acting under other banners, and finally, armed conflict, which flared up in full force after long years of suppression.

When Bertrand Russell visited the new Soviet Union in 1920, he commented that communism bore certain similarities to Islam. This impression now seems more correct than official Soviet theory, according to which the Communist Party succeeded in making the leap from feudalism to socialism in the Central Asian republics without the intermediate stage of capitalism. Indeed, Tajikistan's first freely elected president, a former Communist Party head and apparatchik of the old style, Rakhman Nabiev, took his oath of office on the Koran. But, above all, the power structures and methods of rule scarcely changed from one regime to another. The leap from feudalism to socialism failed, and the more recent attempt at a "suicide leap" from totalitarianism to democracy or from a command economy to a market economy seems just as perilous. The methods of rule employed by the new (read old) rulers seem closer to those of feudal lords than to those of a pluralist democracy in the modern age.

In Kyrgizia, the hierarchical power structures of the Communist Party regime were dismantled. Regional and district Party secretaries were replaced by the *akimos* (chairmen), appointed by the highest bodies of the state, to which they were solely answerable. True, the former local councils were certainly no bastions of democracy, but the top politicians, elected by the councils, had to account for their actions if they wished to be reelected. These councils were dismantled, however, without being replaced by other democratic bodies. The *akimos* are subject to control from above but not from below.

The transition to market mechanisms, "farmerization," and "privatization" are in the air in Kyrgyzia as well. However, the manner in which privatization has been pursued is more reminiscent of the old methods of nationalization than what would normally amount to handing over state property to qualified enterprise managers or to joint stock companies, in which the former economic nomenklatura would have a say in proportion to their share in ownership. The state farms and collective farms were dissolved from literally one day to the next without conditions created to establish functioning private farms.

A *Pravda* reporter commented on the *akim* of the Narynskin region: K. Ashiraliev was quoted as saying that certain farmers had received fifty to sixty sheep, while others had received a tractor or some other farm machinery that no one knew how to operate.[7] The expropriated state enterprises did not fare much better. Whole factories were snatched up at ridiculous prices by the powerful who had ties with the state apparatus. In one example, the administrator of the Osh region summoned the bank people to him and told them to remit 120 million rubles to an enterprise he was promoting. The bank managers complied without the least resistance. Cars were transferred from state to private ownership at almost no cost because it was officially claimed they had already been 95 percent amortized, even when they bore the year 1991 as date of manufacture.

Given such chaos, it was no wonder that the Republic's economy was headed for collapse. Askar Akaev, who rose from president of the Academy of Sciences to president of the Republic, stated that 1993 would be even worse than 1992. Even if the less pessimistic forecasts should fail to be confirmed, commented the president, the Republic would still have to use 80 percent of total revenues in the current year to pay for fuel. The extremely unfavorable terms of trade seemed to be the principal concern of the Kyrgyz government: prices for imported goods rose fifty- to one-hundred-fold, while prices on exported raw materials rose only fifteen to twenty-fold, and, moreover, with traditional economic ties destroyed, even grain imports had to be paid for in hard currency. But the steadily dwindling accessibility to agrarian products was also a cause of concern. Purchases of meat and milk decreased by 50 percent in 1992, reported Prime Minister T. Chrenyshev to the Republic's local leaders. In face of continuing economic decline, the government of Kyrgyzia decided to follow in the footsteps of the governments of Russia and the Ukraine and reactivate state mechanisms rather than push forward with reforms. But, above all, on January 28, 1993, Kyrgyzia introduced its own currency, the *som*, and thereby withdrew from the ruble zone. As reported by the Kyrgyzia news agency, *Ria*, this measure had become necessary in light of the decisions of other successor states to introduce national currencies as well.

The worst development of all, however, transpired in early 1993, when the civil war raging in neighboring Tajikistan spilled over into Kyrgyzia. Tajik irregulars crossed into Kyrgyz territory, killing and taking hostages. In January a curfew was imposed on the Osh region to staunch the flow of refugees from Tajikistan. Tajikistan and Uzbekistan had raised claims to the Kyrgyzian portion of the fertile Fergan valley. Kyrgyzia, in turn, claimed the Pamir region, which is partially populated by Kyrgyz people in the Berg-Badagashan in eastern Tajikistan.

A bloody civil war raged in Tajikistan between ex-communists wearing their new political colors and the Moslems, between the "rich" north and the impoverished south, and among the powerful clans and *seils*, in their struggles for power and influence within the newly emerging power structures. The democratic opposition wanted to bring about a radical change as quickly as possible, but not a few of them dreamed of a return to the *ancien régime*. After all, many had attained status and title in the Soviet system and, having risen socially, they wanted to hang on to their privileges. They identified with the communist system and still do.

Former President and former Party head R. Nabiev, feeling his power threatened, fled to the north. Since the power elite had traditionally come from that part of the country, he felt more secure among his own kind. There he gathered forces for a new power struggle against his principal rival, Hezbi Nazati, the Party of Islam. But the clan and the *seil* meant much more in this part of the Republic than mere party membership. "A cousin will never do another cousin wrong even when the one is a mullah and the other is a Communist Party secretary," goes the saying. In the Soviet era, former Moslem feudal lords became Party secretaries and state officials. Now, in times of change, the same people who had in the interim become Party dignitaries wanted to hang on to their power. They encountered strong resistance, however, from the democratic movement as well as from the Islamic movement, both of which were growing in strength. The rich north, occasionally referred to as Tajikistan's Switzerland, found an ally in the southern part of the country in the impoverished Kuliab region, where communist leaders who also came from the north still had the last say. Also, the terrorist groups from whom Rakhman Nabiev derived his support had their mass bases in the south.

The cotton-producing Kurgan-Taube region, which borders on Afghanistan, also had aspirations to power. From there, it is easy to cross the border in order to establish political contacts for there are Tajiks living over the border as well. Furthermore, the winners of the Afghan war, Ahmed Massud and Afghanistan's President Burhannudin Rabbani, were Tajiks.

The greatest opponent of the current regime, the khasi (the highest Islam dignitary) Khaji Akhbar Turadshanzadeh, a parliamentary deputy, professed his commitment to a lay state, but considered a law that prohibited the clergy from engaging in politics utter nonsense. He also wanted the Koran and Sharia to have a greater influence on legislation. But radical circles in the Islamic movement went even further. For them a lay state was their minimal program as long as their ultimate objective of establishing a divine Islamic state remained unattainable.

When Rakhman Nabiev returned from the north and Dushanbe in mid-November 1992, tens of thousands of supporters of the Islamic opposition fled to Afghanistan or to Iran. Many of them drowned in the Amur-Daria river, which forms the border. There is no lack of fuel for conflict in Tajikistan. According to some commentators, the "assistance" of certain bordering countries had played a role in provoking armed conflict.

The unending succession of governments made fundamental reform difficult, if not impossible. The economy and standard of living declined steadily. In early December 1992, the OECD gave Tajikistan and the four other Central Asian republics the status of developing countries. Although this classification does not automatically mean aid from the developed industrial nations or international organizations, it is nonetheless an important precursory stage and secures more favorable conditions. But aid can only be a contribution toward self-help.

The Other Successor States

Armenia, Georgia, and Moldova also aspired to the OECD status of developing countries, and with good reason: their economic situation was no better, fundamental reform lagged, and there was no end to the armed conflict in sight. The war between Armenia and Azerbaijan over Nagornyi-Karabakh (which declared itself independent on September 2, 1991) had successive periods of relative calm only to flare up again, but the war between Georgia and the autonomous province of Abkhazia shows some signs of abating.

Hardly a month had passed after the situation in southern Osetia had been pacified before armed conflict broke out with Abkhazia, an autonomous republic within Georgia situated on the Black Sea. Abkhazia declared itself independent on July 23, 1992, but only three weeks later, on August 14, the Georgian Army invaded and took back Abkhazia's capital city, Sukhumi, the most important harbor on the Black Sea. The president, Vladislav Ardsinba, and his government fled to the fortress Gandaty. Georgia's justification for the invasion was that only 17 percent of Abkhazia's half-million inhabitants are Abkhazians; 48 percent are Georgians and the rest are national minorities. Eight percent of Georgia's total population (5.5 million) are Russians. The Abkhazians do not accept this argument inasmuch as Stalin's henchman, Lavrentii Beria, who was himself a Georgian, is claimed to have settled vast numbers of Georgians here in the 1930s in order to alter the demographic structure of the region.

The fires of conflict were further fanned when volunteers from the Confederation of Caucasian Organizations, which was part of Russia, came to Abkhazia's aid. The conflict escalated into a confrontation between Moscow and Tbilisi when on September 25, 1992, the Russian parliament directed an ultimatum to Georgia to "cease acts of war immediately and withdraw the Georgian Army from Abkhazia." Tbilisi's immediate reply was: "This is a blatant and unprecedented interference in the internal affairs of a sovereign state." The conflict became even more critical when Boris Yeltsin announced that Moscow would take appropriate measures if the safety of Russians should come under threat in conflict areas. The following reply was made to Yeltsin on October 3, 1992: "Georgia is confiscating all Russian Army equipment still on Georgian territory." At this point Georgia's former president Zviad Ghamsakhurdia stepped in. After being overthrown, Ghamsakhurdia fled to the neighboring Autonomous Chechen Republic where he was killed at the end of 1993. Edvard Shevardnadze (who had in the meantime returned to the Orthodox faith) was elected president of Georgia on October 11, 1992, with a vote of 95 percent on the strength, so it was claimed, of his campaign slogan, "Not to yield an inch, even if it means that every single Georgian will die on the battlefield."

Systemic reforms were easier for Georgia, since even during the period of Soviet power it was one of the most commercialized regions of the Soviet Union. Georgia's private merchants supplied the large cities with fruit and flowers from the south. Ninety-five percent of the former Soviet Union's tea came from Georgia. More than a third of Georgian light industry was in private hands at the end of 1992, and a national currency, the *Lavi*, had been introduced. During a visit to Germany in late September 1992, the Georgian prime minister, Tengis Signa, announced that with the aid of foreign capital, the country hoped to tap and exploit the republic's natural resources, including manganese, zinc, lead, and copper. The joint venturers, however, could own no land.

Armenia's economy has been much more severely affected by the lingering armed conflict over Nagornyi-Karabakh than Azerbaijan's, even though the per capita income in Armenia was $2,320 (for a population of 3.5 million), while in Azerbaijan it was only $1,221. Armenia's developed machine-tool industry and chemical industry were hard hit owing to persistent breakdowns in the power supply. The oil pipeline leading to Armenia through Georgia was cut by Azerbaijan, while Turkey stopped supplying power at the request of Azerbaijan, following an agreement made in December 1992. There had been thoughts of resuming the operation of the nuclear power station twenty-eight kilometers from the capital Eerevan (operations had been halted after the 1989 earthquake), but this idea was abandoned on the advice of the IAEA, the U.N. atomic energy authorities. In the winter of 1992–93, the population had power for no more than two to three hours daily, and often even less. Discontent among the population continued to grow. On February 6, 1993, a hundred thousand people demonstrated before the presidential palace of the once so popular Ter-Petrosian.

The three Baltic republics are faring no better, although they had ranked first, second, and third economically in the former Soviet Union, with per-capita incomes of $3,182 in Estonia (1.5 million inhabitants), $2,989 in Latvia (2.7 million inhabitants), and $2,758 in Lithuania (3.7 million inhabitants). With their degree of industrialization, proximity to Europe, above-average market mentality, and best developed infrastructure, these three successor states scored 10 out of 10 possible points on the ranking list and accordingly were considered to have the best chances of reaching Western Europe's level of development. But events proved otherwise. As their economic ties to the other successor states collapsed, the Baltic republics were forced to pay for their raw materials and fuels with foreign currency. But exports were not large enough to procure the amount of foreign currency needed. Estonia's largest commercial banks were forced to declare insolvency after only a short time in operation.

The systemic changes that were introduced progressed erratically. At the beginning of 1993, privatization of former state industries was only 26 percent in Lithuania, 10 percent in Estonia, and only 7 percent in Latvia.[8] Lithuania's positive experiences were discussed at a symposium organized by the Mare Balticum society in late December 1992 at Vilnius. According to the experts, Lithuania owed its success with privatization to the following circumstances: unlike Estonia and Latvia, Lithuania was not plagued by strife over who were favored and who were disfavored citizens. Everyone who had been a citizen of the republic on the critical day of November 3, 1989, had the right to acquire private property. Thus, the legal basis had been prepared, in February 1991, a year and a half earlier than in the neighboring republics. In 1992, investment checks were distributed. How much a person received depended on age: citizens eighteen years old received a check for 1,000 rubles, those between the ages of eighteen and twenty-five 3,000 rubles, those between twenty-five and thirty-five received 4,000 rubles, while citizens over the age of thirty-five received a check for 5,000 rubles. The check was deposited in investment accounts in the bank. The account balance could be increased to 120,000 rubles through savings and insurance deposits. Because of the ruble's devaluation, these investment funds were indexed. The value was eight times higher in late 1992 than at the time of issue. Administration of privatization was assumed by central and regional committees. Anything valued at less than one million rubles was sold at auction, and anything of higher value was converted into joint stock corporations, with 30 percent of the shares offered to the employees.

But 1992 was not a good year even for newly privatized firms. The reason was the same throughout the economy: delivery delays, broken economic relations with the other successor states, and a lack of foreign exchange.

Economic activity and the standard of living of the population fell dramatically in Lithuania as well as in the other two Baltic republics. Vitautas Landsbergis, the Sajudis leader, paid a high political price for this: in the parliamentary elections of October 1992, he received no more than 19 percent of the votes. The big winner was the former head of the Communist Party, Algirdas Brazauskas, who not only gained a convincing majority in parliament, but was elected president of the Republic on February 14, 1993, with 60 percent of the votes. Lithuania's citizens bestowed their trust on this politician not because he had remained a communist, but because even before Lithuania had declared independence and while he was still chairman of the reform wing of the Lithuanian Communist Party, he had broken with Moscow, and had thus dealt the death blow to the at-that-time-still-omnipotent, CPSU.

Concluding Comment

The systemic reforms in Russia, the Ukraine, and in some of the former successor states have suffered severe setbacks. An unmistakable shift of course was evident. State enterprises were removed from state control but conditions had not been created for market mechanisms to work. The hope that price liberalization would create the preconditions for a functioning market economy was not realized. The consequence was continued economic decline, hyperinflation, and a precipitous fall in the standard of living. One reason for the decline was the disrupted economic relations among the former Soviet republics. In 1991, Russia delivered 117.1 million tons of oil, 92.2 million cubic meters of natural gas, 14.9 million tons of coal, 7.3 million tons of ferrous metals, 14.9 million cubic meters of wood, and 1.725 million tons of fertilizers to the other republics. After the collapse of the Soviet Union, these figures had fallen to 61.7 million tons of oil, 85.2 million meters of natural gas, 12.3 million tons of coal, 3.5 million tons of ferrous metals, 5.3 million cubic meters wood, and 996,000 tons of fertilizers. Bilateral deliveries among the former republics declined even more drastically.

Instead of stepping up the reforms, the republics decided to reactivate the levers of state control. The consequences cannot yet be discerned. The political consequences, however, are evident. In the Russian elections of December 1993, the gains went to the nationalists and the ex-communists. In April 1994, the ex-communists gained an absolute majority in Ukraine. Similar results obtained in Lithuania and Belarus. The conflicts among the former Soviet republics are aggravating. Here are only some of them: between Armenia and Azerbaijan about Nagornyi-Karabakh; between Georgia and Abkhazia as well as Osetia; and between Russia and Ukraine about the oil deliveries, the Crimean peninsula, and the Black Sea fleet.

The following opinion of CIA Director R. James Woolsey has grounds: "We have slain a large [Soviet] dragon, but now must live in a jungle filled with a bewildering variety of poisonous snakes, and in many ways the dragon was easier to keep track of."[9] Instead of a single Soviet nuclear force, the West is now confronted with three. Ukraine has sent only 180 of its 1,800 nuclear warheads for dismantlement to Russia. The amount demanded from the West by former Ukrainian president Kravchuk for the nuclear disarmament and for shutdown of Chernobyl was $7 billion.

The peace of the world will depend on the peaceful relations among the order Soviet republics. The imperial tendencies of Russia, long an empire, are strong. The Western world will do well to support the common Eastern market, but strive against the imperialist longings that are certain to present themselves in Russia.

Chapter 4

The Velvet Revolution and the Thorny Path Thereafter

Autumn 1989 in the nations of Central and Eastern Europe is occasionally compared with Spring 1848. The pace of revolutionary change was just as breathtaking. Then as now, 140 years later, seemingly solid governments, institutions, and citadels of power were swept away like so many houses of cards. The February revolution of 1848 brought down the bourgeois king Louis Philippe of France, and established a republic, albeit short-lived; the March revolution in Vienna brought down Metternich's government; and the uprisings of March 13 and 18 in Berlin led to the fall of the arch-conservatives and the establishment of a liberal government. The pan-German parliament, the National Assembly, convened in Frankfurt, marking the first, if failed, attempt to unite all the German principalities.

The 1989 events of Central and Eastern Europe unfolded at the same dizzying pace. On June 4, Poland's government concluded a historical compromise at a round table with the Solidarity movement. The first consequence was a partial relinquishing of power (65 percent of the parliament's seats were allotted to the United Polish Workers' Party) and Mazowiecki's government, the first postcommunist government of Eastern Europe. Then came the mass flight of East Germans in Summer 1989 after the Iron Curtain was dismantled by the regime of the Hungarian reformist Communist Party and, as an immediate consequence, Honecker's regime in the GDR collapsed. Next came the Velvet Revolution in Czechoslovakia, the bloody transfer of power in Romania, the solemn reburial and rehabilitation of the leader of the crushed October 1956 rebellion, Imre Nagy, and free elections in Hungary; the fall of the Zhivkov regime in Bulgaria, and the unification of the GDR with the Federal Republic of Germany, with the currency union of July 1, 1990. The fall of the Berlin Wall, the most brutal and yet at the same time the weakest link in the chain of barriers securing Soviet interests in Eastern and Central Europe, was symbolic of this entire process.

As in 1848, the worldwide constellations of political power disintegrated: then it was the *Holy Alliance*, established by the Vienna Congress of 1815; in 1989, it was the balance of power and its crucial component, the outer ring of the Soviet empire, created in Yalta and Potsdam.

The late twentieth century, however, is not the same as the mid-nineteenth century: the rebels of Berlin, Paris, Vienna, Budapest, or Prague were struggling against an absolute monarchy for a constitutional monarchy, for freedom of press and assembly, for more rights for a nascent bourgeoisie, against the socage, and for more rights for the peasants. In 1989 the peoples of Central and Eastern Europe were struggling against an inefficient social system imposed upon them from without, and against its one pillar of support—Soviet hegemony. Yet there is a deep-lying connection between the Spring of 1848 and the Autumn of 1989. The 1848 revolution was a bourgeois revolution par excellence: its objectives were in the first instance more freedoms for the bourgeoisie in order to pave the way for a free market economy, even though Marx and Engels were already by that time writing the *Communist Manifesto* at the behest of the Congress of the Communist League held in November 1847. It was one of the paradoxes of history, however, that the uncompromisingly anticapitalist tone of the *Manifesto* and its long-term objective of a proletarian revolution were taken more seriously in feudal Russia, which was untouched by the 1848 revolution, than in the developed industrial countries of the West. Marx and Engels had another vision of the future: in their preface to the second edition of the first translation of the *Manifesto* (done by Mikhail Bakunin in the early 1860s), they wrote that a capitalist development in Russia might be seen as a curiosity in the West. A few years earlier Marx had written a letter to the Russian revolutionary Vera Zasulich that Russia would probably experience a unique development of its own rather than a traditional capitalist development, which was confined exclusively to the West. But it was in Russia, where the proletariat made up no more than 5 percent of the total population, that Lenin split the socialist movement in 1903, created the Bolshevik Party of professional revolutionaries, and embarked upon the path of anti-capitalist revolution. Later on, Stalin would carry that revolution into Central and Eastern Europe on the bayonets of his victorious soldiers. The same economic model was adopted in the industrially developed countries, such as Czechoslovakia and East Germany, as in the backward monarchies of Albania and Bulgaria, and the semifeudal agrarian countries of Poland and Hungary. Although Czechoslovakia's population was 14 million in 1938, its share of the world's industrial potential was 1.28 percent, while Poland, with a population of 32 million, had a share of only 0.82 percent. Industry accounted for 58 percent of the total product in Czechoslovakia (1938), but only 34 percent in Hungary and Bulgaria.

Czechoslovakia accounted for 1.6 percent of world exports, but Poland only 0.9 percent, Hungary and Romania 0.7 percent each, and Bulgaria 0.3 percent. The share of manufactured goods in Czechoslovakia's total trade was 72 percent, while this figure was only 10 percent for Poland, 4 percent for Bulgaria, and 1 percent for Romania. These discrepancies were even more patent when per-capita national incomes were compared. In Czechoslovakia, per-capita income was 56 percent less than in the five major regions of the later GDR, and this figure was 67 percent for Poland and Hungary, 77 percent for Bulgaria, and 80 percent for Romania.

Absorption into the military-industrial complex of the former Soviet Union had grave consequences for all the countries. The chronic, exorbitantly costly confrontation of the Soviet superpower with the far better economically developed West tied down their most valuable resources.

Immediately after Clement Gottwald's coup d'état in Czechoslovakia in February 1948, which brought that country into the Soviet social system, the indicators for the five-year plan were corrected and reoriented to heavy industry and armaments. A structural model based on iron and steel was imposed everywhere, independent of the traditional production system or of the work force's qualifications. This model, with the enormous capital investments it required, had devastating consequences for the consumer goods industries and for the population's quality of life. Their abnormally high level of participation in arming the Soviet superpower, as well as "fraternal assistance"—that is, the establishment of military bases throughout the world—which the Soviets forced upon the countries in their sphere of influence, stretched their capabilities to the extreme.

But the circumstance most fateful for further developments was that so little consideration was given to the ever more frequent protests from workers and intellectuals, and that the reforms hesitatingly embarked upon in the mid-1950s were never carried through to completion. They were either brought to a halt by respective governments, or stifled from without by brute force. The workers' uprising in East Germany on June 17, 1953, the October uprising in Hungary in 1956, and the Prague Spring of August 1968 were all put down by Soviet tanks.

The "third way," envisaged by some reformers today, was already tried by some former regimes, albeit without success, with the more radical of them blocked by the Soviet Union. The reform attempts remained unfinished probably because of the nomenklatura's justified fear that true liberalization would shake the entire regime to its foundations.

In Bulgaria as well, which owed more to the Soviet system than the other Eastern countries, such half-hearted reforms were the rule. Khrushchev's model of transferring economic powers to the territorial authorities was introduced there in 1958, but was abandoned after his fall, just as it was in the Soviet Union. On December 4, 1965, the guidelines of the "new system of planning and managing the economy" were published, but nothing in these reforms pointed to any fundamental change in the existing steering system. The published thesis of the Politburo spoke of "improved coordination," better steering by central planning, but not of shifting decision-making powers to the microlevel. The newly formed industrial associations were given broader powers, especially in regard to capital investments. Radical reforms were introduced in the banking system. The economic management thought this reform was not radical enough, but the party leadership thought it was too dangerous.

At the July 1968 meeting of the Central Committee, the Party leader spoke of the disproportionalities that had to be promptly eliminated, as well as of material, financial, and foreign currency reserves needed to bring about an effective economic reform. Decree no. 50 of the Council of Ministers of November 6, 1968, projected further improvements, but decision-making powers were to be centralized rather than decentralized. The government resolution of December 3, 1970, stripped the industrial associations of their independence and on December 12, 1970, the banking system returned to its traditional structures after a brief experiment with the structures of a market economy. The above-average growth rates began to fall: the average annual national income increased by 8.1 percent during the five-year period from 1965 to 1970, by 7.5 percent from 1971 to 1975, by 6.1 percent from 1976 to 1980, and finally by 1.8 percent in 1985. The more moderate growth rates might have been satisfactory, but not the quality of goods. In an interview with the Bulgarian periodical *Poglev* on August 26, 1985, Leonid Grenost, the Soviet ambassador in Sofia, complained that "many workers in Bulgaria have houses, gardens, vineyards, and even cattle. When they return to their factories, it is natural that they might need to take a rest after working so hard on their private plots. . . . Bulgarian workers are not sufficiently proletarianized." The Party leader responded with the decree of October 10, 1985, on "Measures against young people who offend against socialist morals."

Ed Hewett of the Brookings Institution stated that, although we know how the modern market functions, we do not know how to create it. Of course there are now advisers, some of them very prominent, from the best universities of the West. But their advice comes from textbooks, as Ralf Dahrendorf, former FRG minister and now Master of St. Anthony's College, Oxford, remarked in an interview with the Polish weekly *Polityka*.[1] Theirs are proposals for things that do not exist, scenarios from their own economies that have nothing in common with the real functioning of an economy. Hence, they lead to schematized solutions in economic policy and to unexpected consequences. Even worse, Dahrendorf went on, the solutions being proposed might perhaps have some prospects in Third World countries, but not in Central and Eastern Europe where they cannot be accepted by a highly educated and highly skilled population.

The reforms undertaken by the GDR regime, Moscow's loyal ally, were inconsistent and half-hearted. Their primary emphasis was not so much on decentralization of economic powers but on the perfection of central planning and administration. It hardly needs to be pointed out that in the industrially developed regions of East Germany, the Soviet model was least suited for promoting economic efficiency and raising the quality of goods to world levels. The problem in East Germany was not that of making the transition from an agrarian to an industrial society. Yet the reform attempts differed very little, if at all, from those that had been carried out in the other less developed Eastern countries. The first attempt commenced with the *new economic system* ratified by the Sixth Party Congress of the SED in January 1963. Its objective was to improve and perfect the practical and organizational aspects of the economy, and then to transfer economic powers from the macrolevel to the microlevel across a broad front. The *new economic system* ratified in 1963 was later renamed the *economic system of socialism*, but this was done more with the intention of stressing that there would be no departure from the traditional central administrative system. The main content of this reform was a reduction to a minimum in the number of binding indicators in the economic level.

Principal responsibility for productivity was transferred to the associations of state-owned factories, henceforth transformed from purely administrative authorities to "economic steering organs" operating on the principles of "economic accounting."

The "economic system of socialism" had ceased to function without having been officially abolished. When acute bottlenecks in energy supply arose in the late 1960s, causing disruptions in agriculture, in the construction industry, and in transportation, the meeting of the German Communist Party's Central Committee in September 1970 decided on a more rigid centralization of economic management and reduction of the decision-making powers of production units.

The law on reorganizing planning of the GDR economy in the five-year period from 1981 to 1985, adopted in February 1980, offered not much that was new. Greater emphasis was placed on streamlining planning by adding more binding indicators as well as on "the conceptual underpinnings of five-year plans" and on "the exact planning of science and technology." The new indicators, "final product" (sale of industrial output minus the value of the material input) as well as "material costs per 100 marks of goods output," were intended to put an end to the "ton ideology" and to shift concern to reducing the inflated material costs.

There was no shortage of attempts to streamline the management of the economy in the 1980s as well: the Eleventh SED Party Congress in 1981 made the giant combines the most important administrative unit in industry and construction. Their purpose was to create a closed cycle of production, sale, and research: 175 combines were in operation, each employing 20,000 to 40,000 people.

But the difference in the quality of life between the two German states remained considerable down to the very end of the GDR. Skilled labor emigrated to West Germany so long as it was possible. Altogether, about 2 million people had emigrated before the Berlin Wall was built on August 13, 1961. The manifest objective of reaching the level of West Germany was as unrealistic as Khrushchev's target of reaching the per-capita income of the United States by 1980. Once the Berlin Wall was torn down, unification was a foregone conclusion; the enormous difference in productivity would have bled even a democratized GDR through emigration. Thus, Gorbachev's glasnost and perestroika were the catalyst for the later collapse.

In Czechoslovakia, which economically was on a par with Western Europe between the wars, a command system was just as inappropriate as it was in the GDR. Czechoslovakia was also the only country of Eastern Central Europe in which a democratic regime had been established under the two most prominent politicians of the prewar period—namely, Tomas Masaryk and Eduard Benes. There were no illegal parties in Czechoslovakia—even the Communist Party was legal. At the time of the Munich Accord of September 30, 1938, it had 90,000 members. This denoted a considerable decline compared with 1921, when Bohumil Smeral split the Social Democratic movement and 350,000 members switched their allegiance to the newly founded Communist Party. But some recovery was discernible after Clement Gottwald had reduced the Party to 25,000 members with his dogmatic, ultraleft politics. In August 1945 the Communist Party was already the strongest party of Eastern Europe, with 712,776 members (Poland's Labor Party had no more than 235,296 members in December 1945). The Communist Party of Czechoslovakia received 38 percent of the votes in free elections of 1946.

The Communist Party gained the sympathies of voters with its Kosice program of April 5, 1945, which envisioned nationalization of heavy industry, but not total nationalization, and friendship with the Soviet Union without subordination. Until the historic February of 1948, a mixed system conducive to economic development functioned in Czechoslovakia. The idea was to manage the state sector, already quite large, and the residual private sector by means of traditional market mechanisms and nondirigist planning, and to ensconce this mixed system in a pluralistic democracy.

Gottwald's coup d'état in February 1948 brought the country definitively into the Soviet system after it had performed better than the other Eastern European countries in the first postwar years. Total nationalization of industrial enterprises was soon followed by forced collectivization of agriculture. The Five-Year Plan of 1953 was revised to give clear priority to heavy industry, channeling 37 percent of total investments into that sector. The country was forced at short notice to restructure its foreign trade. Before World War II the share of the Eastern countries in Czechoslovakia's total trade volume was 11 percent, but this increased to 45 percent in 1949 and one year later to 60 percent. The consequences were not long in coming. The inordinate growth rate of the first postwar years of about 20 percent annually shrank to 3.5 percent in 1954 and the refocusing on heavy industry had a negative effect on the living standard. In 1953 the Pilsen workers struck. There was unrest among the students, and Clement Gottwald outlived his great benefactor Stalin by only one week. His successor, Antonin Novotny, hesitated and attempted to improve economic performance by introducing more rigid discipline. Certain changes were made in the system in 1958: the microlevel was left with a negligible margin of discretion in the allocation of basic capital and circulating capital, the number of binding indicators in the state plan was reduced, and material incentives were introduced for management and the work force. But the central plan preserved its directive character. The halfhearted reform created more disproportionalities than it removed. A clear recession set in. In 1963 national income declined by 1 percent, the first decline of the postwar period. The gap between the ruling elite and the people grew deeper. General dissatisfaction and ever sharper criticism from the intellectuals fostered the preconditions for the Prague Spring.

On January 5, 1968, Antonin Novotny resigned his offices as head of Party and state, and was replaced by Alexander Dubcek, head of the Slovakian Communist Party, marking a turning point in the country's history. What was special about the Prague Spring was that it represented the first and only consensus between rulers and ruled on the possibility of socialism with a human face. The Prague Spring contemplated no return to capitalism, although some intervention in existing property relations was envisioned. Most enterprises would continue to be "public property," but they would be freed from state control. Workers' councils were to have been brought onto the management boards of firms. Enterprises were to be given full autonomy and would no longer be under the economic ministries or other state organs. Prices were to be set centrally for only 15 percent of industrial capital goods and for 15 percent of consumer goods.

It is difficult to judge whether the principles of the Prague Spring could have been realized. The Yugoslavian model of socialism with workers' control, which in the end was also not very successful economically, perhaps permits a certain skepticism, even though one must be cautious in making any such comparisons. The invasion by the Warsaw Pact troops on August 21, 1968, rendered this question moot. Although the deputy prime minister of the new government, Vaclav Hula, gave assurances that the old outmoded steering system would "under no circumstances" be restored, a central administrative system was introduced once again, and an attempt was made to mollify the discontented population with a bit of consumer favoritism at the cost of capital investments.

The consequences were described by Gustav Husak, head of State and Party, at the December 1979 meeting of the Communist Party: "Supplies were not even guaranteed within the ministry in terms of delivery, range of products or quality." But neither he nor his successor Jakes in the office of general secretary dared to influence any thoroughgoing reforms. After his replacement, Jakes commented that Mikhail Gorbachev had warned against overhasty reforms. Vaclav Havel, long Husak's prisoner, became his successor as head of state.

The brutal suppression of the Prague Spring doubtless had a decisive influence on the history of Czechoslovakia during the last twenty years, and accelerated the fall of the communist regime, even though the funereal peace of the "normalized" country lasted far into the hot autumn of 1989. Romania, on the other hand, provides an example of a regime's slide toward a one-man dictatorship, with devastating consequences for the country's economic and social development. Romania freed itself from direct aggression by the Soviet Union quite early on, in the late 1950s. In 1958, its leaders succeeded in achieving the withdrawal of Soviet troops from Romanian territory. The long-smoldering crisis in Romanian–Soviet relations reached its high point on April 26, 1964, when the then-Party chief Gheorgiu Dej issued the following declaration:

Every party has the exclusive right to establish its political line, its concrete objectives, and the ways and means of achieving them, independently . . . no party has a privileged place nor can it have . . . the constellation of class forces in one of another country. The shift in forces, the mood among the masses, and a country's particular internal and external political circumstances can be known by no one more exactly and more thoroughly than by the Communist Party of that country.

His successor Nicolae Ceausescu made no secret of the fact that he would continue along the path of national independence embarked upon by his predecessor. This was followed not only by declarations but also by deeds. In the middle of June 1966, when relations between the Soviet bloc and China were still "extremely tense," Zhou Enlai was received in Bucharest with a twenty-one-gun salute. Romanian Prime Minister Jon Maurer spoke of an unshakable friendship with China. On January 11, 1967, Romania established diplomatic relations with Bonn on its own. Romania also refused to sign the Near-East Declaration of the Eastern countries of June 9, 1967, or to break off diplomatic relations with Israel. On July 24, 1967, Ceausescu declared before the great national assembly that "world problems are no longer exclusively the affair of the great powers." Romania refused to lend its troops to the invasion of Czechoslovakia to suppress the Prague Spring. Ceausescu's declaration of August 21, 1968, sounded extraordinarily tough: "It is unthinkable that socialist states should trample the freedom and independence of another state under foot. . . . The Romanian people will never allow the territory of our fatherland to be violated." In December 1972, Romania became the first East European country to join the International Monetary Fund and the World Bank.

But liberation from direct Soviet interference was not used to free the economy from the centralist intervention of the state. Quite the contrary, Romania's economy was steered more dirigistically than the other states of Eastern Europe right to the bitter end of the Ceausescu regime. Although a few vague attempts were made to liberalize the economy, there was never any intention of abandoning central control of the country's resources.

The decision adopted by the National Party Conference in December 1967 entitled, "On measures for improving management and planning and modernizing the local administrative bodies," showed unmistakably that practical and organizational improvements rather than economic reforms had been contemplated. Jon Maurer, then prime minister, made this clear: "It would be absolutely inconceivable to realize socialism without planning, without a concentration of resources, or without a uniform steering of the economy." His deputy Niculescu Mizil was even clearer: "We will not leave the solution of economic problems to the blind forces of the free market."

But the country's productive forces rebelled ever more forcefully against the antiquated relations of production. By the end of the 1970s, Romania's economy was in an acute crisis due to its overinflated heavy industry, its ailing light industry, and its devastated agriculture. There were drastic problems with supply, and a steadily widening gap between production capacities, which literally devoured labor, material, and energy, and shrinking resources. Steel production, with a potential capacity of 20 million tons, received only 12 million tons of domestic iron ore, while the oil refineries, with a capacity of over 30 million tons, received no more than 11–12 million tons of its own oil. In 1980, there was a trade deficit of $2 billion. This former agricultural country had criminally neglected its agriculture. Though 35 percent of the work force was employed in agriculture, their contribution to the total national product was only 16 percent. To avert the deepening crisis, expensive loans from Western banks were contracted: the debt increased from $5 billion in 1978 to $7.2 billion in 1979 and 9.7 billion at the end of 1980. In 1982, heavily indebted, the country declared itself insolvent. The dictator's decision to pay off the whole of the debt to the West had fateful consequences for further development. Ceausescu had signed his own death warrant with his so-called systematization of agriculture, and his plan to create gigantic agro-cities. It drove the already desolate agriculture to ruin and the Hungarian minority—whose villages were to be the first to be destroyed—to the barricades. Members of Ceausescu's own leading elite carried out the sentence.

Poland and Hungary: The Vanguard of the Reforms

Stalin knew better than anyone that the social system he had forged had no chance of being realized in Poland. In 1944, he told the prime minister of the Polish government in exile in London, Stanislaw Mikolajczyk, "To introduce communism to Poland would be like trying to saddle a cow," and he assured him that he had no intention of forcing communism on Poland. But he did so anyway. The regime was totally bankrupted three times: in 1956, 1970, and 1980. The desperate attempt by General Jaruzelski to save Poland by declaring martial law on December 13, 1981, failed, even though he did perhaps succeed in preventing a bloody war of intervention by the Soviet Union. On June 4, 1989, Jaruzelski entered into a compromise at a round table with the *Solidarity* movement, handing over to them complete control of the state a few months later. After World War II, the country, bled dry, was tied to the Soviet Union, although at the time this move had the support of several sectors of society. There was a widespread view that the economy, devastated by war and the occupation (40 percent of the national patrimony was lost and the large cities were in ruins), could only be restored by cooperation with the Soviet Union. The promise of a society without capitalists and landowners aroused great hopes, especially among the workers. Prime Minister Jozef Cyrankiewicz's statement that "we have to be socialist because we cannot build capitalism without any capital" met with comprehension because Poland was a capital-poor country.

Poland was able to regain its prewar potential with a new, Polish edition of the Soviet NEP: in 1945 industrial production was 30 percent lower than in 1938, but in 1946 the difference had lessened to 6.8 percent, and in 1949 industrial production had risen to 48 percent above and agricultural production 10 percent above their prewar levels.

But the NEP period came to an end in 1950. Poland, too, was forced to adopt the Stalinist iron and steel developmental model. The traditional economic branches, consumer goods industries, and especially agriculture, were criminally neglected. In the six-year period from 1950 to 1955 industrial production increased by 2.7-fold but the national product increased by only 90 percent. Collectivization caused immeasurable harm to agriculture, and its output was reduced to a minimum. The disproportionate economic development (capital investment reached 38.2 percent of the total national product in 1953) had a catastrophic effect on the standard of living and on supplies to the people: on October 28, 1950, a price and money reform was implemented for the second time after the war. Money was changed at a rate of 100 : 1. Prices were recalculated at a rate of 100 : 3. Prices increased by another 97 percent because of the two crises in 1951 and 1953. Discontent grew among the population because of permanent undersupply. In August 1956 the workers in Poznan rebelled, and the entire country was thrown into an economic and political crisis.

Wladyslaw Gomulka, the martyr of Poland's Stalinist period, who had to spend six years in prison or in isolation because of "nationalist deviations," returned to power in the historic October 1956, against the will of the Soviet Union. It was thanks to Gomulka that the unprofitable collective farms were dissolved and the church was given more freedom. Within a few months, the number of collective farms dropped from 10,600 to 1,700. Their share of the country's agrarian production dropped to 2.7 percent. However, the Party leadership under Gomulka returned slowly but surely to the usual steering methods. This had devastating consequences on living standards and on the mood of the population. Political and social conflicts reached their peak in early 1968, probably also under the influence of the Prague Spring, with mass protests of young people and intellectuals.

The workers did not let their powerful voices be heard until two years later: strikes and mass demonstrations began on the Baltic coast in December 1970 and spread like wildfire throughout the entire country. On December 19, one hundred enterprises in seven of the nineteen provinces went out on strike. According to official statistics, there were 45 dead and 1,965 wounded. Nineteen state buildings were burned down, including the Party Committee buildings in Gdansk and Szczecin. The workers' uprising brought down the leader of the Polish United Workers' Party, Wladyslaw Gomulka, on December 20, 1970. His successor was Edward Gierek, Politburo member and head of the Party region of Upper Silesia. He assumed the office of general secretary, promising to build a "second Poland," though with the traditional economic strategy. The consequences of disproportionate growth were the same: despite liberalized consumer goods imports, new protests occurred in late June 1976. An attempt was made to eliminate the disproportions by excessive price increases: prices for meat and meat products were to be increased by 50 percent. However, the measures were rejected after mass demonstrations. Gierek built gigantic plants, such as the huge and costly foundry complex in the ecologically utterly polluted city of Katowice, the copper foundry Glogow II, the first coal mine in the new coal basin Lublin, the petrochemical combinate Plock-Wloclawek, and the power plant Belchatow—all were expanded. All these works were undertaken with foreign credit, however, which grew from $7.5 billion in the mid-1970s to $32 billion at the time the Party leader was overthrown in August 1980.

Gierek's economic strategy was evaluated correctly in the draft program for the Ninth Party Congress (July 1981):

> The decision-making process was sometimes criminal; various pressure groups and cliques had gained a decisive influence on economic affairs. The workers' uprising, which once again began on the Baltic coast and then spread throughout the country, brought down the Party leader. But, whereas the resistance movement in 1970 was spontaneous and unorganized, in 1980 it assumed organized form. The *Solidarity* movement under the leadership of Lech Walesa and the country's leading intellectuals gathered ten million members. The Soviet Union attempted in vain to influence the course of events. The Warsaw Pact issued an appeal to Poland's leadership on December 5, 1980, to take the initiative to put an end to the rebellion.

Maneuvers of Soviet, East German, Czech, and Polish troops were announced for the second half of March 1981 under the code name Sojus 81. On April 7, 1981, Brezhnev made a passionate appeal from the podium of the CPSU Party Congress to put an end to the free trade unions. On June 5, 1981, came the sharpest letter theretofore from the CPSU Central Committee, with its implacable attacks and allusions to the seriousness of the situation. General Jaruzelski, minister of defense and Party leader, decided under the pressure of the circumstances to proclaim a state of emergency on December 13, 1981. He thus delayed, but did not prevent, the fall of the regime. Once Gorbachev's perestroika had eliminated the threat of outside intervention, a compromise of negotiating with *Solidarity* was reached on June 4, 1989, securing the Polish United Workers' Party (PUWP) 65 percent of the parliamentary seats. In the event, *Solidarity* won 99 of the 100 seats in the senate elections. The once-powerful Polish United Workers' Party, now under the new name of the Socialist Party of the Republic of Poland, found itself in the position of an opposition party.

The Soviet economic and political system, with its fixation on iron and steel, was suited least of all to Hungary, which has almost no raw material or fuel. Active participation in world trade was a *sine qua non* for this country's existence. The traditional communications mechanisms were, however, reduced to the function of economic accounting, and made any viable cost–benefit calculation impossible. Because of the *forint*'s intrinsic nonconvertibility, foreign trade was cleared bilaterally, and Soviet raw materials and fuels were paid for with finished goods. The consequences of uneven economic development, accompanied by a permanent neglect of the consumer goods industry and agriculture, were more tangible in Hungary than anywhere else. The October 1956 uprising showed how great the discontent among the population was. It was brutally suppressed, but the population's will to resist remained unbroken. The economy continued to develop unevenly, with steadily rising costs: an economic growth of 46 percent achieved in the period from 1958 through 1965 was purchased dearly with a capital investment rate of 27 percent; state subsidies for foreign trade increased by 91 percent in the same period. Not much was left over for augmenting consumption. Janos Kadar, who had assumed the office of general secretary after the October 1956 uprising, well understood that under the existing conditions a reversion to the chaotic state of the early 1950s was inevitable. On January 1, 1968, a reform that had been in preparation for three years, with the modest title "New Economic Mechanism," was put into effect: the central state plan was retained as a guideline to economic development. However, it was henceforth to be more indicative than directive. Planning indicators were no longer to be divided up among the individual production units, but the production units were no longer obliged to account to some superior authority. Relations between enterprises could henceforth be regulated without the mediation of a central distributive apparatus. The sale and distribution of goods was effected through contracts with business partners, in which prices were also necessarily a factor. Firms producing for foreign trade would not be insulated from the rest of the economy. The large enterprises were granted the right to enter into direct ties with foreign partners. They would also assume full responsibility for foreign trade. Some of them were empowered to engage in foreign transactions on a commission basis with permission from the competent foreign trade ministry. The agricultural cooperatives were also freed from daily supervision by the central authorities, and were henceforth allowed to grow crops that promised greater earnings.

While to the liberals this reform seemed too timid, to the conservatives it seemed to go too far. It was implemented under conditions of unremitting conflict between the two. Ivan T. Berend, former president of the Hungarian Academy of Sciences, described events as follows:

The compromises made on the way to reform, then the breaking of these compromises [referring to the years between 1973 and 1977 after the first oil price shock], the abandonment of the "second stage" in the seventies, and the partial retreat in the mid-seventies, created a contradictory system. Within it, both indirect steering and intervention by the central authorities were restored, so that the old and new elements were present at the same time, the one working against the other.[2]

Bela Cikos Nagy, one of the major architects of this reform, described the efforts of his country as follows: "The average is always preferred in everything . . . but when this is applied to an economic mechanism it has resulted in even normative regulations being based on average conditions."[3]

Kadar's model whereby the "politicians would ensure citizens a certain level of prosperity on condition they would restrain themselves politically" (according to Laszlo Lengyel, director of an economic institute[4]) could not work with these contradictions within the system. The growth in real incomes fell by 4.5 percent in the five-year period 1971–75, and to 1.7 percent and 1.2 percent in the next two five-year periods. In the second half of the 1980s, neither the economy nor incomes grew. These developments destroyed the future prospects of the middle layer who had accepted Kadar and his economic policy, and from that time onward they duly set about building mass support for an internal party opposition which, led by Rezsö Nyers, Miklos Nemeth, and Imre Poszgay, finally overthrew the general secretary who had determined Hungary's history for the thirty years after the October uprising. However, the reform communists were unable to prevent the collapse of the regime. In 1989, it resigned without resistance. The Democratic Forum moved to the forefront of political events.

Spring 1989: Not This, But What?

The collapse of the outer ring of the Soviet empire occurred in different ways in different countries. And for each country there were specific national reasons for renouncing the Soviet regime imposed upon it after World War II. What they all had in common were the inefficiency of the centrally administered economy, the monstrous economic structure (fixated on heavy industry and the arms industry—whose purpose was to support the military-industrial complex of the hegemonic superpower—and geared to confrontation with the West rather than to meeting the needs of the population), and finally, the exaggerated expenditure on arms, which had less to do with defending the country's own fictitious borders than with the Soviet Union's falsely conceived ambition to become militarily superior to the West. Another feature in common was the above-average expenditure on state security, which was designed more to protect the regime from its people than to serve them.

Finally, all the peoples of Central and Eastern Europe were fed up with a ruling party that assumed the role of guardian of eternal truth and brooked no opposition. The Party was supposed to symbolize goodness, and to bring out goodness in people. But it failed to do so because the right conditions for the development of the sublime social system it had promised never came about, and the system that was in fact built had to use real people, not fairytale people. This system had ventured onto unprecedented paths in history, and more than any other traditional social system, it needed the opposition of alternative-thinking political forces for precisely that reason. As André Glucksmann, former CP member, later Maoist, and, even later, cofounder of the New Philosophy in France, rightly states: "We must assume that the evil is in ourselves" and that hence we need democracy, that is, "we can be leftists when the rightists make a mistake and rightists when the leftists make a mistake."[5] This philosopher fully understands that there are no ideal solutions, that the choice lies between two mistakes, and that we must always reflect which of them is the greater.

The communist parties of Central and Eastern Europe, like the Soviet Union's Communist Party, anchored their one-party rule in their respective constitutions—which became irrelevant once the peoples of those countries began to cast doubt on both the constitutions and their authors. Full responsibility for every misfortune was placed on the respective ruling parties, even when they were not actually to blame. The officially proclaimed ideology became an empty shell as the gap between itself and reality grew ever wider, and the belief that the parties represented the salvation of the world (a belief which even under Stalinism was enough, at least for an elite of faithful communists, to justify morally the most severe repression) was progressively replaced by cynicism and corruption by the nomenklatura.

The Soviet Union, rightly or not, was made responsible for all calamities. It was, after all, that country that had imposed its own social system on the satellite countries. But the Soviet Union did not always receive blame for things for which it actually was responsible. Most Eastern specialists agreed that prices in mutual trade favored the Soviet Union. But when the CMEA was dissolved and Poland, Czechoslovakia, and Hungary were able to implement their proposals to clear foreign trade with the Soviet Union at world market prices and in convertible currencies, it turned out that this change brought advantages to the Soviet Union as a producer of raw materials, but would have caused each of the partner countries losses of $1-to-$2 billion annually. The price benefits the Soviet Union provided to its CMEA partners were calculated at between $20 and $30 billion for the oil shock period of the early 1970s. The Soviet Union's role as net payer was even clearer in regard to the most recent additions to its empire, Cuba, and then later Angola and Mozambique, Ethiopia, and finally Afghanistan, where it became involved in costly military conflict.

But the Soviet Union was justifiably blamed for having wrenched every radical movement away from the conventional social system by military force or by its mere presence. Although in Central and Eastern Europe this system had for a long time already been rotten to the core, mass uprisings only occurred when perestroika and glasnost had made intervention from outside impossible.

The developments in the historical Autumn of 1989 clearly demonstrated how indispensable a pluralistic social system is: had an alternative political party, with a clear economic and political program, existed at that time, the desired political change could have been made without a "velvet revolution," or a revolution of any other kind for that matter. The mass uprising was narrowly focused on the totalitarian aspect of this system and a pluralistic state became the main demand. The lack of a multiparty system in the past was fateful for the revolution, but not for the later postcommunist period. Party rivalry is just as important for shaping politicians as rivalry in a free market is important for the quality of goods for sale. "People fled the GDR," said André Glucksmann, "not because they knew what a good and perfect society is—it was presumably clear to everyone that Western society was not perfect—but they knew what they did not want for themselves and their children."

As confused as the opposition programs were, two principal currents soon became readily discernible: one—from the very beginning the clearest—whose programmatic objective was to create a better socialism with a human face. It was for emancipation from Soviet hegemony, free trade unions, and decentralization of economic power, and against censorship, but did not aspire to a fundamentally different social system.

The second current saw no hope of reforming the existing regime and aimed at its overthrow and replacement by a pluralistic market society of a Western sort.

The widespread opinion that the revolution of 1989 was a revolution of intellectuals as in 1848 is not fully true: in Poland, for example, mass protest began with the strike in the Gdansk docks, which then spread like an avalanche through the entire country. The intellectuals did not join the workers' protest until later. That rebellion, begun by one social stratum, escalated into a mass rebellion. The Solidarity movement embraced the majority of all levels of the population. The CP elite, in the end totally demoralized, mounted no resistance in any country. There was no trace of the "pride with which Cromwell's Roundheads went underground" as someone signing himself "PBA" wrote in the *Frankfurter Allgemeine Zeitung* of September 16, 1991, and went on, "socialism is no longer defended by socialists. They are literally outdoing each other in their acknowledgment that their cause had been a lost one from the very beginning." Hundreds of thousands of Communist Party members joined the battle against the existing regime. It was no wonder that the opposition carried home an overwhelming victory in the first free elections, in which voter turnout was quite large. The question of direction was no longer asked. "We must build capitalism as fast as possible," declared Josef Antall, head of the Democratic Forum, and the appointed prime minister of Hungary.

Vaclav Klaus declared that his country was striving for a "market economy without adjectives," and it was this path which Leszek Balcerowicz embarked upon with his ruthless shock therapy.

Two essential questions remained unasked: what would be the direction after the change of system, and how to proceed along this uncertain route to capitalism without either capital or capitalists, or without politicians or managers trained in either a pluralist democracy or a competitive market economy? Even less was known of how the population would react to the unavoidable austerity measures after having repudiated a forty-year regime because they longed for greater justice. The path in Western civilization from a feudal to a capitalist system was familiar, but the path from a totally nationalized and centrally administered economy to a competitive economy embedded in the structures of the world market via its economic infrastructure was completely unknown.

An undertaking without historical precedent was being embarked upon: a transition to a capitalist economy that had never been systematically steered from above. This transformation came about in a long historical process with the active collaboration of innumerable human generations and intellectuals. Not even the most famous theoreticians of a market economy have moved along this path. They have only interpreted it—brilliantly.

The First Reform Phase

The first reform phase was supposed to have created conditions for the transition from a distributive economy to a functioning market economy. Two conditions were requisite: first, a price system that provided for an equilibrium between supply and demand without state subsidies; second, a monetary system that restored to money its normal function of a universal means of purchase, enjoying the trust of the population to such an extent that it would drive any surrogate currency out of circulation and undermine the black market in foreign currency. It was no easy task, considering that the prices for food, rent, and services in the overall communal economy were subsidized by the state budget, and that a deep gap between supply and demand had become a permanent breeding ground for a black market operating with organized crime. When prices were freed, in accordance with the rules of the market, the setting of realistic market exchange rates was able to accomplish this task—by no means easy—in the most advanced of the reform countries. Since then, there have been no great departures from the official exchange rate, and so conditions were established for internal convertibility of currencies. The opening up of the market for imports from abroad put an end to chronic shortages in supply. Exporters were allowed to transfer their earnings abroad.

The trade and services sector in Poland was already 90 percent privatized in late 1992. The number of private firms increased from 30,000 in the second quarter of 1991 to 75,000 in the third quarter. Since 1989 until mid-1994, private firms have created 2.2 million jobs.[6]

The situation in agriculture was somewhat different: in Poland, where collectivization was stopped in 1956 and failing cooperatives were dissolved, 14,211,000 hectares were in private hands at the end of 1991. Another 3,489,000 hectares were in state possession, and 696,000 hectares were owned by cooperatives.

No major changes in these proportions have been discernible over the last two years. There had been a negligible increase in private ownership in Czechoslovakia, from 305,000 hectares in 1990 to 331,000 hectares in 1991, whereas at the end of 1991, 2,003,000 hectares were in the possession of the state, and cooperatives owned 4,293,000 hectares. Private ownership increased somewhat more dynamically in Hungary: from 1,289,000 to 1,453,000 hectares. But at the same time state ownership increased from 2,867,000 to 3,057,000, to the detriment of cooperative property, which declined from 5,147,000 to 4,793,000 in 1991.

The transition from highly subsidized prices on the sellers' market was expected to require a drastic rise in prices, considering the great discrepancy between supply and demand. The actual price rise, however, went beyond all expectations. Prices increased most drastically in Poland. The shock therapy initiated in early 1990 brought about a price rise that reached 251 percent of 1989 levels.

In the other two countries of Central Europe, where the reform was not initiated until later, and then at a more tempered pace, prices increased by 1.4 percent and 10 percent in Czechoslovakia in 1989 and 1990, respectively, but by 56.7 percent, 11.1 percent, and 20.8 percent, respectively, over the next three years. In Hungary, prices grew by 17 percent and 29 percent in 1989 and 1990, and by 35.0 percent, 23.0 percent, and 22.7 percent in the following three years. The highest inflation rates during 1991–93 were in Bulgaria (254.3 percent, 79.4 percent, and 72.9 percent) and in Romania (165.8 percent, 210.9 percent, and 237.4 percent).

The deep economic recession that accompanied the transition was the most alarming. It was compared with good reason with developments during the deepest world economic crisis of the 1930s. As the first to initiate the change of system, Poland felt the consequences earlier and more painfully, and more aggressively. The year 1989 was the last year in which the economy grew, if only negligibly (i.e., only 0.5 percent), before a decline. The gross domestic product decreased by 11.6 percent in 1990 and by a further 8 percent in 1991, but in the next two years increases of 1.5 percent and 4.0 percent were registered. In the Czech Republic, which embarked on reform later and more slowly, negative growth was in the years 1990–93 as follows: 1.2 percent, 4.2 percent, 7.1 percent, and 0.5 percent. Bulgaria experienced similar trends: GDP declined during these years by 13.1 percent, 29.4 percent, 12.4 percent, and 6.2 percent. In Romania the declines were 8.2 percent, 13.7 percent, and 15.4 percent until 1992, while in 1993 GDP increased by 1 percent.

The setbacks experienced by Poland's economy in the last decade and especially in the first years of the 1990s considerably increased the gap between it and the other two countries of Central Europe: Poland's per-capita national income was estimated by the World Bank at $1,590 in 1990. Czechoslovakia's was estimated at $3,140 and Hungary's at $2,890, although these countries had similar industrial structures. The share of the electrotechnical and machine industries in total industrial production was 31.5 percent in Poland, 38.6 percent in Czechoslovakia, and 32.9 percent in Hungary; the share of the ferrous metal industry was the same in Poland and Hungary, 5 percent, and was 7.5 percent in Czechoslovakia. Polish industry was hardest hit by the recession, declining by one-fourth between 1989 and 1990 and by a further 14 percent in the next year. The sale of industrial output in 1991 was 40 percent lower than in the preceding two years, while in Czechoslovakia and Hungary it fell by 19 percent and 18 percent, respectively, in 1991. Bulgaria's industry suffered the greatest decline: 28 percent.

Most alarming of all is the traumatic decline in investments that set in during 1991: in the former CMEA region and in Yugoslavia, the decline was 16.5 percent compared with the preceding year. But the decline was greatest in the Czech Republic, 31 percent, followed by Romania at 27 percent. The real income of the population also showed a steady decline: in Poland, by one third compared with 1989. The average wages in Czechoslovakia increased nominally by 16.3 percent in 1991, but real wages had decreased by 24 percent compared with the preceding year. It is worth noting that the rapidly growing stratum of nouveau riche prefers to consume its profits rather than invest them. The Polish journal New Europe reported that Poland had become the most important market for the sale of Western cars. The number of imported cars had increased from 106,000 in 1990 to almost 500,000 in 1991. The leading importer was Volkswagen (65,900), followed by Ford (55,600), Opel (42,200), and Mercedes (29,300)—in conditions, one might note, where almost half the population lives below a subsistence level.

The decline in production is causing a rapid rise in unemployment: in Poland there were 2,238,000 unemployed as of March 5, 1992, but by mid-1994 there were nearly 3 million jobless people. In Hungary this figure was 460,000 in 1992, but it grew to 750,000, or 15 percent. In the other Eastern countries the unemployment rate is 6 to 7 percent. The Czech Republic reported a decline in the rate of unemployment from 4.14 percent in February 1992 to 3.2 percent in 1993. In Slovakia, it is almost three times as high. The Ministry of Labor and Welfare expects that the forthcoming privatization will increase the number of unemployed in the Czech Republic to 500,000. According to the reports of the International Labour Organization (ILO), the number of unemployed in the former CMEA could increase to 22 million. This would already constitute a "danger for social cohesiveness," commented ILO General Director Michel Hansenne in a joint conference held in Paris by the ILO and OECD in mid-April 1993. Hensenne therefore spoke out in favor of an active employment policy for the state, through, among other things, training programs and better coordination of employment by the state, employers, and employees. OECD General Secretary Jean-Claude Paye felt that the reform states should not abandon the economy to its own mechanisms.

The economic crisis, the abnormally high rate of unemployment, and the population's fall in real income were caused by more than just the rapidity of the system's unprecedented upheaval and a transition model that was not always the most appropriate; the disintegration of the CMEA economic community was also in large measure responsible. The countries of Central and Eastern Europe had over a period of forty years coordinated their economies, and the bulk of their foreign trade was among themselves. The core of this trade was represented by the exchange of Soviet raw materials and fuel for manufactured goods from the smaller countries. Remarkably, the smaller countries had in fact been pushing for foreign trade to adopt world market prices and to switch to the use of hard currency. The Soviet Union finally conceded to this wish only after it had been persuaded that it would be the only beneficiary of the transition. The smaller countries not only had to swallow losses of $1 to $2 billion, but also had to accept a dramatic decline, above all in oil imports: Soviet exports to the former CMEA countries decreased from $52.2 billion in 1990 to $23.1 billion, while imports declined from $67.9 billion to $23.9 billion.[7] In this way, the

Soviet Union was able to reduce its debit from $16.9 billion in 1990 to $0.8 billion. The partner countries, on the other hand, not only saw their balance of payments in trade with the Soviet Union deteriorate, but also were forced to replace at least half of the cutback in oil orders by importing from the Arab countries at high prices, and moreover to seek out new sales markets in the West. This extremely difficult transition was successful: Bulgaria increased its exports to the OECD countries from $0.8 billion in 1988 to $1.2 billion in 1991: the corresponding increase for Czechoslovakia was from $4.1 billion to $5.9 billion, in Poland from $6.1 billion to $9.5 billion, and in Hungary from $4.5 billion to $6.4 billion. Only Romania indicated a decline from $3.9 billion to $2.3 billion. As of 1990, the OECD share of Poland's exports was 62 percent, while the OECD accounted for 60.1 percent of imports. Exports and imports by Czechoslovakia accounted for 42.4 percent and 42.6 percent respectively, while these figures for Hungary were 52.7 percent and 52.6 percent, respectively. The OECD share in Bulgaria's exports and imports was 8.6 percent and 14.8 percent, respectively; the corresponding figures for Romania were 41.6 percent and 23.2 percent.

The collapse of the CMEA market hit Poland the hardest. Its trade volume with the former Soviet Union was reduced to one-third of the preceding period. The EC countries headed the field in Poland's foreign trade in 1990 with 157.9 billion zlotys (about $12 billion), followed by the Soviet Union, in second place with 35.2 billion zlotys and, much further down, the United States (4.7 billion zlotys) and Japan (2.6 billion zlotys).

Overhasty Privatization: The Main Cause of Economic Destitution

As recently realized in Poland, the principal cause of the deepening economic crisis is the rapid dismantling of nationalized industries, which accounted for almost 80 percent of total output. As expressed by the first head of planning in the first postcommunist government, Jerzy Osiatynski, it was an attempt to hand over "anonymous property with no value to people who had no capital." The total savings of the Polish population was about $8 billion in early 1990, including $3 billion in foreign exchange, while the value of state enterprises was estimated at $100 billion. A large portion of those savings, however, could be regarded as forced savings, inasmuch as there was little to buy. The same situation existed in the other countries of Central and Eastern Europe. Only the former GDR had it somewhat easier: the *Treuhand AG* was able to sell 6,500 out of a total 11,000 of large firms within two years. The buyers were mainly large West German corporations. Capital transfer from Western to Eastern Germany during the period from 1989 until mid-1994 reached 600 billion deutsche marks.

Such possibilities do not exist in the other Eastern countries. The swiftness with which denationalization was taken up is therefore astonishing: 95 percent of Poland's production capacity had to be transferred to private hands, announced the head of state; 50 percent of state enterprises in Hungary were privatized over the next two years, and should rise to 95 percent in the next ten years, considered Martin Tardos, president of the Hungarian Finance Research Institute. Dusan Triska, the head of Czechoslovakia's privatization authority, gave a somewhat lower estimate of his country's privatization capabilities: 40 percent of total assets.

Economics experts and politicians argued that an overburdened privatization process would cause more harm than good where there was an acute shortage of capital, pointing out that Britain's prime minister, Margaret Thatcher, had needed eleven years to privatize twenty-four concerns—moreover, in a functioning market economy with a highly developed infrastructure. Their arguments, however, fell on deaf ears.

Poland, which had introduced the first stage of reform with its unprecedented shock therapy, was also the first reform country to adopt a consistent law on privatization, on July 13, 1990. In the first two stages, buyers were to be selected and enterprise assets evaluated; then, only in a third stage would those state enterprises selected for selling be restructured into joint stock companies. Initially, the shares package would be held by the Treasury, to be auctioned off only two years later. A firm's work force would be offered the chance to acquire 20 percent of the total number of shares at a preferential price, after which 10 percent of the shares would be offered to foreign firms. By the end of November 1991, 12 percent of state enterprises were privatized on the basis of this law, but only a small number of them were capable of assuming effective economic activity. Seventy-five percent of them were on the verge of bankruptcy. Most of them, however, employed under two hundred people. Privatization is continuing basically via bankruptcy. In October and November 1991, twice as many firms were liquidated in bankruptcy procedures than were privatized. It was these trends that led the vice minister for property restructuring, J. Drygalski, to adopt the view that in 1992 denationalization would concentrate mainly on privatization through the bankrupting of smaller and middle-sized firms.

The managers were in favor of denationalization because it would enable them to broaden their decision-making powers. The work force, on the other hand, feared, not without reason, that their say in activities, already moderate, would be restricted even further. They accepted redirection only because wage rises in privatized firms either were totally exempted from taxes, or were taxed at a considerably lower rate.

The element of uncertainty afflicting the largest and most productive of state enterprises dramatically reduced the economic performance of industry as a whole, and many industries were forced into bankruptcy; this resulted in a loss of jobs for their work force. The third postcommunist government, under Jan Olszowski, thus found itself forced to amend the reform plans of the first two governments and to slow down the pace of reforms. The deputies rejected the prime minister's program with a majority of twenty-three votes. Sooner or later, however, this or some other government will have to decide either to continue the reform policy with a restrictive budgetary, monetary, and credit policy, and hence accept a deep recession and unemployment as the price that has to be paid, or to introduce deficit spending in order to breathe some life back into a dwindling economic activity and ward off the accumulating social conflict.

Voices, albeit much more subdued, are also heard in Czechoslovakia over relaxing privatization policy. "Minor privatization" was achieved quite rapidly. Within a short period, 18,000 shops and restaurants were returned to their former owners or auctioned off. The problems encountered with heavy industry, which was wholly in the hands of the state, were similar to those encountered in every other reform country: first and foremost, an acute lack of capital. Foreign investors were mostly interested in showcase firms such as Volkswagen's interest in the Skoda plant, General Motors' interest in the Pilsner works, Air France's interest in the domestic airline CSA, or K-Mart's interest in the Czech commercial network. However, this commitment would not be sufficient to privatize the industrial assets offered (worth 260 billion Czech crowns, or $9.3 billion).

Vaclav Klaus, the principal architect of the economic reform, devised an interesting plan for denationalization: since there was a shortage of capitalists, every adult citizen was to be given the right to purchase shares. Eleven million people had sufficient funds to buy a book of vouchers worth 1,035 crowns for $36; 8.6 million citizens had availed themselves of this right. Two thousand firms were to be denationalized in this way. The coupon holders had to decide when to exchange coupons for shares. This was no easy task: no detailed information was available on the activity and performance of individual firms. The finance minister's advice was, "Ask your friends" how firms are run and whether they are prospering; yet this advice could not be relied upon because the friends were in no position to know very much.

But a more important problem was that, though these "popular shares" (hardly an unknown phenomenon in the world economy) turned many people into owners, this minuscule bit of ownership was not sufficient to grant any say in a corporation. The problem of genuine ownership—that is, large-scale ownership, which gives the right to a say and to a share of responsibility—remains to be solved.

A law establishing two securities markets, one in Prague and one in Bratislava, was passed on April 21, 1992. The share of foreign capital was not to exceed 30 percent. The finance minister declared on that occasion that about two to three thousand corporations would exist by 1993. The American Securities and Exchange Commission (SEC), the stock market watchdog organization, announced that it was willing to provide "technical assistance" to Eastern Europe in building capital and stock markets. Specifically, the SEC would assist in the organization of investment funds, as well as in the formulation of the rules for the registration of shares and for exercising supervision over stockbrokers, according to SEC head, Richard C. Breeden.

Hungary, which has had since 1968 a more consistent reform model than the other Eastern countries, and has been more intimately engaged in the world market, opted for a privatization program based on closer cooperation with Western firms, eschewing the short-sighted alternative of getting rid of state enterprises as rapidly and as cheaply as possible. Hungary has not had much positive experience with small firms. Though small firms can be privatized quickly, their net profits declined from 306 billion forints in 1990 to 140 billion forints in 1991. The tax authorities find it increasingly difficult to collect taxes. Unpaid arrears have already reached a volume of 400 billion forints. The state budget deficit, which was projected to be about 70 billion forints ($930 million) in 1992, rose to 48 billion forints by early in the first quarter of 1993. The International Monetary Fund strongly advised the country to introduce a frugal budgetary policy.

The privatization of large Hungarian firms proceeded much more cautiously. The idea of purchasing state property with coupons met with little enthusiasm: these coupons were used solely for the recovery of assets expropriated by a law passed on June 8, 1949. Claims for compensation had reached 650 million dollars by late 1992. The intention was to pay off these claims with coupons that could later be used to acquire shares. But it was felt that state firms ought to be purchasable at a fair market price. By early 1992, 10 percent of nationalized industrial assets, worth a total of about 100 billion forints ($41 billion), had been sold by the Hungarian Assets Agency. Twenty large state enterprises were taken over wholly by large Western firms such as Nestlé, Electrolux, or Messer-Greisheim. Shares in two hundred firms were sold slightly below the 100 percent limit, and two hundred other firms were transformed into joint ventures with various kinds of foreign participation.

As in Poland, the uncertainty introduced into Hungary's state enterprises, which had been kept alive by huge state subsidies, led to mass bankruptcies. Ivan Szabo, the minister for trade and industry, announced that 40 to 50 percent of industrial enterprises would declare bankruptcy following the law that came into force on April 8, 1992. The idea, set out by the well-known Hungarian-born Harvard economist Janos Kornai in his 1990 book, *The Road to a Free Economy: Shifting from a Socialist System—the Example of Hungary* (New York: Norton, 1990), that it made no sense to give away state property, gained increasing support. In Kornai's opinion, it was a question of handing over state assets to "better owners" who would be more efficient administrators than the preceding ones had been. Kornai believed that state property must be sold at existing market prices and that the transformation of state firms into corporations would achieve its objective if it led to effective privatization—that is, only if a big shareholder or a financial group were willing to bring sufficient sums of capital with it when it obtained a joint stock company. Kornai's conclusion was that "overhasty denationalization," carried out on the principle of

"Enough of this, let's get rid of all state property," could not serve as a guideline for an undertaking of such importance for the state. His conclusion appeared to be aimed not only at national policy makers but also at international groups that were impulsively pressing for rapid privatization of state property.

Western Aid

Two opposing views can be heard over the question of Western economic aid: international financial institutions, such as large banks, repeatedly stress that what is lacking is not so much a willingness to finance as an adequate economic infrastructure and the desire to invest in the reform countries. But their opponents counter that these countries need not just financial aid but also technical aid, in order to set up the mechanisms for modern economic communication.

It should be stressed that the countries of Central and Eastern Europe were deeply in debt even before they began their reforms: at the end of 1989, Poland owed $40.6 billion, and this figure had risen to $48.4 billion by the end of 1991.[8] Of this figure, the countries belonging to the Paris Club (government-provided or government-guaranteed credits) accounted for $31.5 billion, the commercial banks in the London Club for $11.7 billion, the countries of the now abolished CMEA for $2.5 billion, and other creditors for $2.7 billion. On April 21, 1991, Poland concluded an agreement with the Paris Club to halve the debt, which would reduce its credit burden by $16 billion. The procedures for writing off the debt were already agreed with the biggest creditors of this club (Germany $5.9 billion, France $5.06 billion, Austria $3.65 billion, Canada $2.99 billion, Great Britain $2.51 billion, and United States $2.1 billion). Poland then initiated negotiations with the creditors of the London Club, with sights set on an agreement similar to the one concluded with the Paris Club. The result was the same.

Like Poland, Bulgaria announced insolvency in March 1990. Its debt was $11 billion. The country did not even have sufficient resources to pay the accrued interest. Bulgaria's financial situation, however, was extremely tense because over 80 percent of foreign trade was with countries of the community partners even before the dissolution of the CMEA. The OECD countries' share in total exports was no more than 14.6 percent in 1991. The negative balance was abnormally high: it increased from $1.1 billion in 1989 to $1.4 billion in 1993.

Hungary is the most indebted nation of Europe in terms of the per-capita population. Total debt at the end of 1993 was $21 billion. However, the country announced its commitment to service this debt: interest alone was $1.3 billion in 1991. Hungary shifted its orientation to world trade to a much more significant degree than the other countries of Eastern Europe. The OECD share of Hungary's total trade in 1991 was 52.6 percent, while exports to the OECD countries increased from $4.5 billion in 1988 to $6.5 billion in 1991. Hungary's government believed that it was essential to have the reputation of a reliable debtor if it was to attract foreign capital. This was a proper calculation: more foreign capital has flowed into Hungary than into all the former states of Middle and Eastern Europe put together.

The credit policy of Czechoslovakia has been extremely cautious, both before and after the country embarked upon radical change. The reform process was started with a debt of $1.9 billion, which increased by only $0.9 billion over the course of 1991 and 1992. At the end of 1989, Rumania's foreign debt was only $0.9 billion, since it had completely paid off its debt under the Ceausescu regime. No more than $1.5 billion in loans was contracted in the next two years.

All the Eastern countries had an enormous need for capital: production plant was obsolete and worn out, and the economic structures had to be totally reorganized under conditions, moreover, of a very difficult transition from a command economy to a competitive, functioning market economy.

A Marshall Plan would not be enough to reestablish economic equilibrium in Eastern Europe. At the end of World War II, although a significant part of the production capacities of Western Europe was destroyed, the economic infrastructure was intact and there were enough persons with managerial skills ready to begin the process of reconstruction. Between April 4, 1948, and June 30, 1952, the twelve countries of Western Europe therefore received financial aid of $16.4 billion under the Marshall Plan (some $70 billion in today's dollars). The post-1989 situation in Central and Eastern Europe was different.

The available statistics on contemplated financial aid, however, seem to bear out the opinion that one of the chief reasons for the still moderate input of foreign capital is the continuing frailty of the economic infrastructure and a reluctance to invest, especially on the part of the demolished state enterprises.

The G–24 industrial nations, as well as international financial institutions, approved an aid package for capital investment projects, technical assistance, development of the private economy, and the accumulation of credit guarantees for export credits. The package totaled 36.6 billion ECUs: the European Community's contribution to this was 18.3 billion ECUs, including 55 percent from Germany, 16 percent from France, 12 percent from Great Britain, 6 percent from Italy, and 4 percent from Spain. Poland received the greatest financial help of 12,933 million ECUs, followed by Hungary with 5,642 million ECUs and Czechoslovakia with 3,774 million ECUs. The financial aid to Bulgaria and Rumania is also considerable: 1,554 million ECUs and 3,039 million ECUs, respectively.

But the recipient nations were not tardy in expressing their dissatisfaction over the fact that the promised financial aid has been slow in coming. The Polish president, Lech Walesa, addressed the following dramatic comment to the European Parliament in Strasburg, presumably on behalf of the other Eastern countries as well:

> If the West fails to support the fundamental changes begun in the Eastern part of the continent, and abandons it to its fate, the other shore will never be reached. No one wishes to return to the status quo ante, so we will remain stranded midstream, exposed to the rough waves and currents.

Walesa's words to Germany's industrialists during a visit to Bonn were even more dramatic:

> The West is maintaining a wait-and-see attitude. But the states of the former Eastern bloc are not capable of reaching European standards through their own efforts. . . . You might find your peace somewhat disrupted when ten million hungry, unemployed people turn up on the Polish border. . . . Your helping us helps you as well.

Richard von Weizsäcker's answer was: "We need Poland in Europe." Helmut Kohl added: "We have confidence in Poland as a European country." The response of Heinrich Weiss, president of the German Union of Industrialists, was more blunt: Poland will only be attractive to German investors if it pays interest on the loans it has not paid back, if it comes up with an austerity program, and if wages and prices are kept down to a permanently low level. "But," added Weiss, "Poland and the other countries of Central and Eastern Europe above all need the confidence and economic aid of Western industrialists and bankers. They need not only your capital but also your qualified management."[9]

Joint Ventures

Many consider joint ventures the best form of economic cooperation between the modern Western market and the nascent market in the Eastern countries for which this engagement means aid. And with capital comes skilled management, which is perhaps needed most of all. For Western investors, on the other hand, who bring in management experience with their capital, aid is neither here nor there—their purpose in importing capital is to open up tremendous and very promising sales markets as well as whole regions boasting a relatively cheap labor force that is as skilled as the labor force in the developed industrial countries. Experience over the last four years also clearly showed that Western firms did not in the least regard their engagement in the East as aid to the economically weaker partner. They were investing their money not where it was urgently needed but where they could expect greater profitability and wider possibilities of sales. These are the considerations that determined the choice of business partner.

The net flows in joint ventures and direct foreign investment in Eastern and Central Europe grew from $573 million in 1990 to $2,302 million, $3,055 million, and $3,548 million in the next three years. The main recipient was Hungary, with the capital input in the years 1990–93 of $311 million, $1,459 million, $1,471 million, and $3,325 million, followed by the Czech Republic, with $135 million, $310 million, $983 million, and $409 million. The capital transfer to Poland during the same years was $88 million, $117 million, $224 million, and $330 million. The next largest recipient was Slovenia, with $2 million, $41 million, $113 million, and $110 million, respectively. These four relatively advanced economies received over 90 percent of the total capital invested in the region.[10]

The main problem identified by a survey of these investments[11] was that the capital flowed predominantly into existing assets. Potential foreign investors were deterred from investing in many cases because they encountered a range of operational problems that increased risk and uncertainty. In addition, there has been uncertainty over the macroeconomic outlook and the future level of demand in the transition economies.

Hungary has been the country of choice for foreign investors, especially because Hungarian firms have been cultivating direct and closer contacts with Western firms since 1968, and were far more open to receiving foreign capital. The share of foreign investments in Hungary's industrial capital is about 9 percent, but Hungary is willing to increase the foreign share to 30 percent—that is, to the pre–World War II level. The second in preference is Czech Republic. The difference between it and Hungary, however, is enormous. The per-capita input in Hungary was $226, and in the Czech Republic only about $4 million.

Western investors determine their preferences on the basis of their assessment of the economic situation, technical equipment, and the infrastructure. The U.S. magazine *Chief Executive* gave an extremely interesting picture of the state of the individual countries in its July 1992 issue. These items formed the basis of its evaluation: the debt, the banking system, labor productivity, the work force, the infrastructure, technology, management skills, supplies of capital goods, and the possibility of transferring profits. Each of these items was rated by points on the following scale: 1—very poor, 2—poor, 3—average, 4—good, 5—very good. The maximum score was fifty. The former GDR was rated as the most attractive country, with the highest score of forty-one points, followed by Czechoslovakia and Hungary with thirty-two points each, Poland with twenty-two, Romania with eighteen, and Bulgaria with seventeen. The former USSR, however, scored only ten points. Hungary received good scores (four points) for its banking system, work force, infrastructure, technology, and capital goods supplies, but a low score (two points) for debt. Czechoslovakia scored very good (five points) for the quality of its work force, and good (four points) for the banking system, the infrastructure, and quality of management. Poland received a "very poor" score (one) for debt and "bad" (two points) for infrastructure and technology. The other items were scored at three points. Bulgaria had a "very poor" score (one point) for management, capital goods supplies, and profit transfers, and a "poor" score (two points) for the other items.

Romania had a rating of "good" (four points) for debt, and scores of one or two for the other items.

A Munich consulting firm came up with similar evaluations: Hungary received 9.5 points out of a possible 10 for the attitude of firms to a market economy and free enterprise. Czechoslovakia received a similar score for the cost of wages. Poland received relatively good scores (7.5 and 6.8) for market mechanism and access to land and real estate. All other thirty-four of the forty items studied were rated as "very poor."[12]

What the Peoples of the Reform Countries Think

To address the question of what the people of the reform countries think about their own situation and where the reforms are going, the results of two representative surveys are available: the Paul Lazarsfeld Society of Vienna conducted a survey in November–December 1991 and January 1992 in seven countries of Central and Eastern Europe (the New Democratic Republic [NDR] barometer for the new democracies in 1991), while the London Gallup Institute carried out a survey at the request of the EC Commission in Autumn 1991 in seven countries of Central and Eastern Europe and in the three Baltic countries. It was published under the title *Central European Eurobarometer*.

The answers to this question varied from one country to another. But both polls clearly showed that Poles and Bulgarians were most dissatisfied with the consequences of the change of system. Czechs were more positive about the general course of events. The NDR question, "How would you rate the present situation of your family?" elicited the following responses: 18 percent of Poles responded "quite satisfactory," but 56 percent and 26 percent responded "not very satisfactory" and "not at all satisfactory," respectively. Thirty-seven percent of Bulgarians rated the family situation as "quite satisfactory," but 34 percent responded "not very satisfactory" and 28 percent responded "not at all satisfactory." The figures for Czechoslovakia were 54 percent "quite satisfactory" and only 8 percent "not at all satisfactory"; for Hungary and Romania 49 percent responded "not very satisfactory" and 17 percent and 26 percent, respectively, responded "not at all satisfactory."

The response to the question concerning the "probability of a putsch against parliament and democratic parties" was unsettling: 45 percent of Poles, 35 percent of Czechs, 28 percent of Romanians, but only 21 percent of Bulgarians and Hungarians responded "it could come about."

The London Gallup Institute wanted to know how the people rated how the reforms were going as well as the economic situation in the last twelve months. The figures showed that 58 percent of Poles, 47 percent of Hungarians, 38 percent of Czechs, but only 20 percent of Bulgarians and 37 percent of Romanians thought that the path taken by the reforms was wrong. Rating of the economic situation ranged from skeptical to pessimistic: 26 percent of Hungarians thought that the economic situation would remain unchanged and 31 percent thought that it would get worse. The figures for the responses to these questions were 26 percent and 30 percent, respectively, in Poland, 21 percent and 36 percent in Czechoslovakia, 18 percent and 19 percent in Bulgaria, and 17 percent and 18 percent in Romania.

After the Euphoria, a Sobering

The Autumn 1989 revolution took a gentle course, but the goal was unprecedented; most especially, the transition marked out was not from feudalism to capitalism, but from a social system that called itself postcapitalist and was anticapitalist. It did not have private ownership of the means of production, nor was the economy steered by a stratum of proprietors and managers but by an all-powerful state bureaucracy. This state of affairs would be crucial to the course of the reorganization to come. Not only was it necessary to build an infrastructure suited to a market economy, with a modern monetary and financial system and price structures determined by the market, but an entirely new stratum of industrial managers would have to be trained. This would be a social layer whose activities were not directed toward the fulfillment of planned directives handed down from above, or toward a seller's market, but would be steered by the imperatives of a competitive national and international market. The path embarked upon would be necessarily difficult from the very outset, because the peoples who overthrew the old regime had set their gaze on the prosperity of the industrial states of the West, without knowing whether they would be capable of achieving that level. When *Newsweek* asked Ewa Letowska, former government spokeswoman, how long Poland would need to reach the level of civilized Europe, her response was, "Fifteen years, but not in all domains." Other experts are much more pessimistic. Such timeframe calculations do not take into account that the wealth of the highly developed industrial nations is the result of long experience with management and marketing. And the adaptation of economic structures to the needs of the domestic population is the result of a long process of perfecting production methods, as well as of a historically evolved, relative harmony between workers and employees. The Krupps, Thyssens, Fords, and Rockefellers acquired their abilities not in the universities—or not only in the universities—but through the experience of countless human generations. It is also often forgotten that Great Britain and Belgium owe at least part of their wealth to irretrievable sources—their colonies, now free, which had once supplied the metropolis with cheap fuels and raw materials.

The transformation will also be difficult because the training and skills of the peoples of Central and Eastern Europe were formed not during the transitional phase from feudalism to capitalism but at the end of the twentieth century. This level is therefore often even higher in the former socialist countries than in the highly industrial countries—which does not necessarily mean higher labor productivity. The transition in this domain is not from less freedom to more freedom, but vice-versa—and under circumstances in which only a small social group will improve their material situation, while the bulk of the population will have to endure privations indefinitely. It is by no means certain, given the democratic ideals of a well-educated, intelligent population, that the underprivileged and sometimes even undernourished will look on passively as a small privileged group enriches itself in the midst of economic disintegration, as the Polish scholar, Jozef Robek writes, squandering its gains on consumption, while demonstrating little willingness to invest.[13] It is also doubtful whether this society, which had enjoyed social services as well as free education and health care, despite a lower living standard compared with the West, will accept a market "without adjectives"—that is, without social security.

Of course, pluralism in the exchange of ideas and among political parties is valued highly, although current practices elicit little enthusiasm. The economy is highlighted rather by a truncated market, as wrote Marten Bardosi, the faction head of the Hungarian Free Democratic Party. Moreover, the disadvantages rather than the advantages of Western democracy have punctuated people's everyday experience in Eastern Europe so far. The institutional structures of a multiparty system were created in an astonishingly short time. But too many parties sprang into existence and none were able to create a mass base for themselves. There are more than one hundred parties in Poland, and the party spectrum presented in Czechoslovakia just before the election on June 6, 1992, was just as diffuse.

An unknown, exiled Pole, Stan Tyminski, won 25 percent of the votes in the Polish presidential elections and came in second, ahead of the then–prime minister, Tadeusz Mazowiecki, only because he had promised voters the high living standard found in countries like Canada, where he had built up a prosperous business.

Voters became disillusioned before a pluralistic democracy could gain a foothold. Only 11,887,999 persons out of a total number of eligible voters of 27,516,166 (42 percent) voted in the October 1991 elections to the Polish parliament. The strongest of the twenty-four parties represented in the parliament, the Democratic Union, gained no more than 5.5 percent of the total number of eligible voters and no more than 10.5 percent of the valid votes. In a poll commissioned by the newspaper *Rzeczpospolita*, 60 percent of the respondents felt that democracy was not being correctly administered in Poland, and only 16 percent felt that democratic principles were being respected.

Four years is too short a time for a fair evaluation of the reforms and their expected consequences. Joseph Schumpeter once observed that no revolutionary transformation has yet succeeded in maintaining order in the midst of change. The transformation in Central and Eastern Europe has so far proceeded relatively smoothly, considering its scope. Criticism of the first stage of the reform was relatively mild. Considerable price rises were expected, since prices of farm products and foods were everywhere heavily subsidized by the state. If this stage had required a shock therapy in Poland, this was mainly because Poland's market was more deregulated and the discrepancy between supply and demand was greater than elsewhere. This stage was rather successful if one considers that Poland had in fact succeeded in replacing the distribution practices of a command system with normal market relations. But because of the drastic reduction in buying power, all the reform countries are still a long way from an authentic market economy and a functioning economic infrastructure. The director of the Center for Economic Policy Research in London, Richard Porter, correctly observed that the stabilization achieved in the first stage only demonstrates how inflation can be stopped, not how a communist economy can be transformed into a capitalist economy.[14]

But the second stage of reform has been validly criticized. The contemplated forced privatization of state enterprises had necessarily to further aggravate the decline of the economy so long as there was no capital and no appropriate managerial corps. Neither "popular shares" nor other methods are suited for achieving a privatization that will at the same time spawn a functional and competent management. Foreign capital is attracted to countries that inspire confidence: 60 percent of Hungary's proceeds from privatization came from abroad and 80 percent of privatized large concerns are in foreign hands. It is fully appreciated that economic decline accompanied by a growing unemployment cannot be tolerated over the long term. But none of the reform countries have so far been able to come up with a model that permits a revamping of the economy in the midst of radical change.

Chapter 5

Prospects: Which Reform Country Has the Best Chances to Effect a Change in System?

Lord Ralf Dahrendorf, ex-minister and former EC commissioner, expressed the opinion that the reform countries of Eastern and Central Europe could well institute political democracy in six months, and a market economy in six years, but that it would take sixty years to establish a genuine bourgeois society.[1]

Since the historic Autumn of 1989, five years have passed—too short a time to verify this long-term prognosis. The short-term prognosis, however, has been confirmed. The command economy has been abolished in an astonishingly short time, and normal commodity and money relations have been introduced; the organizational framework of the institutions of a pluralistic democracy have been set up. However, when an expert such as Ralf Dahrendorf asserts that six decades are needed to establish a social system in order to maintain the present level of civilization, he is probably thinking of what is obvious to any unbiased analyst: that there must be an appropriate organizational and institutional framework within which the preconditions can be created for a market economy and democracy—the basic pillars of a modern civil society. Third World countries also have the organizational framework for a market economy and for democratic institutions. But only in very few cases can one speak of a modern democratic state.

The ex-communist reform countries, however, are located in Europe, and their peoples would like to compare their standard of living with that of Western Europe. A modern market economy of West European standards is not just an organizational framework, it is a socioeconomic system created over the course of centuries by many human generations, and it is constantly adapting to changing conditions of production and trade. This implies not only organizational mechanisms and institutions but also economic structures that befit the times: a market economy mentality among the population and the economic elite, qualified management, complex property relations, modern marketing techniques, and so on. Czech Prime Minister Vaclav Klaus put this most clearly:

> It was easy to dismantle explicit socialism, a one-party system, within institutions such as the planning commission, and to change some of the basic rules of the game. However, it is extremely hard to abolish the implicit socialism in us, our habits, prejudices, and traditions, which were shaped over the course of preceding decades by our political, social, and economic system.[2]

After World War II, the countries of Western Europe developed their traditional economic systems into market welfare economies, and with good reason: if they had not been socially oriented, they would have been incapable of securing social peace, of establishing a partnership between employer and employee, thus ridding the world of brutal class struggle and revolutionary passions. The reform countries of Central and Eastern Europe did not set out on the traditional path toward capitalism from a state of feudalism, nor did they have to pass through the intermediate stage of early capitalism, with its unreined exploitation. In fact, no matter how inefficient their social network was, their education and health systems were not all that bad, and there was no unemployment. But during the years of reform, their standard of living deteriorated drastically, social services were dismantled on a large scale, and the unemployment rate rose by an unprecedented 35 percent in the former GDR, and 15 percent in Poland. However rational may be the reductions in the budget deficit introduced under pressure from the international monetary institutions, or however reasonable Vaclav Klaus's statement that "we want to introduce a market economy without adjectives," it is doubtful whether the citizens of these countries will accept the building of such a social system if it means more deprivations than benefits in the foreseeable future, and if only a tiny group will reap all the profits while the majority have to bear the costs.

But, although political scientist Ralf Dahrendorf is not alone in his pessimistic long-term prognosis, Poland's economic expert Stanislaw Gomulka takes the view that his country will need forty years to reach the living standard of Portugal or Spain. This period of privation, however, could be put to use, particularly if the reform measures are controlled in a way that will prevent a further decline in the economy and standard of living, so that Eastern Europe does not fall even further behind the industrial countries of the West.

Attempts to establish a parliamentary democracy have fared no better. The peoples of Eastern and Central Europe cultivated no democratic traditions in the four decades of Soviet communism or for that matter during the period between the wars, with the exception of Czechoslovakia. Poland and Hungary had authoritarian regimes under Pilsudski and Horthy, and Albania, Bulgaria, and Romania were still monarchies. The protagonists in the popular uprisings of 1989 knew that the way to a civilized society was not necessarily through a capitalist market alone, as was the case in Chile under Pinochet or in Spain under Franco, but via a market that had to be firmly rooted in a parliamentary democracy of the Western type. Of course, they knew their limitations, as M. Duverger, the French expert on the theory of elites, demonstrated most clearly: "Rule by the people must be replaced by rule of the people by an elite that has risen from the people." Oxford Professor A.C. MacIntyre made the following comment on this formulation: "An elite that has risen from the people is still an elite and an elite very quickly becomes professionalized." MacIntyre further invokes the cruel but true point made by Joseph Schumpeter: "Democracy is a partiocracy."[3]

The main difficulty for the reform countries, however, is that their elites, having been formed rather rapidly, are extremely removed from the people. Dozens of parties and groups have been established in this brief postcommunist period, many more than in the developed democracies of the West, but none of them can call on mass support. Aleksander Smolar, member of the executive committee of Poland's Democratic Union, notes that this party, numerically the largest, gained 13 percent of the votes in the parliamentary elections of October 27, 1991, but this represents only 6 percent of the electorate—that is, it has no more than 15,000 to 20,000 members, in a country with 40 million inhabitants.

Bulgaria has a similar party spectrum: O. Pishev, the Bulgarian ambassador to the United States, writes:

> Political rivalry is personalized, a circumstance that has led to the formation of thousands of political organizations and groups. Fourteen political parties and alliances participated in the elections of October 13, 1991, but only three of them managed to achieve the minimum of 4 percent of the votes. In Eastern Europe, it is easy to proclaim democratic ideals and values, but former Communist practice is very hard to eradicate. It is easier to advocate individual rights and freedoms than to implement them in a society which is only just beginning to grasp its newly-created political structures. We have many political leaders, but it is somewhat questionable how close they are to the people.[4]

The party scenario in Romania is similar: in the elections on September 27, 1992, 90 parties vied for 328 seats in parliament and 90 seats in the senate.

The hope that a plurality of political parties would bring about democratic pluralism has not been fulfilled. The same applies to the hope that the liberalization of prices and the establishing of a few of the institutions of a market economy would bring about a modern competitive market. The population has little understanding of the rather vague party platforms, and a large segment of the population make no use of their hard-won democratic rights. No more than half the citizens eligible to vote took part in the Polish parliamentary elections in October 1990 or in the local elections in Hungary in March 1992. Somewhat greater was the participation in the September 1993 elections in Poland and in 1994 elections in Hungary. Trust in politicians who are not answerable to party members and merely make thunder in internal party struggles is as slight as people's liking for the nouveau riche. The latter have emerged in part from the former nomenklatura after managing to salvage some of their privileges for the new era, and have built up lucrative businesses thanks to connections old and new.

Not one of the many political parties has an attractive program that is realizable under present conditions other than the slogan "away from communism." But the decline in the economy and in living standards continues, and the parliaments confine their discussions to problems of secondary importance, preferring to debate their shameful past rather than discuss how to work out a viable future. The charismatic leaders of the founding period have been knocked off their pedestals of honor, yet no replacements have been found for them. The uncontested hero of the Velvet Revolution in Prague, Vaclav Havel, was elected to the post of president of the Czech Republic with only 109 deputy votes out of a possible 200, and the legendary leader of Solidarity, Nobel Prize laureate and now President Lech Walesa, is steadily losing his authority and respect among the citizens. The formerly powerful Solidarity union, which with its 10 million members contributed to the fall of the Communist Party regime, is slipping ever deeper into insignificance and now has no more than 2 million members.

Dissidents, who pointed the way to political change—many of whom were held in prisons and concentration camps by the communist regime—knew exactly what they did *not* want: no totalitarianism, no police state, no command economy, and, above all, no subordination to Soviet imperialism. Their visions of the future, though, were rather vague. Most of them were striving for reformed socialism with a "human face" without knowing what form this could take. The present governments are different. Vaclav Klaus, the last finance minister of Czechoslovakia, and now head of government in the Czech Republic, wrote: "We no longer wish to embark upon new social experiments; we have had many experiments in the past. We would like to act according to the traditional rules of the game and accept traditional values. We need neither a third way nor the dream of a socialist market."[5]

Henryk Goryszewski, former vice-premier of the Polish government under Hanna Suchocka, is clear: "It is not important whether we have capitalism, or whether there is freedom of speech, or whether there is prosperity in Poland; what is most important is that Poland remains Catholic."[6] Jozsef Antall, former head of government in Hungary and chairman of the government party, Hungarian Democratic Forum (HDF), outlined his program quite succinctly when he assumed power: "to build capitalism as fast as possible." Ultranationalist writer Istvan Csurka set out his notion of democracy quite clearly shortly before the congress of the Democratic Forum in late January 1993; he called for the creation of a healthy, joyful, and genetically pure nation. This is completely in line with the *Pfeilkreuzler*, the Hungarian Nazis of the 1930s and early 1940s. Istvan Csurka, a member of the Democratic Forum, was reelected to vice-president of the HDF with 536 out of 700 delegate votes.

Miklos Jancso, the Hungarian film director and winner of many international prizes, including those from Cannes and Venice, commented: "The political elite have to propose something new to the people, since mutual accusations and the spread of hatred is not enough for a political program. If they cannot come up with anything positive, the same thing will happen as in Yugoslavia."[7] In a 1993 interview, the filmmaker speaks bitterly of his crushed hopes: "When the new regime was established three years ago, everyone had hopes of something honest and solid coming about; however, the situation is growing increasingly more somber." In Budapest, once considered the most fun-loving "playground" in the East, you no longer hear jokes, says Jancso. The director recalls only one that is told over and over again: "Jozsef Antall managed to achieve in three short years what Janos Kadar tried in vain to achieve in all his thirty years as general secretary of the Communist Party, to wit: to make Hungarians think fondly of communism."

The most bitter criticism of the postcommunist era comes from the ranks of the former dissidents. Miclos Jansos Landsmann, director of a Budapest research institute, and Laszlo Lengyel write:

> Never before has Hungary's political elite consisted of intellectuals to such a degree, and never before has the political elite been so greatly removed from the development of society. . . . Arpad Gäncz, a legal expert and writer became State President; the historian Josef Antall became Prime Minister; the historian Lajos Fur became Minister of Defense, etc. . . . There are writers, doctors, lawyers, and priests in the parliament . . . The intellectual elite, however, lacks a basis for becoming an independent bourgeoisie since they have lived through the past twenty-five years as members of the middle strata.

Lengyel, a scientist, offers the following explanation for the virtually inexplicable plunge of a large part of the Democratic Forum into the abyss of right-wing radical populism: "Because of their isolation, this elite will grasp at anything that promises to give it some social significance. . . . They have fallen prey to political hysteria out of fear that the middle layers might solve their own problems without, or even in opposition to, the intellectuals."[8]

Former dissident Aleksandr Smolar is just as critical of the situation in Poland, writing that the hope that the opposition could count on greater support from the population after coming to power has not been fulfilled. This has happened because the state has taken certain social rights away from some strata (meaning in the first instance workers in the nationalized heavy industries), while other layers of society profit from the civil and political rights that have been granted to them (white-collar workers or intellectuals).[9] Polish popular writer Jozef Hen criticizes the situation even more harshly, saying that the number of profiteers in Poland is equal to the number of unemployed. Senator Andrej Celinski describes the country's politics as follows:

> Our economics policy recalls Gogol [the late nineteenth-century Russian satirist] rather than Silicon Valley or Taiwan. The task does not consist of dividing up the booty among the politicians themselves but of mobilizing the population so as to achieve goals which would be unachievable without proper policy. That is perhaps why people are sick of politics.[10]

Stefan Heym, a respected writer who was one of the earliest dissidents, describes the situation in the former GDR in terms of "making pure new cloth out of old mixed fibers,"[11] a phenomenon that has been spreading throughout the East from centers of power that are even "more powerful than the old Politburo: these are the Treuhand AG (the agency dealing with denationalization of large concerns and combinates) and the Gauck Commission (concerned with the verification of Stasi collaborators and unofficial informants)." Heym, cofounder of the Committee for Justice, which stands aloof from party interests, is merciless in his reproach of the Westernizers, who sell off the little that is usable for the lowest possible price, and who "rationalize East Germans out of existence, while rapidly establishing ties with 'resurgent GDR bureaucrats.' One Treuhand keeps the other clean," Heym concludes.

There are, of course, more optimistic assessments of both the reforms and their chances of success. Leszek Balcerowicz, the principal architect of the economic reform in Poland, is more optimistic than anyone else. After the fateful day of June 4, 1989, when a historic compromise was reached at a round table between the Communist Party government and the trade union Solidarity, and the first postcommunist government was formed under Tadeusz Mazowiecki, the economist Balcerowicz was appointed as finance minister. In a speech on February 2, 1993, he explained: "Provided there are no political setbacks, the East European reform countries have a good chance of putting their transitional path to a market economy behind by the end of the century." He goes on, quite optimistically: "By then Poland, Hungary, the Czech Republic, and Slovakia will have economic structures that are fundamentally no different from those in the Western countries." Only time will tell whether his forecasts are realistic or whether they are only the pious wish of a reformer, who has since returned to his research. If by "economic structures" he means property relations, he may be right, for denationalization is being driven forward dynamically, rightly or wrongly. It is highly unlikely, however, that the countries of Central Europe will have developed modern competitive industrial structures by the end of this century. Indeed, denationalization of the large enterprises have worsened rather than improved the situation. Perhaps he attributed too great a role to the West when he said, "The European Community must offer the Eastern countries clear prospects." He is, however, quite right in pointing out that the imposition of punitive tariffs on steel imports from the East shows how wide is the "gap between Brussels rhetoric and reality." But it would be an injustice to Balcerowicz to say that he does not see the dangers. "The greatest dangers are over, though we still have major problems ahead: in some regions unemployment will still rise drastically, and the restructuring of heavy industry will still demand many victims." The questions Balcerowicz leaves unanswered are whether intolerable deprivation will come to an end by the end of the century, or whether a social market economy—no other economy will be acceptable—can be established, or whether this market, still precarious, will be able to cope with the problems of adapting to and dealing with the continual economic recession with which the industrial countries of the West still have to cope, despite their highly developed capacity for solving such problems.

In a sense, the "big crash" theory of the architect of Poland's reform has been confirmed: galloping inflation has been reined in, the command economy has been replaced by the freer mechanisms of a market economy, and a balance has been reestablished between drastically reduced solvent demand and accumulated stocks, due, among other things, to imports from abroad. The speedy privatization of retail trade and services, as well as of those industrial branches supplying the population with consumer goods, was also beneficial. It would be wrong, however, to think that the exorbitantly high social costs of a market created in this way can be imposed upon highly civilized peoples such as the Central Europeans, only to proclaim three years into the reform that major sacrifices still lie ahead. There is a strong likelihood that Balcerowicz's forecast that the market will be completely in place by the end of this century will be fulfilled. It is not so certain that the majority of the population will continue to accept the privations expected of them for so long. No reform country has yet succeeded in stopping the decline in the standard of living. This restoration is certainly a more difficult one than the mission assumed by the 1917 October Revolution. All the more logical, therefore, would it be to prefer an evolutionary to a revolutionary retreat. Denationalization is more difficult than nationalization, because the bourgeoisie (property owners, managers, entrepreneurs), which controls the economy, has been destroyed. Nor will all the courses given by the most qualified teachers in the most outstanding universities in the world be able to impart to the newly appointed company directors the special qualities possessed by such industrial captains as Krupp and Thyssen, Ford and Rockefeller.

Of course, it would be difficult to create a functioning competitive market if the state sector retained its dominant role. But privatization by means of coupons for every eligible citizen will create neither popular capitalism (shares for the many are a good device for savings, but nothing more) nor any other modern form of capitalism suited to the times. It is an experiment to be avoided—an experiment that will lead directly to "shopkeeper capitalism." Large enterprises denationalized in this way will always come second in any competition with the experienced managers of the developed industrial countries. The solution lies not in finding an "adequate" balance between the state and private property in order to ensure competitiveness on the world market; the decisive factor, rather, will be the relative proportion of hi-tech in industrial structures, as well as the quality of management. This point was made by Alfonso Guerra Gonzalez, the deputy general secretary of the governing Socialist Workers' Party and ex-vice-premier of Spain, during his visit to Poland; he backed up his thesis by pointing out that the state share in Spain's overall economy was 47 percent.[12]

In the light of experience gained throughout the years of reform, the uncertainty created among the management of large enterprises by hasty and ill-considered privatization seems to be a major cause of economic decline and of an appalling, steadily rising unemployment rate. Private firms are sprouting like mushrooms, but, as they are still very small, they will not be able to offer jobs to all those who lost them from the large enterprises, most of which have been privatized by liquidation rather than by sale. It is therefore no accident that the unemployment rate in the reform countries, which can look back on a time of full employment (true, it was grossly inefficient full employment), is much higher now than in the industrial countries of the West, which are themselves now in recession. Perhaps it would not be unfair to mention here the West's failure to participate sufficiently in financing the reform program of Central and Eastern Europe. On the other hand, the reformers in the East do not seem to have considered that the Western countries, burdened by gigantic budget deficits and thus forced to raise money in order to stimulate stagnating economies and to reduce unemployment, cannot do much to help the East. Nor is it unfair to point out the high customs barriers, which have particularly affected the giant foundries in the East. But the protesting foundrymen in Germany and elsewhere in Western Europe are thinking primarily about their own jobs, afraid that cheap steel from the East could place them in jeopardy. Finally there is the support from the EC, which recommended that its member states reduce steel output by 30 billion tons by the end of February 1993 (with a loss of 50,000 jobs), but this is hardly a real prospect.

If money is only trickling from the West to the East, the same cannot be said about good and not-so-good advice. Many talented and very eloquent professors from the most famous universities in the United States and Western Europe, who until now had been offering their advice to the developing countries, are now advising the governments of Russia and Central Europe, and some of them advise all these countries together, on how they can effect the changes in their systems as rapidly and successfully as possible. Most advisers are treated as described by Poland's famous economist Michal Kalecki: "I have offered my advice to five different governments, but it was very rarely heeded. If my advice did get taken seriously, it would only be put into practice in a different way from the one I proposed" (personal communication, 1969). It would therefore be wrong to hold the foreign advisers, rather than those carrying out the advice in their own countries, responsible for the rather moderate success rate. Perhaps they did not even deserve the reproach of Vaclav Klaus in his above-quoted article (although he primarily had in mind left-wing intellectuals from the United States): "These intellectuals, confronted with a shrinking demand for their product, are now looking for markets in the new democracies of Central and Eastern Europe, who are not interested in their advice." And, he goes on quite trenchantly, "I would say that one of the main obstacles to our development was ideological infiltration from the West. This is an endless fight that we have to wage in our part of the world."[13]

The shock therapy model was criticized mercilessly. The view expressed in "The Economic Reconstruction of Central Europe," published under the aegis of the Socioeconomic Department of the Austrian Academy of Sciences, deserves special mention in this respect.[14] Under the motto of neoclassical economist Alfred Marshall, "Nature never leaps" (*natura non facit saltum*), the authors state: "The ensuing consequences resemble the twenties more than the fifties." Then follows a sentence that goes to the very heart of the problem: "There is nothing in the policies currently being implemented and the human discomfort they have engendered that is inherent or even inevitable in a successful transition process." Further, the deterioration of living standards is not only not necessary, it has even been counterproductive, since it might instead be hindering the establishment of a market-based economy. Then comes a proposal of what to do. The compilation of an emergency program should be given top priority, say the authors, for the purpose of stabilizing production and employment, to create the hope of improving living conditions in the future. A precondition is that existing capacities for production and trade relations are expanded rather than destroyed. The view that "the transfer of existing property to private ownership does little in itself to create the conditions necessary for new wealth creation" sounds thoroughly convincing.

Poland's Big Bang: Success or Failure

An observer of the stormy developments in Central and Eastern Europe over the last few years is rather like a seismographer trying to measure the effects of an earthquake with a microscope. The criteria usually used are utterly uninstructive. The following example shows the ineffectuality of analysts: a report published in early January by GATT on Poland's situation states that "the Polish government may have underestimated the economic shock of a rapid market opening."[15] The consequences of the reform processes in all the reform countries are rated just as pessimistically by the *Agenda 1992*. But the conclusions differ greatly: whereas GATT calls on the Polish government to accelerate privatization, the *Agenda* authors take the view that this acceleration of privatization is in fact one of the main causes of the decline in the economy, and recommend that more consideration be given to state industrial enterprises in order to reduce the exorbitantly high social costs of the reform process. In the meantime, the Polish Office of Statistics published a report on the economic results for 1992, slightly dampening the pessimism of these two studies. The gross domestic product increased by 0.2–2 percent in 1992, after declines of 11.6 percent and 7.6 percent in the preceding two years. Progress in industrial production seemed to be even better: after decreases of 24.2 percent and 11.9 percent in 1990 and 1991, respectively, it rose by 4.2 percent in 1992. The GDP rose by 4 percent in 1993. The government spoke of a "breakthrough," or even of overcoming the recession. The opposition, on the other hand, pointed out that the growth rate fell within the range of "statistical error," or that it should even be thought of as a statistical error. The headlines in Western newspapers ("Economic Upswing," "End of the Recession," or "Economic Adaptation in Poland") were more optimistic than the Polish newspapers, which played down the "miracle on the Vistula" with such titles as "Barefoot but Forward." But there was no shortage of voices claiming that Poland, the first reform country in Central Europe, had assumed the role of forerunner in the reform process. It was incontestable that the decline in the economy was brought to a halt at the end of 1992. It was, however, contestable whether the government could regard the arrest of economic decline as a confirmation of the reform course. The answer depends on how one assesses the restructuring of property relations. Investment banks such as Morgan Stanley or Salomon Brothers, as well as many other foreign and domestic institutions, are unanimous in their opinion that Poland's economic indicators are due first and foremost to the private sector. A private share of 50 percent in the gross domestic product in 1992 is much higher than in other reform countries, such as Hungary (35 percent) or the former Czechoslovakia (23 percent).

This assertion is supported by the indicators for the individual branches. Most of the fourteen branches showing growth were already wholly or almost wholly privatized: specifically, the manufacture of construction materials, washing machines, vacuum cleaners, televisions, sausage, beer, or chocolates. But the timber industry also shows a high growth rate (up by 17 percent), as does shipbuilding and auto manufacture. On the other hand, nine industrial branches that are still wholly or in part in state hands (machinery construction, metal-working factories, and mining) show a decline in production of between 8 percent and 12 percent. Crop production in agriculture has decreased perceptibly by 20 percent. There is indeed some basis for the opinion that the causes of the more positive gross national product indicators in Poland and in the former Czechoslovakia or in Hungary are to be found in the accelerated denationalization of large enterprises. The private firms established en masse in the past three years will certainly not be able to employ all the millions of people dismissed by the large enterprises. If privatization continues at the same pace and in the same way, unemployment could reach 20 percent in the coming years, and indeed some forecasts by economists, who tend to be cautious in their estimates, say as much.

Though the private sector may not have been able to make up for the decline in production over the past few years and will be unable to employ the growing number of persons dismissed from state enterprises, there is no doubt that the middle layer in Poland is developing much more dynamically and even functioning much more dynamically than in the other reform countries. Apart from agriculture, which under the communist regime had been run mainly by small farmers, today there are 1.6 million private firms in Poland. Almost 60 percent of the employed population work in the private sector, including 44.2 percent outside agriculture. Half of the 1,495 state farms have been handed over to the Treasury for privatization. It is a striking fact that Poland has succeeded within an astonishingly short time in replacing the loss of the bulk of its foreign trade with former Eastern European countries by new markets. In 1989–92 exports increased by 24 percent, 86 percent of this to the EC countries.[16] But imports grew more than exports. The deficit of the foreign trade and services rose from $0.27 billion in 1992 to $2.33 billion in 1993. Western investors have regained confidence in Poland. According to figures on East European investment, $4.1 billion were invested in Poland, including $3 billion in 1992. A few multinationals, such as International Paper and Fiat, have invested more than $2 billion in Polish industrial firms.

The passing of the state budget in 1993 with a moderate deficit of 81 billion zlotys is considered a success. Although this deficit is greater than the previous year (69.3 billion zlotys), it is no more than 5 percent of the gross domestic product, given the 1992 inflation rate of 44 percent. The opposition demanded a relaxation of the rigid financial policy in order to revitalize the stagnating economy, and reproached the government for succumbing to the diktat of the IMF: in the opinion of the opposition, this was beneath the dignity of a sovereign nation of 40 million people. The government's experts replied that deficit spending made sense only if the inflation rate were no more than 2 to 3 percent, whereas in Poland it was over 40 percent (the zloty was devalued by 39.5 percent in 1992). The budget crisis, said the experts, was a consequence of the "dwindling sources" of budget revenue owing to the steadily declining profitability of state enterprises. The private economy, on the other hand, often avoided taxation by declaring lower earnings than was actually the case, and by expanding undetected the gray area of business activity, which has been estimated at 20 percent of total economic performance. Expenditure, on the other hand, is increasing as a result of the steadily rising cost of growing unemployment.

If Poland complies with the deficit strictures of the IMF, the special drawing rights on the aid package of $467 million initially approved and then suspended in September 1991 may resume. The opposition, however, feared that a further increase in the existing debt of $46.9 billion would imperil solvency. The halving of the debt was accepted by the Paris Club of state creditors (which brought a relief of about $16 billion). The chief negotiator, Deputy Finance Minister Krzysztof Krowacki, estimated that the interest arrears on the commercial debt alone were $2.7 billion.[17] For their part, specialists point out that the problem is not so much a shortage of loan offers, but rather the inability to use the loans offered. Businessmen complain that the main obstacle to expanding credit relations is the banking system, which remains underdeveloped; the banks, on the other hand, complain about the lack of willingness to invest and the rather low solvency of the industrial firms. Both partners in credit transactions are right, but the World Bank loans have remained largely unused. By the end of 1992 these fifteen projects have appropriated $2.64 billion for financing, but as of February 1993 no more than $500 million have been claimed. The existing credit lines, about $638 million, have been used, but only at a snail's pace.[18]

The parliament elections of September 19, 1993, confirmed once again that the people of Poland were discontented with the methods of

the reforms initiated in 1990, with the shock therapy of the four Solidarity governments. The former coalition partners, the Left Union and
the Peasant Party (PSL), received 36 percent of the votes. Because of
the results of the elections, these parties were unable to create a government with an absolute majority. The new head of the government is
the leader of the Peasant Party, Waldemar Pawlak. The left-oriented
government is inclined to continue the reform policy started by the
prior governments. However, privatization of the state-owned enterprises will slow down.

Czechoslovakia's and Hungary's Reform Problems

Although the two parts of Czechoslovakia are now separate, separatist
tendencies have persisted throughout their seventy years of common
history as a state. For the six years under Hitler's rule, Slovakia had
been, if not a sovereign state, independent of the Czech protectorate.
The "Bleifuss" theory, according to which subsidies were passed from
the economically stronger to the economically weaker of the former
allies, was not totally applicable in this case since the two parts of
Czechoslovakia were also economically closely intertwined through
many years of a shared division of labor. It may well be true, however,
that the split had become inevitable since Slovakia did not want or
could not support Vaclav Klaus's reform model, and given the resur-
gence of nationalist feelings in both parts of Czechoslovakia, that a
separation offered a better solution than an uncertain "cohabitation"
that was continually rocked by crises. The Central Office of Statistics
calculated the following monetary value for the loss caused by separation: the decline in the Czech GNP would be 17.3 billion crowns ($750
million) while the Slovak GNP would fall by 20.7 billion crowns (–5.7
percent), but state budget revenues would also fall by 10.7 billion
crowns (5.7 percent). Separation, however, would harm both. Experts
insisted that the separation would cause a decline in production by
several percentage points in both republics.

But the wave of nationalism stirred up in Slovakia proved most
decisive for the split. A speech by the ex-communist Michal Kovac
after his election as president of the Republic will serve as an example:
Kovac celebrated the fascist leader Andrei Hlinka as a national hero
who "kept the torch of freedom constantly alight." The forecast that
the Czech Republic would halt its economic decline in 1993 but that

the Slovak GNP would continue to fall by a further 4 percent was confirmed. The GNP of the Czech Republic declined in 1992 by 7.1 percent and in 1993 by 0.5 percent; the indicators for Slovakia were −7.0 percent and −4.7 percent. Slovakia was economically the weaker of the two: 5.3 million Slovaks had generated 29 percent of the Czech industrial production, while 10.4 million Czechs produced 71 percent. The switch to a market economy evolved more slowly in Slovakia, as evidenced by the smaller proceeds from privatization. In 1989, privatization yielded no more than $170 million in Slovakia, but $1.6 billion in the Czech Republic. The social costs of the transformation were much higher: whereas the unemployment rate in 1992 was 2.6 percent in the Czech Republic, it was 11 percent in Slovakia. Most of the armaments industry was in Slovakia, where it employed more than 100,000 people. This figure fell to 40,000, however, as a result of shrinking demand and obsolete technology. Conversion to civilian production was more difficult than expected. The 1.2 billion crowns allocated in the 1993 state budget to subsidize the costs of conversion were not enough to prevent a further decline. Four to five thousand jobs would be lost yearly. Slovakia has other vulnerable economic sectors. Foreign firms therefore preferred to invest their money in the Czech Republic rather than in Slovakia: only 7 percent of the foreign capital invested in the former Czechoslovakia came into Slovakia. One of the reasons for the poor level of engagement was the flimsy infrastructure.

The legacy of the communist regime was a burden for both republics, as may be discerned from a comparison with Austria, which was economically on roughly the same level as Czechoslovakia in the interwar period. As of 1993, however, the per-capita GNP of the Czech Republic was only 40 percent, and that of Slovakia only 32 percent of Austria's. It will take many years to overcome this backwardness. Experts estimate that, by the turn of the century, these figures will have deteriorated further, to 60 percent and 40 percent.

Slovakia's prospects of progress in reform and of economic recovery are rated pessimistically by the experts. According to the former prime minister, W. Meciar, economic performance in 1992 was 30 percent lower than in 1989.[19] The financial situation of the young republic was especially precarious. According to the economic minister, Ludowik Cernak, Slovakia was forced to seek help from the Czech Republic in the form of loans. At the Davos forum, Vaclav Klaus, the prime minister, denied this news: "That is a false alarm put out by journalists." Yet, in late January 1993 the Slovaks not only confirmed that the report was true, they also made a request for further aid.[20]

The Czech Republic, in contrast, shows growing signs that the economic recession is ending. Whereas economic performance was 7.1 percent lower in 1992 than in 1991, it was 3.8 percent higher in the fourth quarter of 1993 than during the same period in the preceding year. The unemployment rate was no more than 2.6 percent at the end of 1993, while the inflation rate of 12 percent was lower than that of the other reform countries. The private sector's share of the GNP rose from 10.6 percent in 1991 to 19.5 percent. Although this was more than 50 percent lower than in Poland, the World Bank praised the reforms in the former Czechoslovakia as "well structured and well implemented" in a report published in late January 1993. The study credits their success to the "well structured price liberalization, long-term financing facilities, and access to foreign markets." According to the World Bank data, that private firms were given equal legal status to state firms was conducive to the reforms' success. The former Czechoslovakia also received high praise in an Eastern Europe study published in late February 1993 by the University of Kiel for its "effective resolution of the property question."

But people in Prague are especially conscious that the solution to some of the very complicated problems of transition still lies ahead, especially where privatization is concerned. The so-called coupon privatization received mixed reviews. Experts are dubious whether the investment funds can keep their promise to citizens (about 8 million Czechs and Slovaks each bought 1,000-crown coupons at a cost of about 31.6 dollars), specifically, that returns would be more than ten times the investment after one year. It was feared that those who acquired the coupons, meanwhile converted into shares, would want to sell them as quickly as possible but would be unable to find buyers. The division of the country gave rise to other problems: Slovaks acquired 18.6 million shares in Czech firms, and Czechs acquired 4.5 million shares in Slovak firms; the legal ramifications of this are not totally clear. A tax reform introduced in early 1993 also caused problems. The ensuing price rises announced by the government were higher than originally expected. Merchants increased the price of food by up to 40 percent, though the projected increase was a maximum of 7 percent. Rents, energy, and transport prices were also raised. The

Economic Institute of the Prague Academy of Sciences forecast many redundancies in the machinery industry, light industry, and mining, as well as on the railroads. Even cautious estimates spoke of a tripling of the unemployment rate in 1994–95.

These unclear prospects have deterred foreign capital investment. Dow Chemical annulled its contract to buy the Sokolow chemical factory. Dow had agreed to acquire 90 percent of the Sokolow assets, worth $100 million, and later to invest $150 million to expand production capacities. The annulment of the contract came as a surprise in view of the effort Dow had expended to push its offer through in competition with the French petroleum company Société Nationale Elf Aquataine. Observers conjectured that the severance of relations with Sokolow was due not to the purported "high price," but to a loss of confidence, after the huge Czech firm, the Skoda works, with its 28,000 employed in Pilsen, filed for bankruptcy because it had to discard locomotives worth about 35 million crowns and was no longer able to pay its debts of $140 million.

The financial situation was more favorable than in the other reform countries. The collapse of the traditional distribution markets was compensated within a short time. The percentage of Czech exports to Western industrial countries increased from 36 percent in 1989 to 51 percent in 1991, with Czech exports to Germany for 1992 at 33.3 percent and imports from Germany at 26.3 percent. The CIS countries, on the other hand, accounted for only 8.5 percent of exports and 20.2 percent of imports (mainly fuels). Foreign exchange reserves were above average: on February 6, 1993, the day the currency union with Slovakia was dissolved, the foreign exchange reserves of the Czech Commercial Bank were $2.9 billion, while the reserves of the central banks were $540 million.[21]

Germany leads in direct foreign investment. By the end of 1993, its share had grown to 31.2 percent, followed by the United States with 27.8 percent, France with 12.7 percent, Belgium with 7.2 percent, and Austria with 6.2 percent.[22]

**The Government of the Democratic Forum
and the Hungarian People**

According to a study by the German Institute for World Economy at the University of Kiel, Hungary is the best place for business among the five Central and East European countries. The legal system, the rules governing competition, the freedom of markets, the modification of property relations, and other factors were all considered. In all these areas Hungary took first place. The Economist Intelligence Unit, a Vienna consulting firm, came to the same conclusion: it surveyed eighty-seven multinational concerns together with the Creditanstalt-Bankverein. The most zealous investors according to its study, *East European Investment Survey 1992*, were Americans, Germans, and Austrians.

The share of foreign capital in privatized state firms was 7 to 8 percent.[23] Western firms had already invested the following amounts: $311 million in 1990, $1,359 million in 1991, $1,471 in 1992, and $2,325 million in 1993, according to the United Nations Economic Commission for Europe (ECE). The Hungarian government would like to reduce the state share of the economy from 70 percent to 35 percent. For smaller firms, which are being released to their employees or to former owners, leasing models and various forms of partnership are under consideration. Large firms are as a rule being deconcentrated and offered to foreign investors. By the end of 1993 there were about 800,000 owners. One hundred and fifty-seven of the two thousand large firms will not be privatized but incorporated into a holding company comprising public enterprises, cultural enterprises, and infrastructural enterprises. The state will hold 50 percent plus one share in the airline Malev and in telecommunications. The proprietor will be a ministry, though it will have no power to intervene in management decisions. The government is trying to attract the population's savings (estimated at about $10 billion) to its privatization plans, in order to avoid the sale of state assets to foreign countries. Favorable credit opportunities are also being offered. The Central Bank is offering commercial banks credits at a rate of 12 percent, which will be made available to interested citizens or private firms with a supplement of 3 to 4 percent. In practice, however, the interest rate is set in each concrete case depending on creditworthinesss and other factors. The state of Hungarian banks, which are still in a transformational stage, is rather precarious. The proportion of credits with uncertain repayment is as high as 21 percent according to data of the State Banking Inspection: out of a total volume of credits already granted—1,270 billion forints (about $15 billion)—about 260 billion forints are ranked as "uncertain." The Banking Inspection therefore suggests that the banks' own funds should be backed up by state money in order to strengthen their influence on credit policy, and only later should privatization continue.

The social costs of the revolution of the system are no smaller in Hungary than in the other reform countries. The unemployment rate was 50 percent higher in 1992 compared with the preceding year, and reached 12.2 percent by the end of 1993 (UN/ECE Economic Survey of Europe, 1993–94). The number of registered unemployed rose from 653,000 by the end of December 1992 according to statistics of the Ministry of Labor: by mid-1994 this figure rose to 750,000.

The burgeoning budget deficit, due to growing state expenditure on unemployment benefits, is worrisome. The budget deficit increased in 1992 almost threefold compared to the planned objective, and rose to 197.1 billion forints (about $2.2 billion), while 69.8 billion forints was planned. A deficit of 175 billion forints was reached in 1993. One of the reasons for the deficit was the recession-induced decline in tax revenues and the ever-growing gray economy where tax evasion is all but the norm.

The decline in the economy slowed to 4 percent in 1992, compared with 12 percent in 1991, and to −2 percent in 1993. Hungary succeeded in increasing the share of total exports to industrial countries from 40 percent in 1989 to 57 percent in 1991, while hard currency exports grew by 7.4 percent, to $10.7 billion in 1992. The deficit of trade balance rose, however, from $0.4 billion to $3.6 billion in 1993. Hungary is the most indebted country in Eastern Europe per capita. For this reason, Hungary is interested in good relations with the IMF in order to maintain its creditworthiness with the commercial banks.

The falling standard of living and dwindling hopes of raising it again anytime in the near future have provoked the spread of unrest among the population. "Since we have been in government, so much that has taken place has not been to our advantage," said Erzsebet Pusztai, secretary of state in the Ministry of Health and Welfare.[24] It simply was not acceptable, she said, for large enterprises to put their entire work force in the street. Already 2 million of Hungary's 10.6 million people are forced to get by on a subsistence minimum of $160. Citizens living below the poverty level confronted the government with 170,000 signatures demanding a referendum to dissolve the parliament. The government decided under public pressure to help three hundred state firms threatened with bankruptcy with loans worth a total of $1.2 billion to $2 billion.

Capitalist Dissatisfaction with Hungarian Capitalism

Industrialist Peter Zwack, head of Hungary's Industrialists' Party, voiced his discontent over the lack of morality in the burgeoning Hungarian capitalism in a newspaper interview:

> The kind of capitalism that has not existed in the West for some time is raging right now in Hungary. This new eagerness, in itself perfectly natural, for self-enrichment is degenerating into a real gold fever and is driving business fairness and social sensibility into the background. . . . A market economy must not discredit itself with unedifying excesses in the eyes of the man in the street.[25]

But Zwack, a liqueur manufacturer, is wrong to compare the Hungarian capitalism of primitive accumulation with the mature capitalism of the United States from whence he had just returned. The real danger is that the above-depicted ways and means for self-enrichment that have developed in Hungary are also available in the other reform countries. The possibility of avoiding the manifestations of early capitalism is, however, rather small—it is essentially a pious wish that has no chance of coming true.

A study of the Hungarian Institute of World Economics prepared for the European Union at the beginning of 1994 stated that the real recovery will start no sooner than in 1997 and that the standard of living of the better-developed countries could be reached no sooner than in 2005. The disappointed Hungarian people manifested their dissatisfaction with the reform policy of the first postcommunist government in the parliamentary elections of May 1994. The Democratic Forum was voted down and the ex-communists tripled their share in the parliament, reaching a 54 percent majority.

Bulgaria and Romania

At the tail end of the former CMEA, Bulgaria and Romania were not only economically weaker, they were also worse run than the other Eastern countries. Bulgaria was more dependent economically and politically on the former Soviet Union than was Romania; approximately 80 percent of its total trade was with the Eastern countries. Both of these formerly agrarian economies built huge industrial enterprises in accordance with the CMEA specialization project; however, because of their backward technology, none of these enterprises were competitive in the world market, despite considerable capital investment. Their traditional area of economic activity, agriculture, was neglected in favor of badly thought-out undertakings. Bulgaria destroyed its prosperous farms that belonged to Turks whom they forced into mass emigration. Romania made the inefficiency of its system still worse by building unproductive agrarian complexes. Their minorities (the Turks in Bulgaria and the Hungarians in Romania) were discriminated against, increasing conflict. Both countries allowed their debts to the West to increase beyond tolerable limits, even to the point of insolvency. But, whereas the Romanian dictator repaid the entire debt at a cost of irreparable damage to an already devastated economy, the Bulgarian reform government assumed the heavy legacy of an $8.5-billion debt, which it had no way of servicing. Its political and economic structures were the most undeveloped of all the CMEA countries, which made conditions for transforming the system all the more difficult.

The GDP decreased in Bulgaria in 1993 by 6.2 percent and in Romania by 2 percent. An end to the economic decline is not yet in sight. Above all, the decline in state enterprises that had previously been kept going by budget subsidies drove unemployment relentlessly upward. In 1992 one-quarter of Bulgaria's employable population was unemployed. A further increase in the unemployment rate to 28 percent was projected for 1994. In Romania, according to official statistics, 750,000 were unemployed. Another half-million, mostly young people, attempted to keep their heads above water through dubious business dealings. Thousands upon thousands emigrated to Germany through Poland, the flow increasing in pace with rising prices: prices in Romania went up tenfold between 1989 and 1993. In Bulgaria, the 1992 rate of inflation was 79.4 percent. Dwindling budget revenues due to the decline in state industry and the growing costs of supporting the unemployed drove the budget deficit skywards. Bulgaria, deeply in debt yet seeking new loans, was pressured by the IMF to reduce its budget deficit to 5 percent of the gross domestic product. The deficit proposed by the finance minister Alexandrov to the parliament of 18 billion levs

(720 million dollars) should have produced a rate of 7 percent of the gross domestic product, but the real deficit in 1993 was 11 percent of GDP. Because Bulgaria did not fulfill the conditions set by the IMF, the G–24 countries did not release the promised $100 million in loans, and the second tranche of the structural adaptation loan from the World Bank, as well as the grant-in-aid promised by the European Union remained up in the air. The most important financier, however, is a standby credit of $220.3 million from the IMF.

Bulgaria's greatest problem is its foreign debt. It ceased servicing the debt in March 1990 and began to pay the first interest installments in October 1992. Meanwhile the total debt rose to $12.3 billion. The German banks, with 21.5 percent, had the largest share, followed by the Japanese at 19.5 percent, the British at 12.7 percent, and Austrian banks at 12.5 percent. Bulgaria's proposal for transforming the debt into shares in industrial enterprises is still being taken seriously, but so far no agreements have been taken on this account.

Both countries have slowed their reforms under the pressure of the severe economic crisis and the falling standard of living. The Bulgarian government decided to convert 22 billion levs of enterprise debts into state debts. Romania refrained from a further freeing of prices and further reduction in subsidies to unprofitable enterprises. The price increase for gasoline agreed by the previous Stoloian government was rescinded. The hole in the state coffers became even bigger.

Everything indicates that Bulgaria and Romania, trapped between the ruins of a state economy and a truncated market, will be suffering under an ever-deepening economic crisis for a long time to come.

The Former German Democratic Republic in Confrontation with the Industrial Giants of West Germany

The reunification of East and West Germany constituted a unique political act: "What belonged together has now grown back together," said Willy Brandt. Economic integration, however, has proved a slower and more costly process, involving the union of a weak economic organism and its antiquated structures with Europe's most technologically advanced industrial state whose population enjoys an above-average standard of living. Living side by side for many years and becoming more intertwined gradually might have been more rational economically, but with open borders this option could not have been realized, owing to the deep social discrepancies between these two peoples of a single nation. After the currency union was formed, it was inevitable that the technologically backward East German combinates would be swallowed up by the Western giants. The employment structure of the East German economy in 1989 was equivalent to the West German structure in 1965. The shock resulting from the collision of the economic leader of the former CMEA with the leading country of the EC was much more violent, and the consequences of the ensuing transformation were far graver, than in the other reform countries, for the latter had not set themselves the unattainable goal of reaching the technological level or standard of living of the West German industrial giant. Those countries would have been unable to gather the resources to do this, and in any case they were far more backward than was the former GDR. Monetary transfers to the East exceeded all estimates: rising from 46.2 billion DM in 1990 to 131.8 billion DM in 1991, 163 billion DM in 1992, and in 1993 it was only 2 billion DM less than in the preceding year. Of course, it would be wrong to consider this tremendous sum one of the costs of adjustment to West German levels. It may well be that West German concerns acquired East German assets at prices that were far too low. The difference had to be met by the state: in the first instance, the vast human army of workers who lost their jobs when works were shut down had to be supported. Industrial output in the five new provinces decreased in the fourth quarter of 1992 to 48 percent of the level of the last quarter of 1989. The number of employed decreased from 10,000,000 in late 1989 to 6,112,000 as of the end of 1992. The manufacturing industry's contribution to the GDP diminished from 44 percent to 1989 to 34 percent in 1992.

Specialists agree that within ten years, Germany will succeed in integrating the economy of the former GDR into the modern developed structures of Western countries—the greatest challenge since the 1948 monetary reform—despite the enormous expenditure of money and energy this will entail. The other reform countries are unlikely to overcome their backwardness within the next decade, even relative to the peripheral areas of Western Europe.

Comments

Transformation has shown greater progress in Central Europe than in the successor nations of the former Soviet Union, but it is still far from

complete. The economic results achieved by the transforming economies are summarized in the appendix. The difficulties lie in the idio-
syncrasies of the transition to capitalism. This is not the usual historical
transformation—from a lower to a higher stage of civilization as from
feudalism to capitalism—but rather is a transformation from a system
that defined itself as socialist. Actually, what is taking place is a reversion, a restoration, a correction of what might be considered a historical aberration for which not one of the reform countries has found an
appropriate remedy. In a system that was supposed to be, but could not
be, socialist, and that had evolved into an Asiatic mode of production,
not only the traditional institutions—the steering mechanisms and traditional property relations created over the course of innumerable generations by collective human wisdom—but also the creative stratum of
proprietors and entrepreneurs were destroyed. The proletariat was proclaimed the demiurge of society, yet administration of the state's assets
was placed in the hands of a state bureaucracy that had a monopoly on
decision making—concerning production, distribution, what was con-
sumed, and what was invested, and so on. The economies of Eastern
and Central Europe were incorporated into the huge military-industrial
complex of a superpower (regardless of traditional economic and social structures) that was determined to permit no deviations from its
economic and political system.

Unlike the former Soviet republics, the reform countries of Central
Europe were able to develop a buyers' consumer market in an astonishingly short time by freeing prices and the internal convertibility of
the national currency. The transformation began to veer off course
when the shock therapy turned to heavy industry, which had been
totally in the hands of the state. Unlike small businesses, commerce, or
even the service sector, there was not enough capital to purchase these
huge assets, and not enough managers to manage them properly. Un-
conventional methods of denationalization, such as the infamous coupon privatization or citizens' shares, were introduced. Disputes arose
over whether just the 27 million adults or the 10 million children as
well could have a share in the denationalized assets. Poland's powerful
Peasants' Party (PSL) carried things to absurdity: it proposed delaying
the implementation of the relevant law for nine months in order to
allow children who had been conceived but not yet born to take part.

In the meantime, nationalized enterprises were thrown into such
uncertainty that denationalization took place more through bankruptcy

procedures than through actual privatization, whereas the price for establishing a consumer market was the impoverishment of a large portion of the population, many work collectives had to pay for the started but uncompleted process of denationalization of the large companies with the loss of their jobs.

Unexpected difficulties arose in the transition from totalitarianism to a pluralist democracy: a plethora of parties was created, none of which, however, had much backing among the disappointed population. Disillusionment with politics set in before a pluralistic democracy could become established. Half of those entitled to vote did not do so. After three years of reform, 53 percent of Hungarians and 30 percent of Poles thought they had a better living under the old system, while 34 percent and 18 percent, respectively, felt they had a better living under the present system.[26]

What was once said about the leaders of the French Revolution applies equally to the protagonists of 1989: they knew what they did not want but did not know what they wanted. But, whereas the Enlightenment and the French Revolution produced a wave of emancipation that spread over the whole of Europe, today a destructive nationalism is spreading an infectious kind of decadence. It will be a long time before the positive consequences of the Velvet Revolution are likely to make themselves felt.

Chapter 6

Soviet Communism Is Dead: In China It Survives with "Chinese Features"

At a press conference held upon his return from China on December 30, 1992, Boris Yeltsin said, "We would like to send at least one communist to China to learn from their experiences." But now it is too late, said the president, for "China has been engaged in reform for fourteen years, we for only one year." The powerful leader of the Association of Industrialists and Businessmen, Arkadii Volskii, took a different view: for him, China's reform model was still of interest today because it was propelling the economy forward rather than driving it to ruin.

Yeltsin did not meet Deng Xiaoping, the architect of reform, not because Yeltsin left Beijing a day earlier than planned, but because Deng could make no time for Russia's leader. It should not be forgotten that Deng never had believed in a rapprochement with the former Soviet Union. A month after his comeback in September 1977, he gave the following reply to the German MP Wörner: "I am now seventy-three years old and will never live to see a rapprochement; Comrade Hua Gofing [then General Secretary of the CP] is fifty-six years old, and he will witness the end of the century, but not a rapprochement with the Soviet Union."[1] Mao Zedong was more concrete: "China's conflict with the Soviet Union will last ten thousand years," he said to

British Foreign Minister Anthony Crossland just one month before he died on September 9, 1976.

Mao had already begun to distance himself from the Soviet Union in the mid-1950s. He could not tolerate Soviet hegemony and its interference in China's internal affairs and foreign policy. The conflict became more acute when Nikita Khrushchev recalled Soviet specialists from China in 1956 and stopped supplying the huge projects that were being built with Soviet aid. This caused serious damage to China's economy and its population.

For Mao the Asiatic mode of production which the Soviet Union had established under the banner of "socialism" was by no means unacceptable—quite the contrary. He himself had pushed things so far with his Cultural Revolution and Great Leap Forward that the ten years of "acceleration" utterly ruined the devastated and underdeveloped economy, and decimated its cadres. Jiang Zemin, then general secretary of the Central Committee, commented at the Fourteenth Party Congress on October 12, 1992: "The ideological, political, organizational, and economic chaos left by the Cultural Revolution was very bad."[2]

One of the countless victims of the great purges was Deng Xiaoping: in 1966 he was expelled for the first time from the top Party committees for a period of seven years, and three years after his comeback, in 1973, he was removed from all his offices. In August 1977 he returned, initiating the crucial "Reform and Opening" with a resolution to the Third Plenary Session of the Eleventh Central Committee of the Communist Party in 1978.

As Jiang Zeming reported to the Fourteenth Party Congress, the purpose of the reform was to "transform China into a wealthy, strong, democratic, civilized, socialist, and modern country." Deng was realistic enough, however, to know that a great leap forward can lead straight into an abyss. His goal was to achieve a per capita income of $1,000 by the end of the century. This would still be 2.5 less than the per-capita income in Russia in 1989, but only half as low as the per-capita income in Russia in 1992, after the big crash.

Russia and China differ not only in the aims of their reform but also in the means they have used to achieve it: Boris Yeltsin, former head of the Communist Party in the industrial region of Sverdlovsk (now Ekaterinburg), came to ban the Communist Party in which he had risen to be a deputy Politburo member. His ultimate goal was neither a developed socialism nor any other kind but, as he put it, "a return to the civilized world." Deng, a martyr of the Cultural Revolution, when asked on a trip to Southeast Asia in 1978 whether China would still be communist in the year 2000, answered: "I do not know. I will remain at any rate a Marxist-Leninist to the end of my life."[3] Yeltsin's declared goal is a competitive market economy of the Western type. Deng's ultimate goal remains a "socialist market" in a socialist social system with "Chinese features," even though his vision of socialism has become more pragmatic and less ideological than it was at the time of the Great March. On October 17, 1992, the official Chinese news agency presented his definition of socialism: "The essence of socialism is to liberalize and dynamize the forces of production, to eliminate poverty and drastic contrasts, and to ensure prosperity for all." The official ideology now is "Marxism-Leninism and Mao Zedong's thoughts." Deng commented elsewhere on another occasion, however, that one cannot live by "ideology alone."

The attitude of the Communist Party leadership to planning and the market has undergone a fundamental change. The report to the Fourteenth Party Congress states: "A planned economy is not equivalent to socialism and a market economy is not equivalent to capitalism. . . . More plan or more market—that is not the essential difference between socialism and capitalism." The attitude to property has also changed: individual businesses, private economy, and entrepreneurs with foreign capital should complement common property. The report then states even more clearly, "We are convinced that a market economy could and should function better under conditions of socialism than a market economy existing under conditions of capitalism."

Deng Xiaoping and John Kenneth Galbraith

The reforms introduced in Russia and China had different tasks to resolve. Russia was bent on a transformation that would raise the economic performance and standard of living to the level of the Western industrial countries. Hunger and poverty were not the issue. China's revolutionary reform of the economic system within the existing political framework together with its opening up to the world were undertaken in order to free the country's population of 1.1 billion people from hunger and to give them better clothing. The days when millions of people were dying of hunger were not so far in the past. Deng was doing what John Kenneth Galbraith, formerly "price tsar" in Franklin

D. Roosevelt's war cabinet, recommended to the postcommunist states: first, privatize small businesses and the service sector; then lift price controls, initially in the service sector and then gradually in the remaining economic sectors.[4]

Before China's great architect began his price reforms, he instituted a historic change in' agriculture. The inefficient agrarian communes were abolished and the land was leased in perpetuity to the peasants (who comprised 80 percent of the total population). This revolutionary act enabled China, with only 7 percent of the world's arable land yet 21 percent of its population, to feed its own population and free 1.1 billion Chinese from the threat of hunger. In Russia, on the other hand, collective farms and state farms still determine the fate of agriculture and force the country to import grain. Russia is still discussing conditions for the sale of land to foreigners; China has already cleared the way for foreigners to lease land for up to seventy years.

Abolition of the Agrarian Communes

China is still a developing country, but the emancipation of the peasants from the diktat of the commune bureaucracy increased their performance to such an extent that there is no longer any threat of hunger. Between 1978 and 1990, the per-capita income of peasants increased 4.7-fold from 134 to 630 yuan, and that of the urban population by 4.3-fold from 316 to 1,387 yuan. Allowing for inflation (6.7 percent per year), the threefold increase in peasant incomes and the twofold increase in the income of the urban population are quite considerable, even if very moderate in absolute terms.

China only began to liberalize its price system after it could guarantee to supply its population with farm products. One cannot yet, however, speak of complete liberalization. Fifty percent of the volume of goods and services were traded at prices freely agreed between industrial enterprises and at free market prices; 15 percent of the prices for goods were still totally controlled by the state—particularly where firms were unprofitable and subsidized by the state; and on about 35 percent of the prices the state authorities set an upper limit. Prices for agrarian products have gradually been liberalized as forced deliveries have gradually been abolished and replaced by normal market relations.

The second most important reform measure was to free industrial enterprises from the diktat of the state and to decentralize decision making. The most important economic decision-making powers were transferred to the large enterprises. The principle of separating ownership from administration is being systematically introduced, and state and Party are gradually being eliminated from enterprise management. The powers of management are being progressively broadened, and managers have increasing powers of decision over production and sales, which are now regulated by contracts with the business partner. Central planning continues but, whereas before the reform, the manufacture and distribution of three hundred products were centrally planned, afterwards the central planning authorities regulated only fifteen products of importance to the state.

The next reform measure was a progressive privatization that went beyond services and commercial shops to include large enterprises. It is claimed that denationalization of the latter had gone further in China than in the reform countries of Central and Eastern Europe; this is no exaggeration—thanks largely to the massive commitment of foreign capital. Family firms employing fewer than eight people now have an aggregate of 25.5 million employees; 120,000 firms with more than eight employees provide jobs for 2 million people. Of 153 million employees in municipal enterprises, 107 million work in nationalized companies. Between 1980 and 1991, the proportion of the output of state enterprises in total industrial production fell from 78 percent to 53 percent, while the share of cooperative output increased from 21 percent to 36 percent, and that of private firms rose from 1 percent to 11 percent. Forecasts for the year 2000 are 27 percent, 48 percent, and 25 percent respectively.[5] China's economic structure (in which agriculture, forestry, and fisheries together accounted for 27.5 percent of gross domestic product in 1990, while heavy industry and the service sector accounted for 45.3 percent and 27.2 percent respectively) still resembles that of a developing country. Between 1978 and 1990, however, the share of the service sector increased more rapidly than that of other economic spheres—namely, from 23 percent to 27.2 percent. In early March 1993, the *Business Times* (March 5, 1993), China's English-language newspaper, provided an indication of how the private sector was growing: China now has 500 millionaires. The newspaper writes: "Some people have perhaps grown rich in questionable ways, but it must be recognized that they have an excellent spirit of enterprise."

The Losses of State Enterprises

Nationalized enterprises function no better in China than anywhere else: 20 percent of budget spending goes to subsidize unprofitable state enterprises, and 80 percent of total loans goes to finance their poor economic performance. Between 1988 and 1990, profits and, at the same time, taxes paid to the state decreased from 177.5 billion yuan (about $30 billion) to 150.3 billion yuan, while production costs increased by 30.8 percent. The proportion of unprofitable enterprises out of the total number of firms increased from 10.9 percent to 27.6 percent, while losses increased from 8.19 billion to 34.88 billion yuan. In 1991, losses increased by 19.3 percent while profits shrank by 5.3 percent. Thirty-six percent of firms operated at a loss, so that unsalable stocks reached a tremendous volume ($16.2 billion).

Opening Outward

The goal of "opening up" is one of the pillars of Chinese reform. China wants finally to end its isolation from the world. Its leaders would like to make use of foreign capital and qualified foreign management to expand its domestic industries and especially to equip them with modern technology. Foreign capital has confidence in Chinese firms' stability and is pouring in at a growing rate in the form of loans and capital investments. New firms are being built with foreign capital and old ones are being modernized.

Foreign trade started to grow dynamically once the shock of the Tiananmen Square massacre was overcome. In 1991, joint ventures totaling $17.6 billion were agreed, 46.7 percent more than in the preceding year, and at the end of 1991 there were 37,215 registered joint ventures with a total capital of $46 million. I have seen at first hand when visiting the China-Schindler Elevator Company that these are efficient industrial concerns. The Swiss firm Schindler, which is involved with a fixed capital of 25 percent, committed itself to providing the most advanced know-how. Ten percent of the work force were trained in Europe. The profitability rate is 9 percent to 10 percent, according to Deputy General Manager Dieter Taubert, and there are no problems transferring profits abroad.

Foreign trade volume increased by 17 percent in 1991 to $137.5 billion, and again in 1992 to $165.6 billion. Of these figures, exports accounted for $85 billion, which is an 18.3 percent increase compared with the preceding years, while imports accounted for $80.6 billion (an increase of 26.4 percent). Imports of the most modern technology increased by 172 percent to $3.5 billion. Japan is China's most important trading partner, with a volume of $22 billion. Trade with Europe increased by 11 percent to $17.3 billion, and trade with the United States increased by 17 percent to $14.2 billion.

China established close economic relations with Germany and Austria: in early July 1992 Germany received a delivery order amounting to $500 million, while Austria in turn received one of approximately $30 million. China's total import volume is projected to be about $300 billion over the next five years. Credit relations are growing. The total value of contracted loans increased from $15.8 billion in 1985 to $52.6 billion in 1990.

The Four Small Dragons

China's "four small dragons" are situated on its Pacific coast: these areas have been given the status of special economic zones and are now engaged in a lively foreign trade with neighboring countries, with no restrictions whatsoever. Thanks to this opening to the outside world, China has been able to reach the level of effectiveness of the four Asian tigers (South Korea, Singapore, Taiwan, and Hong Kong), and even to exceed that level in certain areas.

Within a short time, a market-friendly infrastructure with security exchanges and commercial banks has been set up, creating the preconditions for a progressively growing trade in shares and state securities. Special value is attached to expanding the industrial city of Shanghai, with its population of 12 million, and it is hoped that foreign capital will accelerate this undertaking. According to the head of government, Li Peng, it was envisioned that Shanghai would become the most important economic, financial, and trading center not only of China but of the whole of Asia. Ten billion dollars have purportedly been earmarked for this purpose over the next decade. Major significance has been attached to the Pudong zone, which lies in the Shanghai region. In order to expand it, China wants to draw investors and specialized personnel from abroad, and some investment projects have already been completed (660 with the aid of foreign capital).

Foreign Chinese have been active in the Pudong zone. The All-Chinese Federation for Chinese people who have returned home promises advantageous conditions, and especially advantageous land usage fees, to investors who engage promptly in expanding the Pudong zone. Great value is attached to the accumulation of share capital: the commodities exchange established in Shanghai and Shenzhen, as well as the China Investment Fund established in Hong Kong, have promoted the creation of the necessary needed infrastructure. A consulting firm with its base in Beijing was established on April 17, 1992, by the China International Economic and Legal Consulting Corporation, in cooperation with Victor Chu and Co., Ltd., Hong Kong, to advise foreign investors. This firm is expected to play an important role in transforming Chinese state enterprises into shareholding companies.

As of the end of 1991, foreign capital investment projects worth a total of $121.5 billion had been approved, and capital already invested had reached $79.6 billion. But the population's aggregate savings of about 160 billion yuan have been spent on share trading: 40 percent of the shares sold in 1991 were bought by private persons.

In view of Hong Kong's approaching annexation in 1997, special emphasis has been placed on the accelerated development of the contiguous special zone of Shenzhen, which Deng Xiaoping would like to see developed into a "socialist Hong Kong." This zone will be given special rights to promulgate its own laws, which will give it a special status relative to the central government in Beijing. The authorities in Shenzhen are using their new powers to expand the area sixfold: it now has an area of 328 square kilometers and a population of 2 million. Shenzhen's economy is very closely intertwined with that of Hong Kong. The Hong Kong dollar functions here as an unofficial means of payment.

Special zones have also been expanded in respect of the changed attitude toward Taiwan and Macao. China's government has adopted a model of "peaceful reunification, or the country with two systems," and it is striving to intensify economic, cultural, and political relations between the two sides. The Taiwan government has eased the conditions for visits by relatives and relieved restrictions. As of the end of 1991, 3 million Chinese had traveled from Taiwan to the mainland. The mutual trade volume reached $5.79 billion in 1991. The mainland occupies fifth place on Taiwan's list of trading partners, and Taiwan is the sixth largest market for the mainland. Certain differences, however, exist over Beijing's "peaceful annexation model." Taiwan has proposed its own idea—"two political structures with equal rights."

Stability

China's leadership is holding on to its political regime, with the Communist Party in a monopoly position. In his report to the Fifth Congress of the Seventh National Congress on March 20, 1992, Prime Minister Li Peng said: "We must maintain this line over the long term, and must not diverge from it for one hundred years. . . . Guaranteeing social and political stability is a precondition for reforming and opening and for economic development. . . . Order brings advancement, while rebellion leads to ruin."

In contrast to the reform states of Eastern Europe, China was able to continue its reform policy and to guarantee economic growth as well as a rise in the standard of living, which is still quite modest. In 1991, the gross social product increased by 7 percent and industrial production rose by 14.2 percent. Grain harvest increased by 435.24 million tons, the cotton harvest was 5,663 million tons, 1.09 billion tons of coal were mined, crude oil production was 139 million tons, and steel production 70 million tons. Capital investments increased by 18.6 percent, retail trade by 10 percent, foreign trade by 17.5 percent, and the inflation rate was 2.9 percent. The economic indicators for the subsequent three years were revised drastically upward. Li Ping declared in his opening speech to the People's Congress on March 14, 1993: "The economic reforms which led to economic growth of 12.8 percent in 1992 will be continued." For the rest of the five-year plan down to 1995, the earlier planned target was raised from 6 percent to 8–9 percent.

Of course, stability was the most important precondition for success of the reform policy, provided economic growth was continuous. The charge that human rights have been violated under the given political conditions has been dismissed: the most important right of citizens, according to the official view, is the right to work and to a tolerable existence without great contrasts between rich and poor. And China must feed 1,150 million inhabitants—one-fifth of the world's population—with a further 17 million added every year, despite rigorous birth control.

Whether a one-party regime claiming the exclusive right to represent truth, with inevitable social stratification and a rising general level of education, can guarantee stability over the long term is a matter of dispute in China as well. To this question the most recent developments in Eastern Europe provide a clear answer.

The West and the Revolution in the East

Robert Schediwy

The Historical Background

There is little doubt that the events in Eastern Europe in 1989 and 1990 represent one of the world's great historical revolutions that change the destiny of the nations concerned as well as the long-term international relationships in their area.[1] With the dissolution of the Soviet Union as a unitary power structure and with the full independence of its former satellite states, one of the most important players on the scene of world politics has suddenly disappeared, leaving behind a fractured mosaic that has not yet been rearranged in a stable pattern. At the same time, the whole economic and political balance of Eurasia has been overturned. In a period of globalization of economic and ideological issues, a completely new situation has been created. Roughly five years after the beginning of these revolutionary transformations, we can start to speculate cautiously about the long-term changes in international relationships that will result from these events.[2] Few things are certain as yet, but one aspect is quite clear: Contrary to the misleading and vulgarized Hegelian slogan of the "End of History" that was endlessly repeated by journalists around 1992,[3] we can now be certain of a phenomenon that could be called the "Return of History": Eastern Europe seems about to continue its development path in many ways roughly at the point where it stood before the gigantic, violent, and ultimately unsuccessful experiment in modernization undertaken by communism—with its westernmost areas again fully enjoying the vicinity of highly developed capitalist societies and its more remote areas falling back to the "Balkanic" status of a somewhat anarchic "Wild East." In some fields the heroic, if ultimately catastrophic, endeavor of communism has bettered the previous situation, especially with regard to mass education. In some aspects, however, Eastern Europe is starting with a handicap even compared with its precommunist status. This is especially so for the field of economics because the enormous industrialization efforts of Stalinism and the almost total destruction of private initiative in combination with all-out nationalization have done more harm than good—specifically to this area's most developed regions.

The "return of history" should, of course, not be interpreted in the sense of "historical fatality." Ahistorical concepts (such as model-oriented approaches that ignore the role of cultural heritage, for example, in the building of a functioning market economy) are as one-sided as concepts whose explicative approach is based mainly on "ancient hatreds"[4] (the latter being, of course, an ideal pretext for superpower noninvolvement). Still, the obvious parallels—for example, between the national disintegration of the tsarist empire in 1917 and the present state of decay of the former Soviet Union—make it overwhelmingly clear that the historical background of social development is extremely important. While it should not be overinterpreted in deterministic terms, it is a helpful tool in defining the "possibility space" of current trends. The concluding part of this book focuses on this sort of global, historical perspectives, especially since the six chapters themselves contain a quite sufficient amount of data and empirical information.

Up to the end of the seventeenth century, Russia and the Ukraine on the one hand and the states of Central and Eastern Europe and of the Balkans on the other hand belonged to two rather different sets of international relationships. Bohemia and Moravia were part of the heart of Central Europe. The Balkans as well as Hungary were part of the spheres of power and conflict of the Ottoman empire and the Hapsburg empire. Large parts of present-day Poland (especially Silesia, Krakow, and the Baltic coast) were integrated into the main European trade flows and political developments, with dominant influences from the West (Russia) and the North (Sweden). The great Russian empire, however, remained for a long time in a rather exotic marginal situation, not in the least because of the Swedish and Polish power sphere which at that time extended far to the East. Western influences were transmitted via the Baltic areas that had become part of the Hansa territories in the Middle Ages. For example, the German aristocrats of the Baltic regions were not only estimable soldiers serving the Russian tsars, but would also become the spearhead of scientific development in the Russian empire. Craftsmen and specialists such as Italian architects were already being imported from the time of the late medieval period (the Kremlin Wall was built by an Italian architect). However, it was only Tsar Peter the Great who tried to push for extreme Westernization, not only by his famous order for the Bojars to cut their beards and "Westernize" their dress, but above all by massively importing Western experts and technology. A driving force behind this effort was the tsar's conflict with Sweden. Even though Peter's successors continued in this westernization and modernization effort and in the development of St. Petersburg as a "window to the West," the Russian monarchy remained a great power in a marginal situation. The fall of Napoleon after his attempted conquest of Russia underlined the military might of this enormous mass of land and human beings, and drew it into Central European politics—as one of the main pillars of the "Holy Alliance" and as a mainstay of stability (leftists would call it "reaction") in 1848–49. Already around 1830, the famous French political analyst Alexis de Tocqueville correctly foresaw the United States and Russia as the future dominant world powers.[5] While Western Europe experienced a dynamic development of industrialization and democratization throughout the second half of the nineteenth century, however, the Russian empire fell behind. This great military power, with its underdeveloped social and economic system, appeared to many as a hateful and primitive giant allied to the "forces of the past" in Europe. The way Russia suppressed the Hungarian Revolution in 1848–49, in keeping with its obligations from the "Holy Alliance," and the tough Russian line against insurgent Poland reinforced these conceptions of the European Left. This global perspective explains Karl Marx's expressions of contempt and hatred for the Russia of his time.[6] At the end of the nineteenth and the beginning of the twentieth century, however, the integration of the Russian empire into world trade increased (this held mostly for the grain trade, which was fomented by railway building; thus Russia became one of the world's largest grain exporters). The tsarist monarchy also became increasingly integrated into the progressive polarization of alliances in Western Europe. The tsars showed their interest in gaining access to the warm seas of the Mediterranean and supported their Slavic brethren, the Bulgarians and the Serbs, against the decaying Ottoman empire. This, of course, brought them into increasing conflict with the German and Austrian interests in the Balkans—which ultimately was to trigger the First World War with the assassination of Archduke Francis Ferdinand in the fateful city of Sarajevo. In this way, traditions were formed that still reverberate today as Russian nationalists tend to take the side of the orthodox Serbs in the Yugoslav Civil War while remaining suspicious of Germany's and Austria's sentimental leanings in favor of newly independent Slovenia and Croatia. Also, at the end of the nineteenth century industrialization was starting in Russia, mostly with the assistance of French and English capital. The encirclement of the new industrial power of United Germany and of its vassal, the politically decaying Hapsburg empire, by the French-Russian entente thus became discernible. At the same time, Russia's humiliation in the Russian–Japanese War of 1904 and its consequence, the Russian Revolution of 1905, revealed just how fragile and backward was the political and economic system of the large Eurasian empire. Archduke Francis Ferdinand, the victim of Sarajevo, a leading "dove" in Austria's political elite, had predicted with uncanny foresight that a great war would destroy the Russian as well as his own Austro-Hungarian empire.[7]

The latent weakness of the tsarist monarchy became evident less than three years into the First World War, when it started to disintegrate under the pressure of an insupportable war effort. As this disintegration process, which started in February 1917, turned into a total power vacuum around the end of the year, a small group of extremist Marxist revolutionaries brought in from Germany were able to stage a coup d'état in the so-called October Revolution. It is well known (and documented by the only relatively free election in Soviet Russia under Lenin) that the Bolsheviks (or "majority" socialists) actually represented only a minority inside the Russian Left. The fact that they were able not only to take power but to keep it in a protracted civil war must be credited to the extreme social exhaustion after World War I not only in Russia but also in the victorious countries of Western Europe around 1920.[8] Many people in St. Petersburg probably prayed for a British attack on the city, just as the famous poetess and diarist Zinaida Hippius[9] wished when the new communist regime established its reign of terror there. But the Western powers chose inaction in the form of an ineffective blockade. The marginal situation of the Russian empire was further accentuated by the creation of the new independent states of Poland, Finland, and the Baltic (whose independence was, by the way, not accepted by the "White" side in the Russian civil war—an extremely foolish move that estranged its potential allies, and probably thus contributed to the more than seventy years of communist power). At any rate, this new westward-looking fringe area made it more acceptable to the Western European powers for a totalitarian regime—considered likely to be short-lived anyhow—to assert itself in the main body of the former tsarist empire.

The only military power that might have been able to overthrow the new, essentially weak communist regime was the United States, which joined the World War only during its last quarter. The United States, however, returned into isolationism after 1918. Its European allies, Great Britain and France, tried to support the conservative (White) side in the Russian civil war, but with very limited military and economic means. They realized the political danger represented by the new regime, but their governments were far too weak to convince their population to continue a large-scale war. This also had something to do with the fact that for the first time in history, a Russian regime was able to exert a positive mobilizing effect on a substantial part of the Western European intelligentsia and sizable parts of the working classes. Large segments of the European Left that had been radicalized by the First World War were now looking to Russia with hope, this was true not only for the short-lived soviet republics in Hungary and Bavaria, but also for the creation of important communist parties in almost all Western European states, as a break from the reformist and well-integrated labor movement of the prewar years. These communist parties were able at least temporarily to fascinate many of Europe's most brilliant minds. They were also able to establish a solid proletarian base in many countries. Thus, the great Eurasian power under its new name of the Soviet Union was able to command for the first time in its history a network of fanatic followers in Western Europe. This unique and unrepeatable constellation was to bring the Soviet Union a giant step closer to its desired status of an internationally established world power.

After the failure of Leo Trotsky's "World Revolution," this new great power in the East made it clear to Western Europe that it was not going to follow a foolishly expansionist course. Besides, in technical and economic matters, the Soviet Union collaborated since the treaty of Rapallo (1923) ever more closely with the second outsider of the postwar European power system, the German Reich. This stabilization of Soviet power and influence received an enormous boost during the Great Depression. Though the increasing amount of Soviet terror was obvious to most clear-sighted observers, the fascination of the Soviet model not only for the Western European Left but also for many liberals increased paradoxically at the very moment when Soviet agrarian collectivization was leading into mass starvation and Stalinist totalitarianism. It was mainly the Western experience of large-scale unemployment during the 1930s that made the planned but ruthless industrialization model of the Soviet Union so attractive. Of course, the famous Austrian Marxist Otto Bauer had already formulated in 1931 (at the end of his work, *Rationalisierung—Fehlrationalisierung*)[10] that "the spirit of terrorist dictatorship permeates the whole life of the Soviet Union," that "fear creates opportunists," and that the highest positions were taken over by "spies, denouncers, and careerists." There was also ample testimony by exiled Russians about the horrors of the civil war and of War Communism.

Still, some of the most prominent representatives of the political and cultural establishment of Western Europe were ever more fascinated with the Soviet Union of the five-year plans. It was not only George Bernard Shaw who congratulated Stalin's regime on its "balanced budget" and Hewlett Johnson, the "Red Dean" of Canterbury, who praised it from the pulpit. H.G. Wells, who was a guest of the dictator during the summer of 1934, proclaimed that he had "never seen a more open, just and decent person" than Mr. Stalin. Truthful information on the Soviet Union, of course, was available, such as Malcolm Muggeridge's famous three "nonauthorized" reports for the *Manchester Guardian*.[11] These showed in the spring of 1933 Stalin's "war against the peasants" and the terrible famine associated with agrarian collectivization. But such reports were usually dismissed by devoted believers as "enemy propaganda" coming from "renegades."

The "spirit of the time" in the West was probably better represented by Walter Duranty, the Moscow correspondent of the *New York Times*, who was then winning Pulitzer prizes for his stories about a thriving Soviet agriculture—much to Muggeridge's dismay and scorn.[12]

Simply put, there was a very important school of thought in the West that *did not want to know* the truth about what was going on in the Soviet Union. It was not just the selective Soviet information policy that effectively closed access to the Ukrainian hunger areas. Even the knowledge of scholars and intellectuals is strongly colored by what they *want* to believe. And Sidney and Beatrice Webb's giant volume on the Soviet Union (1935), proclaiming it to be a "new kind of civilization,"[13] was not just a document of the credulity of two aging icons of the British labor movement, it was a symbol of an era when many people in the West were desperately looking for signs of hope in the midst of a world depression. The Webbs were not the only ones who found many excuses for the KGB terror, which they were obliged to acknowledge to some extent. Nobel Prize-winning scientists such as the Curies and artists including Pablo Picasso were also "friends at disposal" whom the agents of Stalinism were able to use in propaganda even through the early 1950s (and this in spite of the fact that the Curies, for example, were well aware that even top-ranking scientists were kept in the Gulag, and they even tried to rescue them, as in the famous Weissberg-Cybulski case[14]). The role of ideologically committed Western scientists in the development of Soviet nuclear technology after 1945 and the famous Cambridge spy ring attest to the very real information and power bonus the Soviet Union was able to reap from its intellectual friends in the West into the mid-1950s.[15]

The attempt to create a planned economy in the Soviet Union was in some ways true to the totalitarian nucleus of the concrete measures proposed by Marx and Engels at the end of the *Communist Manifesto* of 1848 (centralization of credit, militarization of production, etc.). However, the details of this plan were not copied from Marx (who had always remained evasive about "painting the future" in detail). Lenin's concrete model was the German war economy. In this context, the fascist as well as the Soviet experiment with their voluntaristic economic policies that were to fascinate the crisis-ridden interwar period were related to the emergency period of 1914–18 and its administrative authoritarianism. At the same time, Stalin's slogan, "Socialism in one country," was greeted as a sign of moderation in the West compared with the prior official ideology of a world revolution that, however, even Stalin did not drop completely. Inside the Soviet Union, Stalin's ascent was due not only to his favors to the party apparatus but also to his "centrist" policies. (Trotsky, with the Red Army behind him, inspired even more fear of dictatorship inside the Party at the beginning of the 1920s than the far less colorful Stalin.) When the Soviet Union signaled that it would act as a solid and reliable partner in international trade, it also started to prove its attraction for certain maverick Western businessmen, such as "Lenin's friend," the legendary Armand Hammer.[16] The very inefficiency of centrally planned Soviet socialism offered fabulous profit margins for Western firms with privileged contacts with the Eastern empire's top officials.

The enormous expansion of the Soviet sphere of influence was started in 1939 with the German–Soviet understanding concerning the division of Poland and the extension of the Soviet empire to include (again) the Baltic states and Bessarabia. The eastern half of the German Reich, the Balkans and Eastern and Central Europe, traditionally an area of economic and political competition between Germany and France, became part of the Soviet power sphere after the Allied triumph of 1945.

Again, this enormous expansion of the Eurasian autocracy would not have been possible without indifference and tolerance of the leading world power, the United States, whose leaders still felt they needed the Soviet Union in order to win the war against Japan with a minimum of American casualties.

Thus, there was no Western offensive in the Balkans (as Churchill had advocated), and the technologically and economically still backward post-tsarist empire was able for more than four decades to dominate capitals of Central European civilization such as Budapest, Prague, and half of Berlin.

It was only the ruthless "sovietization" of this vast conquest after 1945 that drew the United States into a permanent active role in Europe. The economic stimulus of the "arms race," started during the Cold War, contributed to the West's postwar prosperity by stabilizing aggregate demand (quite contrary to the development after 1918), while the heavy armaments burden became more and more intolerable for the much weaker economies of the Eastern bloc. Thus, the apogee of Soviet power around Stalin's death also became the turning point after which the communist empire slowly began to crumble.

Paradoxically, the Marxist thesis of the primacy of the economic basis over the political superstructure in this context verified its long-term validity. It was the inability of the Stalinist bureaucratic regimes to deliver economic welfare in a comparable amount to neighboring Western countries that eventually caused the demise of "Real Socialism"—and this economic inferiority was due not only to lower levels of productivity and innovation but also to an extremely oversized defense sector.

While economic inferiority made it difficult to foster mass loyalty in the citizens of countries newly subjected to communist rule, the intellectual elites in the West who had been fascinated for decades with the model of dictatorial socialism also became progressively disaffected with the Eastern regimes after 1950.[17]

The first shocks had been the Stalinist show trials of 1937–38 and the Hitler–Stalin pact. The latter was hardly acceptable to those many idealistic followers of communism of a Jewish background. The construction and perfection of the "Iron Curtain," the East German uprising of 1953, the Hungarian Revolution of 1956, the erection of the Berlin Wall in 1961, and the occupation of Czechoslovakia in 1968 were then the main symbolic events that undermined the attraction of the communist model to the intellectuals of Western Europe. The Eastern bloc's bureaucratic authoritarianism and its sham democracy became an ever clearer indication of fatal weakness in political and, above all, in economic terms. (With the exception of extreme terror and war, mass emigration is generally more indicative of economic problems than of political disenfranchisement.) Poland's state of war declaration in 1981 (probably a last alternative to Soviet occupation) was another fatal blow. When Hungary decided in 1989 to pull down its part of the Iron Curtain, the mass exodus of East Germans via Hungary finally brought the entire satellite system to its collapse.

By this time the lack of economic competitivity of "Real Socialism" compared with the market economies of Western Europe had become evident even to the political elites in Eastern Europe. It is ironic but very telling that Donald Maclean, the master spy from Cambridge who defected in 1951 and died in 1983, had become an ardent advocate of liberal reform inside the Soviet nomenklatura:[18] thus, in the Soviet system as well as in other totalitarian regimes, intelligence officers with their privileged view of the world were among the most eager reformers in a system bogged down by its own parochial and bureaucratic spirit. But when Mikhail Gorbachev's perestroika tried a limited last-minute reform of the ossified, totally corrupted system, the "movement" that had long fallen into a standstill proved in fact unreformable. De Tocqueville's wise remark that revolutions do not occur at the height of tyranny but rather at a time when repression has eased and well-meaning attempts at reform are started puts Gorbachev in the bizarre role of a luckier cousin of France's ill-fated King Louis XVI.

Basically, the collapse of the Soviet empire, which started in Afghanistan and then led to the liberation of the satellite countries and—almost contemporaneously—to the dissolution of the dominant empire itself, simply meant a return to "historical normalcy": the advance of an economically as well as socially underdeveloped power right into the heart of a region with much higher economic and cultural potential could only be temporary, just as the hegemony of Sparta over Greece and the hegemony of nomadic tribes over sedentary civilizations could be nothing more than relatively short historic interludes.

Proclaiming the end of Russian hegemony over its satellites as a "return to normalcy" could, of course, be regarded as a trite ex-post prophecy. Thus, such a characterization should be used as a basis for falsifiable hypotheses. One such hypothesis would be the expectation that traditional investment rivalries in Eastern Europe should fill the vacuum left by the end of Soviet domination in this area.

Despite the positive development of the European unification process after the Maastricht Treaty, we have to expect that the main industrial nations of Western Europe will try to conquer Eastern European markets along similar patterns as before World War I and during the interwar period. Compared with the latter, however, German industry seems to be taking the lead. Its present dominance is evident even in areas that were favored by French investment after the First World War under the political auspices of the "Little Entente." Volkswagen's deal with Skoda and the giant investments by Siemens make it clear that France so far has been playing a secondary role in the Czech Republic, at least during the first round of this giant monopoly game. However, the historically difficult relationship between Germans and Czechs, notably the Czech fear of becoming a "German colony" again, could influence future Czech governments to play the anti-German card for populistic reasons.

The investment activities of reunified Germany are to be seen, however, not so much under a nationalistic angle, but rather under a mostly economic one, and the specter of a return of the Sudeten Germans is in fact totally unrealistic: these people are, if still alive, mostly retired persons without any plans to give up their settled life. Even if there were indications that some elderly German industrialists or top managers still dream of a strong Germany as a dominant power in the Balkans and Eastern Europe, the immediate motive for the extremely strong German investment activities in the Czech Republic, Hungary, and Poland is probably mostly due to the attractive wage differential of these countries compared with the former German Democratic Republic. (In spite of numerous tax breaks, the latter has become relatively unattractive as a place for investments and thus an economic problem area due to its integration into the mark currency zone.) Even if we take into account all proclamations of a European spirit, we have to face the fact that there are deeply rooted traditional animosities in Western Europe regarding a strong German position in Eastern and Central Europe.[19] Thus, German investment activities in this field are regarded with considerable mistrust in Paris, Amsterdam, and London. The appearance of extremist Czech chauvinist parties in the former Sudeten areas and Poland's misgivings about the conceptions of the "Euroregions" (as a "new way of partitioning Poland"), as well as certain conflicts regarding the German minority in Silesia, make it clear that there is also a certain sensitivity about a strongly increased German economic role in the areas concerned. A return to historical normalcy that would mean a return to economic rivalry among the European industrial nations in Central and Eastern Europe could create considerable tensions within the European Union—notably since the latter is still only a relatively weak confederation without any democratically elected top officials.

In the core area of the former tsarist and communist empire, the Commonwealth of Independent States, a certain return to historical patterns is visible as well. The process of disintegration of a multinational empire, which was started under the terms of the treaty of Brest-Litowsk and was largely "corrected" by Trotsky's Red Army, seems to have started again. This is an effect that Otto Bauer again was aware of in 1931 when he wrote, "The fall of the Soviet dictatorship would lead to bloody civil war in the Soviet Union. Civil war would create national secessionist movements in the non-Russian areas of the union."[20] (Bauer, however, was overestimating the capacity and willingness of other powers to intervene in this chaos.)

A Czech caricaturist has coined this phrase regarding the peaceful separation of Slovakia from the Czech Republic: "Each people has the right to enjoy its own nineteenth century." This process of a belated formation of nation-states is equally valid for the former Soviet Union, which was basically a multinational empire rather similar to the structure of the 1918 deceased Austro-Hungarian monarchy. The great danger of such a process, of course, is the temptation of "ethnic purification" in areas where different nationalities settle side by side. The attempt to create clearly defined nation-states with a minimum of ethnic minorities has always shown fatal affinities to tragedy: the massive expulsion of Germans after 1945 may be understood (if not justified) as a consequence of the most terrible of all "ethnic purifications," the Jewish Holocaust (even though the populations concerned had little direct relationship with the criminal war machinery that was committing the crimes of extermination, and even Jews returning from concentration camps were often driven out of Czechoslovakia if they entered "German" as their mother tongue in a peacetime census). The present outrage in what was Yugoslavia, however, cannot even be explained as an immediate counter- and overreaction. It has to take its "justification" from crimes committed half a century ago. Besides, a separation of ethnic groups is as impossible in the Caucasian regions as it is in Bosnia—unless executed under the most atrocious terms. Furthermore, this return to the national concepts of the nineteenth century appears curiously atavistic at a time when all the industrialized states are experiencing enormous immigration of new ethnic and religious minorities. However, where hatred has started to speak, the voice of the intellect (which Sigmund Freud rightly called low) probably stands little chance.

A Commonwealth of Independent States appears to be necessary on rational grounds of economic cooperation, of course. Nevertheless, the mere rational conviction that this cooperation across boundaries would be reasonable, especially in terms of the strong interrelationships created by the monopolistic economic structure of Stalinism, will not be sufficient to guarantee a minimum of unity. A certain economic nostalgia after the Soviet Union (even in its most stagnant phase) may be helpful, as the recent election turnouts in the Ukraine and Belarus indicate. Still, peaceful reunification seems unlikely, and reunification by force, as accomplished by the Red Army at the beginning of the 1920s, is much more difficult to imagine today than it was then, notably because of the nuclear arsenals of the Ukraine and Kazakhstan.

One thing, however, seems almost certain: the disorders of the post-

Soviet breakdown will be acted out without notable foreign interference.

Democracies have always had difficulties mobilizing their military potential (unless the risk is as minimal as, say, in the case of the U.S. invasion of Grenada). This fact is borne out not only by the United States' massive isolationist tendency after World War I and up to the Japanese attack at Pearl Harbor (remember that Franklin D. Roosevelt was elected in 1940 on a platform that promised to keep the United States out of the war in Europe and that the claims of the American political right that Pearl Harbor was a desired result of his skillful maneuvering may be justified).[21] The trauma of Vietnam, the withdrawal of American forces after a suicide attack on the U.S. marines in Lebanon, and the present unwillingness of all leading democratic powers to engage in a land war in the former Yugoslavia attest to the same tendency. Thus, if Russia and its neighboring states should fall into political and economic chaos again, such a tragedy would most likely marginalize Russia's role in Europe, just as happened after the catastrophe of Mongolian domination.

One may, of course, argue that this kind of isolation would be impossible under today's network of international communications and enormous mobility of refugees. But again, the former Yugoslavia, which is so near to the centers of European power and prosperity, is a sobering counterexample. It is perfectly possible for a people to live in relative peace and prosperity at only a short distance from massive chaos and terror (Switzerland's neutrality during the world wars is another example of this capacity to "seal off" modern societies from neighboring catastrophes). We are, of course, not advocating that the West turn its back on the destinies of states with hundreds of millions of inhabitants fewer than a thousand miles from the center of Europe. In fact, one objective of this book is to argue against this tendency to ignore the difficult and "unpleasant" situations in areas few West Europeans and even fewer Americans have ever seen in person. We have to admit, however, that especially during a period of economic uncertainty in the West, the tendency for the most developed countries to mind their own business might be growing.

From Euphoria to Disillusionment?

Crucial historical events have psychological effects that transcend their immediate importance. The revolutionary changes in Eastern Europe during the second half of 1989 have created enthusiasm not only in the countries concerned but—via the media—in the whole of Europe and even throughout the world. After decades of stagnation and an icy confrontation of rigid military and political blocs, all of Europe seemed to be "on the move" again. A new wind of freedom seemed to blow away the barriers between East and West. Unforgettable moments like the opening of the Berlin Wall and the jubilant demonstrations around Vaclav Havel in Prague made 1989 one of the historical cornerstones of the twentieth century.

Of course, these moments of enthusiasm cannot last, and many problems that may be swept aside in a wave of high spirits will show their faces again when the festivities end. Thus, the initial phase of euphoria is followed by a phase of disillusionment, in the countries concerned as well as in the West. Indeed, the five years since the end of "Real Socialism" have brought for most of Eastern Europe (with the exception of its westernmost fringe) mostly negative short-term economic effects—namely, a process of disintegration and inflation, unemployment and criminal insecurity. Western Europe has been disillusioned by the unpleasant surprise that old, half-forgotten prejudices and national confrontations have reemerged after the demise of the official solidaristic ideology. The increasing role of religion in Eastern Europe that was already obvious during the last years of communist rule, while it meant increasing opposition to the old regime, was rather popular in the West. Then, however, the extreme conservatism of parts of the clergy (e.g., in Poland) and religious confrontations such as in the Western Ukraine accompanied the ascent of the religious institutions to a powerful position in postcommunist Europe. Violent conflicts between nationalities that had previously been kept in check by police-state methods and open manifestations of racism (e.g., against Jews or gypsies) frightened the Western media. The people whose liberation from totalitarianism was greeted with such enthusiasm turned out to be all too human. Cultural patterns that had been suppressed but not eliminated by the official Marxist-Leninist ideology resurfaced. Still, the unsurmounted barrier between West and East should not be increased unnecessarily by emotional reversals. The apparently popular stereotype of the "ugly Eastern European" ("he is lazy, criminal, without initiative and chauvinistic") is unjust. Again, the concept of a return to "historical normalcy" can serve to put this understandable disillusionment in perspective.

It is evident that everywhere in Eastern Europe a certain nostalgia for the old regime is emerging. This is quite natural. Despite their long-term disastrous effects, the communist regimes were able to guarantee modest economic survival and social security for their people. This is no longer true. The years 1993 and 1994 have witnessed strong electoral showings of more or less democratized ex-communist parties in the East. While the new leftist governments in Poland and Hungary are by no means a return to the *ancien régime,* Westerners seem to be increasingly viewing such events as a disillusioning retreat ("These people yearn for the yoke they have just shaken off"). The West, however, should not forget that to some extent Western institutions and individuals are to blame for the disappointment that has spread throughout Eastern Europe. This is specifically true for those prophets of a "great leap forward" into capitalism that seriously underestimated the real difficulties of such a transition process and thereby contributed to the lack of realism that was all too visible in Eastern Europe after the glorious revolutions of 1989.[22]

Today there are already many economists and politicians in Western and Eastern Europe commenting with a certain touch of cynicism on the role of foreign counselors in Eastern Europe around 1990. To be fair, however, we should admit that while promises of a fast and painless transition into a market economy were not very realistic, they represented powerful desires in the West as well as in the East. Their message was illusory from the beginning but it was effective because the ground had been prepared for a gospel of instant salvation. Amid the immediate postrevolutionary euphoria, many spoke of an equalization of economic potentials and welfare levels east and west of the former Iron Curtain within five to ten years. Such a view was contrary to the experience in all of economic history, which has shown a great stability[23] of regional income differentiation over many decades even under rather similar capitalist structures. Economies whose growth potential in terms of a market economy was almost intentionally destroyed by a disproportionate focus on heavy industry and armaments as well as by absurd hypercentralization, economies where the human capital of entrepreneurship was willfully annihilated, can of course make up for such disadvantages neither in five nor in ten years, with or without foreign help. That concepts of an "instant transition" toward a market economy have played such a strong role in the West may have something to do with the ahistorical model-oriented approach that has dominated economics for a long time, but especially during the 1980s.

Eventually, this kind of *tabula rasa* thinking had to show its illusory character. A wonder cure that would spare the reform countries the long labors of a gradual transition had its fatal attractiveness. Mass privatization via coupons as now realized or promised in a number of postcommunist states is a typical child of this sort of thinking. Such ideas may be politically popular in the short run but it is highly doubtful whether they would be successful in the long run: while concepts like these create the appearance of a democratic and capitalist ownership structure they supplant the disastrous absentee ownership of communism with a new absentee owner: the helpless, ill informed, poor, small shareholder who has been lured into "capitalism" by completely unrealistic profit expectations and then deeply disappointed by experiences such as the fraudulent MMM fund run on the pyramid scheme. Of course, we can still hope that most of the funds that will actually play the ownership role will engage in reasonable investment and marketing policies. (There are some indications of this in the Czech Republic, for example.) But these funds may also turn into strongholds of political camarillas or into agents of a dubious casino capitalism. Western examples (even the attempts of a highly profitable IBM company in the 1960s with its elite work force)[24] indicate that small shareholders will sell out rather soon even if offered advantageous access to attractive shares: either cashing in on modest gains or, more probably, giving up in disappointment with unfavorable price developments on the stock markets. The latter process may lead to exactly those kinds of robber-baron capitalism or of foreign domination in industry that the coupon schemes were created to avoid. At any rate, we should be aware that the economic rise of the most important industrial states was not the effect of an anonymous capitalism of the stock-exchange model but largely the effect of powerful Schumpeterian entrepreneurs and enterprises with stable ownership structures (even today, unfriendly takeovers are practically unheard of in Germany, Sweden, or Switzerland). Idealization of the "perfect market" of the stock-exchange type in some Eastern European states since 1989 should be interpreted as a psychological reaction against the extremely regulated or totally suppressed markets under communism. The anecdote about the Central Committee building of the Polish Communist Party being turned into a stock exchange and bank building can be interpreted as a belated reprisal for 1945, when the old Warsaw stock exchange was reportedly turned into a "Museum of the October Revolution." In any event, it has become abundantly evident that stock exchanges will not solve the problems of Eastern Europe.

Impatient enthusiasts for unfettered capitalism in Eastern Europe have pointed out that privatization at the speed of the Conservative Thatcher government in Great Britain in the 1980s would mean, for example, that the Czech economy will be fully privatized within only four hundred years. It has become clear in the meantime that there can be no Great Leap Forward in an economic sense, either from feudalism into socialism (as Chairman Mao had to realize) or from socialism to capitalism. Any attempt to change existing economic structures with a voluntaristic effort within a very short time is greatly at risk of ending in catastrophe.

Western institutions have contributed to the rapid destruction of the economic structures of the "house of socialism" instead of consciously solidifying it via concrete injections of market forces. They have pressed for rapid liberation of prices even though the monopolistic ownership structure, in a perfect sellers' market, would only create inflationary price rises. Other hasty measures—for example, in the view of exchange convertibility—have pointed into the same direction. More perspicacious observers such as Austrian journalist Hans Rauscher explicitly stated at the beginning of January 1992 that "the American neoliberal concepts could turn out to be a catastrophe" for Russia.[25] Still, the West must share a certain responsibility for the present chaotic situation, which to some extent offers opportunities to the old communist nomenklatura to seek "democratic" rehabilitation. The minister of the economy of a small postcommunist country once remarked how skeptical he was with regard to those American advisers who came out of certain elite universities selling "wonder drugs" without any specific knowledge of the countries they were advising. He cited an example of some young lawyers who had visited him who were unaware that the American case law system could not be adopted by a small country situated in the heart of Central Europe that has been deeply influenced by Roman law for centuries.

It has become customary today to criticize the lack of entrepreneurial outlook of Eastern Europeans, or to quote callous statements like, "These people didn't want a market economy, they wanted socialism plus video games." It is good in the face of such criticism to remember that the illusion of a fast and painless transition into Western welfare society has been fostered by the West too.

Why Is There No Marshall Plan for Eastern Europe?

Politicians like Lech Walesa, industrialists like Carlo de Benedetti, or economists like John Kenneth Galbraith have often taken up the demand for a new Marshall Plan for Eastern Europe. Unfortunately, this Marshall Plan idea seems even less likely today than it was immediately after the events of 1989, when on the wave of the first euphoria a massive transfer of income from the West to the East via solidarity taxes would have been thinkable not only in Germany but in the whole of Western Europe. Today a real Marshall Plan for Eastern Europe is almost unthinkable because of the same cluster of factors that impeded the equally often proclaimed "Marshall Plan for the Third World": unlike the original Marshall Plan, such new aid programs would not be responding to the urgent economic and political interest of major lobbies in the would-be aid-giving countries.

The original Marshall Plan was conceived as a political and economic instrument to stabilize and possibly roll back the Soviet sphere of influence in Europe after 1945. At that time, the Soviet Union had not only occupied its future satellite states in Central and Eastern Europe and was about to turn them into replicas of Russia's Stalinist regimes, but the strong and well-organized Communist Parties in Italy and France (and, more latently, in Spain) made it clear that a Western Europe that would be destabilized economically for a longer period could also fall prey to the Stalinist model of autocracy. In this extremely dangerous situation, the United States was ready to liberate enormous financial means and real investment in order to contribute to a rapid stabilization of Western Europe. At the same time, the savings due to demobilization in the United States federal budget created a much greater potential for reallocation of resources than is possible today. It may be argued that the military-industrial complex in the United States and to some extent in Western Europe should now also reallocate savings toward the East, but the armaments industry during the Cold War solidified into a big business complex whose sudden "demobilization" could wreak havoc in many economic areas. While President Clinton wanted to reduce military spending much more dramatically than his predecessor had planned, it is already clear that his intentions are not politically feasible. Alarming signs of a negative "peace dividend" have already surfaced for certain parts of the United States where military industries are concentrated.

A situation like the one that unfolded in 1945, which must be interpreted in terms of the containment or rollback of a totalitarian superpower and its ideology, has never existed thus far in the Third World (aggressive Islamism might be considered vaguely comparable today, but on a much smaller scale). And postcommunist countries of Central and Eastern Europe have become paradoxically less important because they no longer belong to a unified repressive system. It was quite rational to favor the most liberal reform countries of the Eastern bloc as long as this Eastern bloc still existed (this includes Tito's Yugoslavia and later Hungary). The political motivation to help these states, however, has paradoxically but logically diminished. Communism has broken down and Poland and Hungary are now debtor countries that tend to be treated on an equal footing with, say, Argentina or Uruguay. Postcommunist Eastern Europe as a whole no longer represents a global political danger and trade relations take place on a relatively modest scale. The area offers substantial uncertainties for the future and thus simply is not very interesting to overseas investors, with the exception of its westernmost fringe. Interest in Eastern Europe seems to be declining with the square of distance on land and with the third power of distance on water. Even the English Channel appears to be a powerful psychological barrier in this respect. France, which is showing less economic presence in Central and Eastern Europe compared to the interwar period, is also witness to this phenomenon. The present detente between the major European powers now assembled inside the European Union makes politically motivated investment drives less attractive. France, now a close ally of Germany, no longer has any political reasons to build up a "little entente" with Poland and the Czech Republic in economic terms as a counterweight against its neighbor. The greatest motivation to invest in Eastern Europe thus is present on the former border states west of the Iron Curtain. This "neighborhood effect" has its problems as well, especially in connection with unsettled historical problems. Japan, which for some time made it very clear that its economic involvement in Russia was largely dependent on a positive solution to the question of the return of the Kurile islands to Japan, is a case in point. Germany so far has avoided similar gaffes, on the one hand because, until the full Russian withdrawal by August 31, 1994, there were still sizable contingents of ex-Soviet troops on its territory. On the other hand, Chancellor Kohl as a historian knows all too well that the allure of being a "great power" has never benefited Germany. One cannot, however, rule out the possibility that similar ideas and attitudes as Japan's in the Kurile question could play a more marked role in Germany in the future with regard to the former Sudeten area or Silesia. This, of course, would not be very productive for East or West.

If we assume that nations and governments are to some extent rational and egoistic actors on the international scene, there is very little hope for a Marshall Plan for Eastern Europe. On the contrary, the interest of large private companies that want to be present as new and promising markets are opening up is quite discernible. Advertisements for typical consumer Western products such as Marlboro cigarettes and Coca-Cola already dominate some Eastern cityscapes, in place of the red and white slogans of the old regimes. This obvious interest, however, is going to turn into substantial real investment only under conditions of a minimum of political stability. (Investors, like tourists, are hypersensitive about social unrest.) Thus, we are witnessing the creation of an economic transition area between Western and Eastern Europe. In 1991 I speculated that this transitional area would probably comprise a strip of 100 to 150 miles of land from St. Petersburg in the north, encompassing the Baltic states and western Poland, the Czech Republic, and the western part of Slovakia, to Hungary west of the Danube and to the northern parts of the former Yugoslavia (Slovenia and Croatia) insofar as they are not too involved in that area's civil war.[26] This prediction can still be upheld, even though St. Petersburg, the Baltics (with the exception of Estonia), and the Kaliningrad area have not yet shown excessive dynamism. The area described can be compared to the traditional transition zone between the highly developed United States and northern Mexico. It will probably involve 10 to 20 percent of the population of the old Stalinist empire, and include some of its most important cities, such as St. Petersburg, Budapest, Prague, Bratislava, and, at the limit, Warsaw. With the exception of this transitional area, which will be favored by industrial investments but also partially by tourism, only isolated investment and modernization centers in areas with valuable natural resources, tourist attractions, and administrative centers will be favored islands of development. In the context of normal development, Austria's sizable experience with traditional trade relations with the Eastern bloc as well as with new investment ventures in postcommunist Europe appears interesting.

The Austrian Experience

Today's Austria is a small remnant of a large Central European empire that has played an important historical role for large areas of the former Eastern bloc: from Poland and Hungary to Slovenia, Croatia, and former Czechoslovakia. Economic and trade relations between Austria and the other parts of the former Hapsburg empire were relatively intense even after 1918, even though the new countries of Central and Eastern Europe tried to sever their "postcolonial" ties by increasing import barriers and other obstacles to trade. Even after 1945, Austria's economic relations with its Eastern neighbors continued, albeit under increasingly difficult circumstances. Austria continued its economic relationship with the countries subjected to Stalinist communism in a way that can be only compared with Finland. At the same time, Austria developed a strongly Western-oriented pluralistic democratic and capitalist economic order in which a sizable sector of nationalized industry was, ironically, built with the help of the Western allies and Marshall Plan money, while Russian occupants opposed nationalization on the grounds that it involved "German property" that should be turned over to the Allies. This nationalized industry, which was thriving and well before the mid-1970s, succeeded in developing stable markets in Eastern Europe and in the Third World, and thus favored Austria's small and medium-sized private subcontractors. On the other hand, Austria's exports to Eastern and Central Europe were largely based on favorable credits to the countries concerned. This led the Austrian state and its specialized banking institutions to guarantee an excessive amount of credits to the East. These credits have created, and continue to create problems, ever since it became clear that Poland, Bulgaria, and Hungary, among other debtor countries, would have difficulties paying back their debts. In spite of this problematic situation, Austria remains a very active investor in Eastern Europe, although now it is mostly the private sector of the economy that is investing across the border. Several hundred miles of border with the Czech Republic, Slovakia, Hungary, and Slovenia, which had been relatively impoverished and depopulated areas during the past forty years, have recently been integrated in a process of dynamic exchange. Austria, thus, is involved in a laboratory of economic development interaction whose first empirical results allow predictions about what are likely to be the most successful development strategies for the establishment of a functioning capitalism in the states of former "Real Socialism."

Austrian enterprises have, above all, invested in the retail trade (so far with mixed results), as well as in shoe and paper manufacturing (the latter is presenting problems because of current European excess capacities and Scandinavian export dumping). Austria's banks have been quite successful in Eastern Europe where banking technology and know-how have been practically nonexistent. The role of Austrian banks in developing the new stock exchanges in Eastern Europe so far, however, has been disappointing. Austrian building industries have invested heavily in former East Germany, but this is a case apart.

It is somewhat too early to talk about the real flops and the real successes of these investment ventures, especially since large investment projects even in the West often have to overcome an initial phase of several years of losses before they reach a breakeven point. Nevertheless, the Austrian example already shows some general patterns. The most successful forms of joint ventures seem to be those developed by small and medium-sized Western firms "right across the border," and where the developed marketing apparatus of the Western firm is used to create employment for an Eastern plant that is essentially benefiting from the low Eastern wages (at present there is still a wage differential of one to ten and more, which, even though productivity in the East is also much lower, offers interesting possibilities for wage-intensive "no-frills" products). Also, some of the most successful East European enterprises are situated near the border and oriented toward a stable customer in the West. Investments in heavy industry are attractive where differentials in wage and environmental protections costs are important—for example, where mass products in the fields of cement, fertilizer, and aluminum are concerned. (Steel is more problematic because of excessive worldwide overcapacities, but it constitutes a primary area of "desperate" export offensives.) Insofar as industrial East European enterprises in these fields are trying to conquer Western markets by themselves, they naturally encounter opposition from West European producers, who complain about environmental and wage dumping. Meanwhile, it becomes obvious that many Western firms, such as those in the cement and fertilizer industries, are already buying up East European companies that are active in fields where export to the West is imaginable. In terms of the home market of the Central and East European countries, the first investments have been made in retailing. This probably has to do with the specific backwardness of retailing and services under communism, and with the countries' populations' characteristic hunger for Western consumer goods. This domination by Western retailing groups, as it has become evident in former East Germany, may create problems for producers that are used to smugly delivering to a peaceful home market. Retailing, which requires relatively little initial capital, is one of the mainstays of the new small business class in Eastern Europe.

Larger Western investors are showing specific interest in the food and drink industry. Breweries and tobacco factories, with their stable and captive markets, have been prime targets for Western takeovers. East European cityscapes are enlivened—at least during the summer months—by masses of "Marlboro" and "Rothman's" umbrellas shading patrons at streetside cafés. As a matter of fact, the Western tobacco giants—encountering increasingly aggressive opposition to smoking on their home turf—are looking toward the Eastern and Third World markets, where health considerations are as yet less developed.

Western knowhow and technology are very important in banking as well as in detergent and cosmetics production. Textile and shoe production could become important export assets for Eastern Europe because of their high wage-cost component.

Outlook on the Future

The "specter of communism" has left Europe but the "specter of nationalism" has come back with a vengeance. In fact, the specter of communism did not really haunt Europe (contrary to the assertion of Marx and Engels in *The Communist Manifesto* of 1848) until the end of the First World War. The only possible exception was the Paris "Commune" of 1871 when, as in 1917–18, the vacuum of military defeat unleashed a formidable revolutionary potential. Since 1917, however, when communism for the first time succeeded in dominating a large empire for a considerable period of time, its specter has been a dominant aspect of West European and later global politics. In spite of Stalin's reductions of Lenin's concepts of a global revolution, for decades the European business classes experienced communism as a very real threat. Without losing ourselves in a maze of historical speculation, it seems indisputable that the fatal attraction offered by "strongman rule" in the interwar years to Europe's upper and middle classes had something to do with this feeling that the creed of revolutionary Marxism was fundamentally dangerous.[27] Besides it was not just paranoia to assume that the well-organized communist movements in the West could be seen as a kind of fifth column of the totalitarian regime in the East. This communist threat seemed to be easing during the prosperous 1920s when Lenin's NEP offered the prospect of a moderate "Mexicanization" of the Bolshevik revolution. The Great Depression, however, and Stalin's five-year plans and increasing terror can be regarded as partially instrumental in Adolf Hitler's ascent to power as a "savior" against communist chaos. After 1945, it was the brutality and consistency with which Stalin's Soviet Union remodeled its sphere of influence according to its own pattern that reinforced the "specter of communism" for Western Europe's upper and middle classes. This threat also finally convinced the United States to assume the leading part in the Western camp during the Cold War. Thus, the challenge from the East became a unifying, integrative factor for the West. The idea of European unity and of an international economic and political solidarity of the democracies East and West of the Atlantic never would have been so effective had there not been this ever-present threat by a powerful and highly armed "Evil Empire" in the East. In this sense, institutions like the EEC (EU) or the OECD and the Council of Europe owe a great debt to the very system they were created to combat. Even the postwar economic stability of Western Europe and of the United States can be regarded as partially dependent on the constant arms race of the postwar years. By the same token, the boom period of the Reagan era in the 1980s had something to do with the enormous efforts to ruin the Soviet Union and its satellites once and for all in a new round of the arms race. (Even though President Reagan made it clear that he was no Keynesian and that he was striving for a balanced budget, the real effect of his policies was an enormous spree of "deficit spending.")[28]

After Stalin's death it became obvious that the mobilizing power of Soviet ideology was on the wane in Europe. Repeated uprisings and attempts at reform in the satellite states made it clear that the Stalinist version of Asian despotism was not acceptable to the populations in Central and Eastern Europe, and that even the brightest of their communist leaders were desperately looking for other models. In fact, the slow erosion of communist voting power in European parliaments or their "social-democratization" (as in the case of Italy) made it obvious that the specter of communism, in the sense of a proletarian revolution, no longer really existed in the Western democracies. Even when the Soviet Union itself had already entered the "period of stagnation" (as Gorbachev described the Brezhnev area), communism again showed its fatal attractive power; only now its attraction was focused on the underdeveloped countries of the Third World. (This is perfectly in line with Lenin's assertion that the chain of capitalism can be most easily broken by attacking its "weakest links," even if it runs exactly contrary to Marx's expectation that revolutions would occur in the most industrialized countries.) The humiliation of colonial France and later of the United States by communism in Indochina, the transformation of the Cuban revolution into post-Stalinist totalitarianism, and the establishment of Marxist totalitarian regimes in Angola, Mozambique, Yemen, and Ethiopia seemed to resurrect the specter of communist expansionism on a global level. At the same time, it was already evident that communism was no longer a centralized bloc because after the minor Yugoslav schism of 1948, the new communist power of China was acting as a second focus of power in the communist world. Still, until the early 1980s, the political system built by Lenin, Stalin, and their successors appeared to be undefeated, if not invincible. Even the last conquests, however, had to be fought and guaranteed by foreign troops. Cuban soldiers played an important role in Angola and Ethiopia, and the Soviet Union had to invade Afghanistan to guarantee the survival of its puppet regime there. All this made it overwhelmingly clear that the draw of communism was on the wane even in the postcolonial world. On the other hand, we must remember that this lack of attraction was evident in Central and Eastern Europe in 1945 too—but it did not present a serious obstacle to the ruthless introduction of Stalinism. Except in Czechoslovakia, there were no sizable communist parties in Eastern Europe at the time. Still, the Soviet system was established by a minority of fanatical communists supported by the military might of the Red Army.

The Soviet invasion of Afghanistan was as related to the traditional dream of Russian imperialism to gain access to a warm sea as it was an "offensive defense" against the spread of Islam. This fatal error, however, made the weakness of the Soviet power machine all too evident. While the United States' humiliation in Vietnam signified a psychologically depressing episode for a nation that nonetheless remained a superpower, the debacle of Afghanistan was much more pivotal for the

Soviet Union, for the Soviet Union had to cultivate its myth of invincibility so much more because its economic achievements were so poor. With hindsight, Gorbachev's liquidation of the Afghanistan commitment can be interpreted in terms of a domino theory: it was the first withdrawal from an occupied territory, the first step toward the gradual implosion of an overextended empire marked by the status of an occupying force practically everywhere, even in most of the non-Russian areas at home. Still, there is some truth in the bitter criticism by Great Russian nationalists and old guard communists that Gorbachev lost the empire won in 1945.

The occasionally expressed suggestion that the events of 1989 came as a total surprise is not really true. Of course, experts like Richard Pipes who were regarded by some as "cold warriors" always had a more critical eye for the weaknesses of the system than more liberal experts—and Western "sovietologists" had a legitimate personal interest in the survival of the object of their profession. But to most unbiased observers, it was obvious that the Soviet power system was ossified, corrupted, and hardly reformable. It was a huge and impressive but evidently shaky structure—and such buildings can crumble tomorrow or stand for another thirty years. The gradual loss of motivation of communist ideology was specifically evident in the satellite countries in Central and Eastern Europe. The human sacrifices of the civil war at the beginning of the 1920s and those of Stalinist industrialization and collectivization were administered by a vanguard of almost religiously fanatical believers who were able to convince the habitual crowd of opportunists that theirs was the future. Similar groups were active during the first phase of the Stalinist reconstruction of Eastern Europe after 1945. Hungarian "goulash-communism," however, after 1956 already showed that the power elites had to resort to bribing the people with promises of depoliticization and more consumer goods. As Timothy Garton Ash has pointed out, the power elite stopped bullying the people in exchange for a minimum of cooperation that would allow the nomenklatura to continue to enjoy its privileges. This return to a private quest for happiness, however, was obstructed by the inflexible economic structures that made a depoliticized consumer civilization extremely difficult to construct. Also, a gradual transition to a more pluralistic system seemed practically excluded. The main political difficulty in this context was that the ruling elite realized that if it started a reform process, it would risk being swept away by a wave of suppressed popular wrath. (This was specifically the case for East Germany and, above all, Hungary, where the "liberal" Janos Kadar was also a symbol of postrevolutionary repression who never quite succeeded in washing the blood of 1956–57 off his hands.) The economic structure of the satellite countries, which had been remodeled according to the pattern of Soviet Stalinism, proved extremely unfit for a gradual transition to a market economy—an unfitness that can be best characterized by contrast with China. The fact that China seems to be doing so well in its transition to capitalism (under the political hegemony of a communist nomenklatura) is probably based precisely on the fact that China's industrialization process never went as far as the one in the Soviet Union and Eastern Europe, and notably, that the Chinese agrarian structure remained largely nonmechanized. That backwardness became an advantage because it facilitated the reprivatization of agriculture and the creation of modern consumer goods industries.

We have to face the fact that the essential weakness of the colossus in the East could only be overlooked in the West for such a long time because the permanence of the Cold War confrontation was advantageous to certain lobbies and segments of the population in the West. The positive effect of a threat from the East on the process of European economic and political integration as well as on the partnership between Western Europe and the United States has already been mentioned. In concrete terms, this meant that certain groups in the West, notably the so-called military-industrial complex (and some professional watchers of the East in academia), began to see the Eastern empire as a "dear enemy" whose strength should not be underestimated—not least because it furnished the argument for lavish government expenditure to counter it. Nobody will be surprised that the CIA estimations of Soviet economic power were for many decades far too optimistic. Of course, the military power of the Warsaw Pact was impressive: especially in the area of conventional armaments, and despite the questionable loyalty of some troops from satellite countries, occupation of Western Europe within a few weeks would have been conceivable without threat of nuclear retaliation. This situation legitimized huge U.S. defense budgets for a long time. This situation, of course, has changed dramatically (and Saddam Hussein has turned out to be a poor substitute for the evil empire in the East). Thus, the U.S. defense budget has entered a squeeze period that is likely to produce serious employment problems on the American domestic scene. President Clinton has proposed to cut the U.S. arms budget over the next five years by almost one-third (this would be more than twice the amount envisioned by George Bush). Whether such reductions can be carried out, especially during a period of fragile economic recovery, remains to be seen.

The most brutal dictatorships of the Stalinist model, like Nicolai Ceausescu's regime, offered a certain attraction for the most conservative Western bankers—their sheer brutality could be seen as a guarantee that the dictatorships would squeeze their population in order to pay back their credits (a hope that failed in the case of North Korea). Basically, it was the so-called reform countries that demonstrated that a slow process of disintegration of a communist governmental system might be a relief for the population, but risky for international creditors. Such a process weakens the kind of rigid central authority that seems to be absolutely necessary for a communist system's survival. Also, it creates a great number of economic decision-making bodies that tend to develop soft budget constraints. The process of chaotic decentralization now so typical for the post–Soviet Union states could already be observed in pre–civil war Yugoslavia. Conversely, relatively strong central coordination—that is, a more or less autonomous central banking system—is characteristic of those reform countries that are now in a more or less acceptable economic condition, such as Hungary, the Czech Republic, Poland, and Slovenia.

Finally, a certain amount of stability was ironically guaranteed by the so-called Iron Curtain. This system of border barriers was an important propaganda asset for the West, while at the same time it precluded the danger of mass immigration that has become such a great concern. West Germany, for example, was able to offer extremely generous conditions to immigrants from the East mostly because relatively few people could emigrate (these were mostly retired people whom the overaged East German state was glad to get rid of because they were only consumers and not producers anymore).

A Western lobby specifically favored by the peculiar structure of the Eastern economies was the agricultural producers' lobby. Before the First World War, Russia was one of the world's largest grain exporters. The inefficiency of collectivized agriculture meant that traditional agrarian export countries like Canada, Australia, Argentina, and the United States were free from the competition of a nation that ought to have been a gigantic producer of agrarian surplus. These

Western agrarian exporters were even able to find customers in the East that were ready to pay good prices for products that otherwise would have offered serious surplus problems. Since it is reasonable to expect massive rises in the productivity of East European agriculture, at least in the medium term, we have to expect almost devastating effects on the world's grain markets—unless major hunger catastrophes in the Third World should justify generous gifts of grain.

The stability of the borders in the Yalta system effectively created the basis of decades of peace in Europe—but not in Europe alone. For some time it seemed that the principle of unrevisable borders, established in Europe after 1945, would hold even in the former colonial areas that were turned to sovereign states in the 1960s. This principle of nonreversibility of borders may seem absurd, especially in Africa, if contrasted with ethnic realities. Still, it was upheld (for example, in the case of the Biafra uprising). One aspect of the Yalta system, Germany's division into two sovereign states, by the way, was specifically acceptable to a number of states and strong political groups in Western Europe (including such disparate figures as Charles de Gaulle and Margaret Thatcher). Thus, there was an unjust but seemingly permanent peace order in Europe. Just as the peace order created by the Holy Alliance after the Vienna Congress of 1815 guaranteed for a number of decades a clear-cut map of Europe with a certain Biedermeier charm, the Yalta system produced a sort of "second Biedermeier epoch" of stability and (gradually reduced) police repression.

There were, thus, sufficient reasons for not believing in a quick demise of the communist bloc and for not wanting to believe in it. These comfortable illusions have been destroyed by the events of 1989 and 1990. We have had to face the fact yet again that no order of peace can be guaranteed for an unlimited time and that long phases of stability in world and regional politics lead to an accumulation of latent conflicts which can become explosive. The peace systems of the Vienna Congress and of the Berlin Congress, as well as that of Yalta, functioned rather well for thirty to forty years. We are now, however, experiencing the liberation as well as the tragedy of an explosive outbreak of accumulated conflicts. The civil war in the former Yugoslavia is the most brutal expression, the separation of Czechoslovakia is the most civilized, but in either case the concept of stable borders in Europe now appears rather shaky. The Yalta system has ended. So far there have been no border changes between existing states and only new "internal" borders have been created. But if Bosnia were to be divided into three parts established partially by ethnic purification, another dangerous precedent would be set. Claims for a "reunification" of Moldavia with Romania and for the sizable Hungarian minorities in Romania and Slovakia with their "mother people" could easily be encouraged. This situation can be regarded as extremely dangerous, especially in view of a potential Slovak–Serb–Romanian alliance against a Hungary trying to strike up a close friendship with the Ukraine, or other possible destabilizing developments.

Thus, there is an enormous potential for latent conflicts in Eastern Europe that have been suppressed and manipulated during the decades of communism that are now coming to the fore under democracy. And just as some are nostalgic for the "modest, orderly" system of Brezhnev's "period of stagnation," some people in the West are starting to feel nostalgic about the dreaded but calculable partner-opponent in the East. Europe is entering a new period of incalculability.

What does this mean for the future? The danger of a true restoration of an old type of Soviet communism is minimal, even though some may dread it and some may wish for it. Some "reformist" ex-nomenklatura members may score electoral successes with their postcommunist parties, but the Hungarian and Polish experiences already show that this will not turn the tide. People like Gyula Horn themselves have experienced the erosion process of an ideology that initially was able to motivate people for noble sacrifice as well as cold brutality, which then turned into meaningless ritual. Communism was able to conquer so widely because it was essentially a secularized myth of salvation. But nobody believes that myth anymore, with the possible exception of its former octogenarian high priests. A system that has confessed its lies and crimes as has happened under Khrushchev and Gorbachev cannot be restored. According to their own logic the old Stalinists were right when they were appalled at Nikita Khrushchev's famous secret speech at the Twentieth Party Congress in 1956. In terms of pure power politics this speech was a mistake. Khrushchev himself realized this. The "river of truth" that started to flow then was frozen after the experience of the Hungarian uprising. But the ice started to break again under perestroika and now there is no turning back. All the crimes and official lies from the Great Purge of 1937–38 to the massacre of Katyn have been exposed. Even the fabulous achievements of the famous miner Stakhanov from 1935 who was to lend his name to a whole organization of socialist worker-heroes were officially declared a lie in 1987 (Stakhanov had two helpers), and the millions of civilian victims of Stalinist repression have become part of public discourse—this fact alone is bound to disqualify Stalin himself from hero status for future mass movements. In this destructive sense, perestroika has been a success, and Boris Yeltsin's special message to Polish President Lech Walesa concerning the murders of Katyn in 1992 marked an important political achievement, even if all it did was to destroy old and monstrous lies.

Of course, there are regions where the old systems remain essentially unchanged (such as Belarus and the Ukraine), and there may be even cases of true restoration. Still, a complete return to the conditions of 1970 or 1950 is unthinkable. Awareness of the level of corruption as well as the insight into the superior efficiency of a capitalist, profit-oriented economy have spread. In many countries the former nomenklatura is trying to form a new oligarchy of capitalists—which would have amused Karl Marx who was so keenly aware of the tendency of an upper class to remain an upper class even under a changing economic regime. (It is quite another question, of course, whether the initial advantages of these new "entrepreneurs" will be sufficient to maintain their privileged position.) The backwardness of the former Soviet Union in this process and the obstructionist tactics of the old privileged groups against truly penetrating reforms are probably due to the fact that the Russian nomenklatura are not as ready to become a "neocapitalist" upper class as, say, Poland's privileged are. The Russian bureaucratic elite still needs its privileges. More problematic than this somewhat ironic transformation of parts of the old into a new upper class, however, is the tendency toward social disintegration and the growing criminal disorder now evident in many postcommunist countries. The reform countries are witnessing spreading instances of organized crime, individual brutality, and massive corruption. A recent anecdote tells of a Slovak criminal clan who engaged in armed robbery and murder in Austria, but whose head was for some time quite a successful politician and founder of a "business party." Even the neighboring Western countries are feeling some of the effects of this transformation process. East European prostitutes and pimps, as well as organized groups of beggars and car thieves, are now as much a part of their neighboring countries' social realities as East European street musicians and illegal immigrants. Even if semi-authoritarian regimes should succeed in creating a higher degree of public order, the virus of so-called Latin-Americanization will not be conquered soon. This is probably the most solid insight that we can formulate five years after the revolutionary changes in the East.

Another clear insight is the development of the above-mentioned transition zone between Western industrialized societies in postcommunist Central and Eastern Europe. The exact contours of this transitional area are, of course, hard to establish, but we can undertake an informed guess: it is rather certain that the westernmost parts of Poland and the whole of the Czech Republic will be favored. The same may be said of the westernmost areas of Slovakia, whose capital city of Bratislava almost forms a double city with Austria's Vienna; a dramatic increase of legal as well as illegal economic cross-border activity is inevitable. The differences between this metropolitan area and rural eastern Slovakia will, however, increase dramatically in this process. Even in Hungary, which has profited most by Western investment and tourism, there is a marked difference in development between the areas near the westernmost border and the eastern half of the country beyond the Danube.

The separation of Slovenia and Croatia from the rest of Yugoslavia was intended to speed up the process of Westernization and economic development by leaving behind the politically dominant but poor, militarized, and bureaucratized Serbia. Things are, of course, more complicated. Slovenia fares best, because it is not involved in the civil war, but the poor south of Yugoslavia and Croatia were the most important markets for its industry. Croatia and Serbia are directly involved in the war in Bosnia, and even though they seem in some bizarre sense to be allies dividing up the territory of multinational Bosnia, their economies have been deeply affected by this brutal and inhuman war.

The Baltic states, which hope to find economic and political help in Scandinavia, face a similarly uncertain fate. They feel still threatened by the former Red Army, which projects itself into the role of a protective force for the rights of the sizable Russian population within these countries, even though the army has been formally withdrawn. Thus, the economic and political fate of the Baltic states is directly dependent on the regime in Moscow and on the capacity of the local governments to engage in consensus politics involving their Russian minorities; it is doubtful that the Western powers would engage in more than verbal protest in case of any Russian "intervention."

Estonia appears to be in a slightly privileged economic position; it will likely profit from relations with ethnically similar Finland. No such parallel situation exists for the other Baltic states. Finland itself, however, as a small country with a traditionally high percentage of trade with Russia, has been severely affected by the present recession in the West combined with the dramatic reduction in exports to the East. Further, St. Petersburg, situated next to the Finnish border, will probably become a formidable competitor against Estonia for Finnish investment, even though Estonia may be the Finns' sentimental favorite.

The Commonwealth of Independent States plays a dominant role in the Baltic states as a source of energy and as a buyer of industrial products, especially for Latvia and Lithuania. This dependency is less marked in the case of Estonia. The basic question in the Baltics, however, is whether the tendency toward confrontation between ethnic Baltic people and Russians will escalate or diminish. Conditions such as the present disenfranchisement for Russians in Estonian elections and the prohibition for Russians to acquire property in Latvia are not cause for optimism.

The Russian metropolis of St. Petersburg is favored by its extreme border position and should profit, like Prague, from its enormous potential for tourism, provided a minimum level of political and social stability can be maintained. The looming question here is the economic status of this city. St. Petersburg was supposed to become a special economic zone according to the successful Chinese model, but so far there has been very little progress in this direction. The same is true for the eastern part of former East Prussia, which is today a Russian enclave. There, too, the promised status of a special economic zone has yet to materialize.

The degree of economic development in this transitional area between West and East depends to a large extent on the economic conditions in Western Europe. Western enterprises that are encountering production bottlenecks during a boom period will be tempted to transfer a part of their activities to postcommunist areas. Industries that are running below capacity and encountering difficult market conditions in their home market, however, will not be easily tempted even by favorable wage conditions to invest in foreign countries. The best thing that could happen to Eastern Europe may well be a long and vigorous growth period in the West.

Still, positive as well as negative developments in the East will to a considerable extent be homemade. How fast and how efficiently will the transformation of the hypertrophied defense economy be carried out? How quickly will domestic consumer goods producers be able to break the myth of Western import products with their own cheap and qualitatively satisfying products? To what extent will politicians be able to resist the temptation to cater to their electorates' chauvinistic tendencies? How much can the independence of central banks be guaranteed? These are decisive questions.

What can the West do for the East? Given a long and rather troubled experience with development aid, we should not harbor too many illusions about the capacity and the will of the Western industrialized states to put Eastern Europe on its feet economically. One of the decisive lessons of postcolonialism is that large investments in the postcolonial areas stopped when those nations were no longer regarded as part of the home country. Without denying the disasters wrought by colonialism (such as the introduction of agrarian monocultures for export purposes), we must admit that it had some advantages, including a certain willingness to invest in infrastructure and the introduction of a relatively high-quality colonial administration that was much less corrupt than its successors. Acceptance of colonies' independence drastically diminished the wish of the former colonial powers to engage in longterm economic development in these areas. Those enterprises that continued their economic activity there did so mostly because they wanted to retain access to specifically valuable natural resources—and they tried to get along with the new elites on a basis of a "minimal payoff."

Such a "neocolonialist" attitude unfortunately appears to be pragmatic for the West's future dealings with large areas of the former Soviet empire. This sort of situation is linked to a fatal inclination not only of foreign investors but of a domestic upper class as well, to transfer the products of domestic economic activity to safe havens abroad as quickly as possible if a political system appears to be highly unstable. Thus, economic and political insecurity and a lack of trust in the future motivate a massive flight of capital. The often criticized practice of Latin American upper classes holding enormous deposits in foreign exchange abroad can already be observed in Russia. No amount of international credits or even gifts can compensate for this fatal practice. Moralizing appeals for international solidarity are also unlikely to be very effective in the rather difficult and unstable situation that prevails particularly in the CIS area.

The role the West can play today in Eastern Europe is a rather modest one. The most realistic hope would be for the West to open its markets to the postcommunistic countries in those areas where they can export competitive products to the West. These are, as mentioned, mass production items and staples such as agrarian products, cement, aluminum, and steel. A sudden flooding of Western markets by low-priced products from the East is obviously not at all popular with the traditional producers of these products in the West. Attempts such as that of France to seal off the Western markets against Eastern agrarian products (by offering subsidies for intereastern trades) are understandable, if lamentable. The same is true of similar actions in the steel area. Poland has rightly criticized the access problems for its steel production to the West. In some ways the situation is comparable to the post–World War I scene, when the Allies wanted Germany to pay enormous reparations but would not allow German industry the export activity that would have allowed Germany to finance such reparations.

The decisive prerequisite for long-term economic progress in Eastern Europe will be the transformation of its productive apparatus. This is an extremely thorny problem: hypercentralized and specialized complexes of heavy industry cannot easily be transformed into productive light industries with a transparent and effective private ownership structure. In fact, this is not just a problem of a change of production structure but of a kind of cultural revolution. Entrepreneurial thinking and active management attitudes were not well thought of during the decades of Stalinist rule; in fact, they were penalized. Insofar as this kind of thinking still manifested itself in marginalized form, it was discredited by the ruling nomenklatura in campaigns against "speculators." While the legal systems of communism marginalized and criminalized individual entrepreneurial attitudes, the minimum survival of these societies was to some extent dependent on this attitude (for example, private kolkhoz markets or small gardening as a main source of fruit production in the former GDR). Admittedly, part of this "underground capitalism" had quite negative effects, such as the pervasive exploitation of "private relationships" to get scarce goods or the enormous volume of theft that became an accepted abuse in a completely socialized economy. The Mafia-type rackets that are extorting money from the new rich in many postcommunist countries echo the traditional disapproval of "speculators" in the older regimes (indeed, within the organizations engaged in such extortion, there seem to be not only groups of certain national minorities but also members of the old over-sized security apparatus). Thus, a major concern today is regenerating a responsible, honest, entrepreneurial class in these countries. Such a new entrepreneurial middle class is needed not only in wholesale and retail trading, which has already been privatized at least in some countries to a surprising extent; it is especially needed in production. And it is in this area that Western governments and Western peoples may have the most to offer. The postcommunist countries are comprised of a well-educated population whose educational standard should enable it to master the challenges of the free market. What this population needs, however, is a practical introduction to a market-economy type of activity. By giving countless bright young people from Eastern Europe a chance to build up their own family enterprises via gifts or cheap leases of old machinery, and by practical training, the Western entrepreneurial middle classes could play an enormous role in Eastern Europe. In short, it is a matter of giving not fish but fishers' nets and teaching the people how to fish. While relatively anonymous institutions such as business schools can participate in this process, more important would be personal relationships. Part of the success of economic development in East Asia and of organizations such as France's Centres Leclerc in retailing has to do with the establishment of personal ties of loyalty between people of different ages and of different economic backgrounds. Western businesspeople who are ready to invest a small portion of their wealth in the companies of bright young men and women from the East whom they have learned to trust personally and whom they have initiated into their own way of thinking and of doing business could be extremely helpful agents of a new consciousness in Eastern Europe. Venture capital subsidies to ex-emigrants from Eastern Europe to become entrepreneurs in their old countries and thus to help with the development process there would allow for a transfer of knowledge and capital. The less anonymous these programs are, the more successful they will be. The United States has an inspiring and successful tradition in creating personal ties, such as the well-known Fulbright programs. With regard to Eastern Europe, the United States would face an important challenge of a similar kind. Capitalism cannot function well without a solid basis of puritan ethics. In a climate of pervasive corruption, where contracts are often not honored and where each individual is trying to maximize his or her own short-term profit at others' expense, capitalism has always shown its ugliest face (as well as its least predictable). Some sort of "puritan ethics," thus, must be re-created in the East. A possible religious upsurge in these areas could do away with the dangerous anomie that is visible in Eastern Europe.

Even without large investments from the West, the ex-communist countries could increase their wealth and decrease their environmental pollution by profiting from the existing slack in an absurdly organized social and economic system. Eastern Europe is in a situation where it could probably save considerable energy and thus liberate resources for production, which could raise the standard of living of the population, by purely domestic efforts. There is also hope that the quantity and quality of agricultural production can be increased dramatically within a relatively short time. A prerequisite for this positive process, however, would be that the existing structures not be shut down totally but that they be superseded gradually by more effective ones. Increased understanding and some help from the West are certainly indispensable. While it is probably best to give up illusions of "instant happiness" in the East, there is still hope that the West will show practicality and solidarity with the complicated path of the postcommunist world back into civilized society, without giving up its own interests and priorities.

In the heart of Moscow, close to the Kremlin, there is a giant circular swimming pool. It was constructed in 1961 on the foundations of the great "Palace of Soviets" which haunted for decades the minds of Moscow's city planners.[29] The building was supposed to be 420 meters high, higher than the Empire State Building, which was then the world's tallest building. It was Stalin himself who ordered that, instead of a relatively small "liberated proletarian," a seventy-meter statue of Lenin should be erected on top of this building. Thus, the totalitarian counterimage to the Statue of Liberty in New York was to be installed on top of the counterimage of the Empire State Building. Stalin's Babylonian tower, incidentally, was to be built on the site of the demolished Christ Savior Cathedral. It is highly symbolic for the fate of communism that its tower was never to rise higher than its foundations. The project is also typical of the absurd competition with the United States, the richest country in the world, which finally ruined the experiment of Russian communism.

In 1961, the swimming pool, a pleasant recreation facility for the hot Moscow summers, had nonetheless to be the "biggest in the world," and Nikita Khrushchev, its creator, had not yet given up the race with the United States. He actually had the hope of overtaking the United States economically written into the program of his party (while his faithful East German followers were stupidly proclaiming at the end of the 1950s that they would soon overtake their arch-rival West Germany). Still, the pool was a symbol of détente and of catering more to the needs of the people than to those of a megalomaniacal bureaucratic elite. Now, after the communist experiment has broken down, these vainglorious pretenses and the burden of competing with the world's richest economies have been finally shaken off. The time is ripe to show the exploited and demoralized population of this region the path to a modest, self-created peaceful state of well-being. Whatever the West can contribute to this sort of development, it would be in its enlightened self-interest to favor it.

Appendix

Table 1

European Transition Countries, Economic Activity 1990–1993 (percentage change with respect to same period of preceding year)

	GDP				Gross Industrial Output			
	1990	1991	1992	1993	1990	1991	1992	1993
Bulgaria	−13.1	−29.4	−12.4	−6.2	−17.2	−22.2	−16.2	−9.3
Czech Republic	−1.2	−4.2	−7.1	−0.5	−3.3	−24.4	−10.6	−7.1
Hungary	−3.3	−11.9	−3.0	−2.0	−4.3	−19.1	−9.2	3.8
Poland	−11.6	−7.6	1.5	4.0	−24.2	−11.9	4.2	7.4
Romania	−8.2	−13.7	−15.4	1.0	−19.0	−18.7	−22.1	1.3
Slovakia	−2.5	−14.5	−7.0	−4.7	−4.0	−25.4	−12.9	−15.4
Slovenia	−4.7	−9.3	−6.0	1.0	−10.5	−12.4	−13.2	−2.6
CIS	−3.4	−13.9	−19.2	−13.0	−1.1	−7.8	−18.2	−14.6
Russia	−2.0	−12.9	−18.5	−12.0	*	*	*	*
Ukraine	−2.5	−11.2	−16.0	−20.0	−0.1	−1.8	−9.0	−22.4
Baltic States	−3.9	−10.8	−31.5	−14.5	−2.5	−4.2	−43.3	−38.2
Total transition economies	−4.8	−12.2	−16.9	−10.0	−3.6	−8.8	−15.7	−13.8

Source: Economic Survey of Europe in 1993–94 (United Nations, March 1994).

Table 2

European Transition Countries

	Changes in Consumer Prices Indices: Percentage Change in Respect to the Preceding Year			Unemployment Thousands and Percent Work Force							
				1990		1991		1992		1993	
	1991	1992	1993	Thousands	%	Thousands	%	Thousands	%	Thousands	%
Bulgaria	254.3	79.4	72.9	72.3	1.8	419.1	11.5	576.9	15.6	626.1	16.9
Czech Republic	56.7	11.1	20.8	39.4	0.7	221.7	4.1	134.8	2.6	185.2	3.5
Hungary	35.0	23.0	22.7	81.4	1.7	406.1	7.4	663.0	12.3	632.1	12.1
Poland	70.3	43.0	36.5	1,126.1	6.1	2,135.6	11.8	2,509.3	10.4	2,839.6	14.4
Romania	165.3	216.9	237.4	150.0	1.3	337.5	3.1	929.0	8.2	1,170.0	10.1
Slovakia	61.2	10.2	23.1	39.6	3.3	302.0	10.1	260.3	13.3	368.1	15.4
Slovenia	117.7	201.3	32.7	33.4	17.1	91.2	24.5	118.7	26.3	137.1	29.6
Russia	100.3	1,468.0	911.3	•	•	61.9	0.1	577.7	0.8	835.3	1.1
Ukraine	83.5	1,240.0	4,474.0	•	•	6.8	0.1	70.5	0.3	83.9	0.4

Source: *Economic Survey of Europe in 1993–1994* (United Nations, March 1994).

Table 3

Transition Countries, Change in Foreign Trade Value and Trade Balances (in billions of U.S. dollars)

| | Growth rates (%) | | | | | | Trade balance, billions of U.S. dollars | | |
| | Exports | | | Imports | | | | | |
	1991	1992	1993	1991	1992	1993	1991	1992	1993
Bulgaria	−34.2	1.6	−13.4	−31.3	27.9	0.2	0.7	•	−1.4
Czech Republic	3.6	3.2	5.5	−7.3	14.6	0.5	0.4	−0.9	−0.1
Hungary	5.1	4.1	−16.8	30.2	−3.2	13.2	−1.3	−0.4	−3.4
Poland	−19.3	−11.4	6.9	24.3	1.8	24.9	•	−0.3	−2.3
Romania	−1.0	5.2	6.4	17.6	8.2	6.1	•	−1.1	−1.3
Russia	−24.6	−25.2	1.4	−35.9	−21.3	−27.1	1.3	5.4	−16.0

Source: *Economic Survey of Europe in 1993–1994* (United Nations, March 1994).

Notes

Chapter 1

1. *Ekonomika i zhizn'* (March 1990).
2. *The Wall Street Journal* (March 11, 1992).
3. *Moscow News*, 2 (1992).
4. Estimates of the U.S. Department of State, *Financial Times* (June 1, 1986).
5. *Neue Zürcher Zeitung* (September 15–16, 1985).
6. *Pravda* (January 27, 1987).
7. *Ekonomicheskaia Gazeta* (February 1992).
8. *The Wall Street Journal* (April 23, 1992).
9. *Pravda* (March 12, 1992).
10. *Moscow News*, 2 (1992).
11. ECE/U.N. *Economic Survey of Europe in 1993–94* (Geneva: United Nations, 1994).
12. *Financial Times* (April 21, 1992).
13. *Welt am Sonntag* (March 2, 1992).
14. *Welt am Sonntag* (April 2, 1992).
15. *Business Week* (April 13, 1992).
16. *The Wall Street Journal* (April 1, 1992).
17. *Financial Times* (April 21, 1992).
18. *Business Week* (January 13, 1992).

Chapter 2

1. *The New York Review of Books* (June 11, 1992).
2. Jeane J. Kirkpatrick, "After Communism," *Problems of Communism* (January–April 1992).
3. Severyn Bialer, "The Death of Soviet Communism," *Foreign Affairs*, 70 (winter 1991–92): 166–81.

4. Kirkpatrick, "After Communism," p. 8.
5. *World Politics*, 44 (October 1991): 37.
6. Erich von Ludendorff, *My War Memoirs* (Berlin: 1919).
7. Lenin, *Selected Works* (Moscow: Progress, 1976), p. 366.
8. Ibid.
9. Ibid., p. 425.
10. *Neue Zürcher Zeitung* (May 15, 1984).
11. *World Politics*, 44 (October 1991): 131.
12. Ibid.
13. Kirkpatrick, "After Communism," p. 7.
14. *Foreign Affairs*, 70 (January 1992):78.
15. Bialer, "The Death of Soviet Communism," p. 174.
16. Dimitri K. Simes, "America and Post-Soviet Republics," *Foreign Affairs*, 71 (summer 1992): 73–89.
17. Ibid., p. 79.
18. *Profil* (Vienna), 2 (January 1992).
19. Simes, "America and Post-Soviet Republics," p. 78.
20. Adrian Karatnycky, "The Ukrainian Factor," *Foreign Affairs* (summer 1992): 94.
21. Martin Wolff, "Breaking Up Is Hard to Do," *Financial Times* (August 29, 1991).
22. Martha Brill Olcott, "Central Asia's Catapult to Independence," *Foreign Affairs* (summer 1992): 108–130.
23. Ibid., p. 109.
24. Ibid., p. 112.
25. Bialer, "The Death of Soviet Communism," p. 170.
26. Olcott, p. 119.
27. *Frankfurter Allgemeine Zeitung* (July 10, 1992).
28. Afanasev, *Profile (Vienna)*. January 1992, p. 53.
29. Ludwig von Mises, *Le Gouvernement Omnipotent* (Paris: Libertarian Press, 1944), p. 90.
30. Petr O. Aven, "Economic Policy and Reforms of Mikhail Gorbachev. A Short History," in *What Is to Be Done* (Vienna: IIASA, 1991), p. 180.
31. A.J. Katzenellenbogen, *The Soviet Union, Empire, Nation and System* (New Brunswick, NJ: Transaction Press, 1990), p. 122.
32. *Izvestiia* (February 16, 1990).
33. *Ekonomicheskaia Gazeta*, 6 (1992).
34. International Monetary Fund, the World Bank, and the OECD, *A Study of the Soviet Economy* (Paris: 1991).
35. *Ekonomicheskaia Gazeta*, 51 (1989).
36. October 2, 1992.
37. *The Wall Street Journal* (October 2, 1992).
38. *Pravda* (October 17, 1992).
39. *Times Literary Supplement* (November 1991).
40. *Pravda* (October 21, 1992).
41. *Problems of Communism* (January–April 1992): 110.
42. Ibid., p. 94.
43. *Pravda* (October 3, 1992).
44. Aven, *What Is to Be Done?*, p. 91.

45. Ibid., p. 90.
46. *Pravda* (October 19, 1992).
47. *Pravda* (October 14, 1992).
48. Aleksandr Yakovlev, *The Opening to a New Civilization* (1992).
49. Friedrich von Hayek, *Fatal Conceit* (Chicago: University of Chicago Press, 1988).
50. *Ekonomicheskaya Gazeta*, 42 (October 1992).
51. *Ekonomicheskaya Gazeta*, 45 (November 1992).
52. *Pravda* (October 22, 1992).
53. *Ekonomicheskaia Gazeta*, 36 (1992).
54. Ibid.
55. *Ekonomicheskaia Gazeta*, 38 (1992).
56. *Pravda* (December 11, 1991).
57. *The Wall Street Journal* (December 15, 1992).
58. *Pravda* (December 11, 1992).
59. *Pravda* (November 17, 1992).
60. *The Wall Street Journal* (December 16, 1992).
61. Ibid.
62. Quoted in Steven Erlanger, "Reform in School," *New York Times Magazine* (November 29, 1992).
63. *The New York Times* (December 15, 1992).
64. *The Wall Street Journal* (December 16, 1992).
65. *Standard* (Vienna) (January 8, 1993).
66. ADN (German News Agency) (December 28, 1992).
67. *Die Zeit* (January 1, 1993).
68. Boris Yeltsin, *The Struggle for Russia* (New York: Times Books, 1994).
69. Ibid., p. 241.
70. Ibid., p. 274.
71. Ibid., p. 291.

Chapter 3

1. *Polityka* (January 2, 1993).
2. Dimitri K. Simes, "America and the Post-Soviet Republics," *Foreign Affairs* (summer 1992): 87.
3. *Pravda* (January 13, 1993).
4. *Pravda* (November 11, 1992).
5. Adrian Karatnycky, "The Ukrainian Factor," *Foreign Affairs* (summer 1992): 101.
6. Martha Brill Olcott, "Central Asia's Catapult to Independence," *Foreign Affairs* (summer 1992): 126.
7. *Pravda* (December 15, 1992).
8. *Ekonomika i zhizn'* (January 1993).
9. *Forbes* (October 25, 1993).

Chapter 4

1. *Polityka* (March 14, 1992).
2. *Europäische Rundschau*, 1 (1988).
3. *Europäische Rundschau*, 3 (1980)

4. *Standard* (Vienna) (September 30, 1991).
5. *Standard* (Vienna) (March 21–22, 1992).
6. *Business Week* (July 18, 1994): 55.
7. *Ekonomicheskaia Gazeta*, 6 (1992).
8. *Voice of Business* (Warsaw) (March 15, 1992).
9. *Wprost* (Warsaw), 15 (1992).
10. ECE/U.N., *Economic Survey of Europe 1993–94* (Geneva: United Nations, 1994), pp. 12, 33.
11. Ibid.
12. *Polityka* (April 25, 1992).
13. Ibid.
14. *The New York Times* (April 2, 1992).

Chapter 5

1. Ralf Dahrendorf, *Reflections on the Revolution in Europe* (New York: Times Books, 1990).
2. *Problems of Communism* (January–April 1992): 73.
3. A.C. MacIntyre, "Recent Political Thought," in *Political Ideas* (London: C.A. Watts, 1966), p. 186.
4. *Problems of Communism* (January–April 1992): 67.
5. Ibid., p. 73.
6. At a mass in the village of Rutka. Quoted in *Gazeta Wspolczesna* (February 1, 1993).
7. In an interview with the Polish newspaper *Polityka* (February 12, 1993).
8. *Standard* (Vienna) (September 30, 1991).
9. *Problems of Communism* (January–April 1992): 70.
10. *Zycie Gospodarcze* (January 24, 1993).
11. Stefan Heym, *Gedanken über Unsere Deutschland*, 1992).
12. *Polityka* (October 3, 1992).
13. Vaclav Klaus, *Problems of Communism* (January–April 1992): 73.
14. Egon Matzner, Jan Kregel, and Gernot Haber, *The Market Shock* (Ann Arbor: Michigan University Press, 1992).
15. *Blick durch die Wirtschaft* (January 13, 1993).
16. Data from a speech by Poland's Prime Minister Suchocka given in Vienna, February 24, 1993.
17. *Blick durch die Wirtschaft* (January 21, 1993).
18. P. Tarnowski, "The World Bank Approves the Credits, but There Are No Borrowers," *Polityka* (February 20, 1993).
19. *Blick durch die Wirtschaft* (January 16, 1993).
20. Reuters (January 31, 1993).
21. Reuters (February 16, 1993).
22. Data of Czech National Bank.
23. *The Wall Street Journal* (December 11, 1992).
24. *Standard* (Vienna) (February 8, 1993).
25. Quoted in *Kurier* (Vienna) (June 19, 1992).
26. *Polityka* (March 6, 1993).

Chapter 6

1. Quoted by Erwin Wichert, German ambassador to China (Stuttgart, 1982), p. 343.
2. *Beijing Observer* (October 27, 1992).
3. Quoted by Wichert, p. 343.
4. In a talk given on the occasion of the opening of the Kreisky Forum in Vienna in March 1993.
5. *The New York Times* (October 19, 1992).

Epilogue

1. That the events of 1989–90 constitute one of history's "great revolutions" is readily acknowledged by liberals such as Sir Ralf Dahrendorf (who wrote immediately afterwards a book with the "Burkean," title, *Reflections on the Revolution in Europe* [London: Random House, 1990]). This will of course be openly contested by all those who would still interpret them (in secret) as a "step backward" because they might consider that "Real Socialism" had—at least in some areas such as ownership patterns—already "surpassed" capitalism. The view that communism represented some sort of "historical progress" despite its obvious "imperfections" is common among many political scientists of the 1968 leftist tradition as well as for many "disappointed idealists" who had turned their back on the system in the 1950s and 1960s.
2. Periodizations are always debatable, but Philippe Schmitter's view on the connections between the world's major waves of democratization seems bizarre. In a June 28, 1993, talk at Webster University in Vienna, he distinguished four historical "waves" or movements toward democracy: the "spring of peoples" of 1848, the developments at the end of the First and Second World Wars, and the period from 1974 (the Portuguese revolution) through the present day. Rarely have I ever heard a more impressive example of distorted historical thinking. Not only did Schmitter omit the first "wave of democracy" at the end of the eighteenth century, comprising the American, French, and Polish Revolutions (and when questioned about these, he minimized their interrelationship, calling Lafayette and Kosciuszko "minor figures"), but grouping the East European "wave of democracy of 1989–90" with the end of dictatorships in Portugal and Spain in the mid-1970s is a rather surprising feat for the coeditor and coauthor of such useful series of books as *Transitions from Authoritarian Rule* (3 vols., Baltimore: Johns Hopkins University Press, 1986, 1989). While the revolutions at the end of the Enlightenment certainly were connected both politically and through personal connections on a high level, Southern Europe in the mid-1970s and Eastern Europe at the end of the 1980s are characterized more by partial structural parallelism (e.g., dictatorial gerontocracy, the necessity for democratic reformers to leave the old regime's repression apparatus unpunished) than by direct influences—even though democratic transition in Southern Europe definitely inspired hope east of the Iron Curtain that the European political system after 1945 was not totally "frozen." The decisive difference was, of course, that Eastern Europe had

(and still has) to reconstitute an economic system based on private ownership of the means of production, whereas "traditional" dictatorships (and even Nazi totalitarianism) left these structures fundamentally intact.

I must note, by the way, that the first years of the Portuguese transition process after April 25, 1974, were actually characterized by strong antidemocratic tendencies of the Stalinist (Cunhal) and the more anarchist type (Otelo de Cavalho).

Schmitter's delineation of periods serves well the purpose of an expert on Southern Europe wanting to turn into a "specialist on transition" in general.

3. The "End of History" as a vulgarized journalistic slogan had relatively little to do with the much more subtle message of Francis Fukuyama's work, *The End of History and the Last Man* (New York: Free Press, 1992).

4. A typical example of ahistoric thinking in economics would be A. Zlabinger's comparison of the two island economies of Singapore and Jamaica, basing their income differences mainly on their integration in world trade and disregarding totally the weight of sociocultural traditions of an ex-slave economy compared with an old commercial settlement (see H. Giersch, A. Zlabinger, and B. Krug, *Kampf der Kontinente: Die Zukunft der Weltwirtschaft*, Vienna: 1990).

The "ancient hatreds" approach has been dominant in recent literature on the war in the former Yugoslavia. See, for example, R. Kaplan, *Balkan Ghosts—A Journey through History* (New York: 1993).

5. Alexis de Tocqueville's famous dictum on the role of the United States and Russia as future world powers is related at the end of the first volume (1835) of his work, *De la Democratie en Amerique* (Paris: Union Generale d'Editions, 1962), p. 214ff.

6. Karl Marx's expressions of contempt regarding reactionary Russia can be found mostly in his letters. See S.K. Padover, *Karl Marx on History and People* (New York: McGraw Hill, 1977). Around 1870, however, "Marx became increasingly aware that alongside the retrograde official Russia, which he so often attacked as the focus and the gendarme of European reaction, a different Russia of revolutionary allies and radical scholars had grown up, increasingly engaged with his own theoretical work" (T. Shanin, *Late Marx and the Russia Road* [New York: Monthly Review Press, 1983], p. 7). "Marx began to study Russian as if it was a matter of life and death" (as his wife complained to Engels; quoted ibid.).

7. Francis Ferdinand, whose assassination was to trigger World War I, was its strongest opponent inside the Austrian ruling class. His dictum that a great war could destroy the tsarist as well as the Austrian empire is documented in R. Kiszling, *Erzherzog Franz Ferdinand von Österreich* (Graz: Boehlau-Verlag, 1953), p. 192 f.

8. Maxim Gorky summed things up quite openly when he concluded (in a series of articles on the postwar situation cited in 1922 by J.M. Keynes for the *Manchester Guardian*) that "a few hundred revolutionaries had seized the power to create an empire of perfect equality and social justice" (quoted in R. Skidelsky, *John Maynard Keynes—the Economist as Saviour 1920–1937* [New York: Viking, 1992], p. 104).

9. Zinaida Hippius, *Between Paris and St. Petersburg*, (Urbana, University of Illinois Press, 1975). Her judgments on the foolish moves of the White side in the civil war are quite pertinent.

10. Otto Bauer's *Rationalisierung—Fehlrationalisierung* has been reedited as

part of his *Werkausgabe* (Vienna: Aufbau-Verlag, 1976), vol. 3, p. 719ff. The quotation is on p. 907.

11. Malcolm Muggeridge's reports ("The Soviet and the Peasantry—An Observer's Notes") appeared on March 25–28, 1933. For typical responses, see the ensuing letters to the editor.

12. Muggeridge recalled his isolation bitterly in a commemorative article in *Guardian Weekly* (April 17, 1983).

13. Sidney and Beatrice Webb, *The Soviet Union—a New Civilization* (London: Longmans, 1935).

14. Alexander Weissberg-Cybulski reported on his experiences in his famous book of 1951 (reedited recently as *Im Verhör* [Vienna: Europa-Verlag, 1993]). Weissberg was an important witness in the Rousset-Lettres Françaises trial, a sequel to the famous Kravchenko trial of 1949. (See *Le Monde*, January 22–23, 1989).

15. The role of Western scientists in transmitting high-tech military technology is exemplified by the Fuchs and the Rosenberg cases. See, for example, I. Philipson, *Ethel Rosenberg—Beyond the Myths* (New Jersey: Rutgers University Press, 1988).

16. See Armand Hammer's obituaries around December 12, 1990, and S. Weinberg, *Armand Hammer—The Untold Story* (Boston: Little, Brown & Co., 1989).

17. A history of how leading European intellectuals tended to break with communism could start in the early 1930s with Panait Istrati; later prewar examples include André Gide, Arthur Koestler, Ignazio Silone, Albert Camus, and George Orwell.

18. Donald Maclean's role as a dissident and precursor of perestroika was recently revealed by the post-Soviet opening of archives (see *Guardian Weekly*, December 6, 1992).

19. Documents of a certain fear of the "German giant" are common, especially in the French press. Similar thoughts are echoed in Margaret Thatcher's memoirs, and one of the most thoughtful German politicians, Joschka Fischer, has recently written a book, *Risiko Deutschland—Krise und Zukunft der deutschen Politik* (Cologne: 1994), pleading for "conscious modesty" on the part of unified Germany. One should remember, by the way, that French President Mitterrand traveled in the summer of 1989 to Berlin in order to exhort the East Germans not to embrace the Federal Republic (see J. Heilbrunn, "Tomorrow's Germany" *The National Interest*, 36 [1994: 44 ff]).

20. Otto Bauer, *Rationalisierung—Fehlrationalisierung*, p. 908.

21. The reluctance of the American people to enter World War II must be seen as the archetypical response of a democratic society, where the fear of losing millions of men in a large war always constitutes a formidable barrier to political activism.

22. The role of the prophets of "instant transformation" in the East after 1990 is exemplified by Jeffrey Sachs of Harvard.

23. The relative stability of per-capita GDP differentials is documented by the fact that from 1860 to 1910 the United States ranked permanently among the top three of a survey of thirteen industrialized countries (including Austria, Belgium, Denmark, France, Germany, Great Britain, Italy, Norway, Sweden, Switzerland). Russia (later the Soviet Union), despite its gigantic industrialization effort, remained below the bottom of this list (*Economic Survey of Europe* [1969], calculations by the Austrian economist A. Kausel).

24. IBM's relatively unsuccessful attempts to turn its employees into share-holders are recounted in Thomas T. Watson, Jr., and Peter Petric, *Father and Son & Co.: My Life at IBM and Beyond* (New York: Bantam, 1990).

25. H. Rauscher, *Wirtschaftswoche* (Vienna) (January 25, 1992).

26. I suggested this transition zone argument at the ICD Conference in London on February 1991 and published it in *Wirtschaftspolitische Blätter* (Vienna), 5–6 (1991), pp. 101ff.

27. The German "Historikerstreit" of 1987 about the precedence and similarities of Soviet totalitarianism compared with Nazi totalitarianism contained some very questionable tendencies to mitigate the crimes of Hitler's regime, but it certainly put justified stress on certain imitative tendencies.

28. The somewhat paradoxical Reagan "strategy" is well illustrated by his former budget director David Stockman in *The Triumph of Politics—Why the Reagan Revolution Failed* (New York: Avon Books, 1986), e.g., p. 356ff.

29. On the symbolic importance of the Palace of Soviets, see, e.g., A. Ryabushin and N. Smolina, *Landmarks of Soviet Architecture 1917–1991* (Berlin: Ernest & Sohn, 1992).

Index

About the Author

Adam Zwass for many years held senior positions in the central banking systems of Poland and the USSR. From 1963 to 1968 he was councillor in the Secretariat of the Council for Mutual Economic Assistance in Moscow, where he was responsible for financial settlements and the work of the International Bank for Economic Cooperation.

Since his emigration to Vienna, Austria, Dr. Zwass was affiliated for over twenty years with Austrian and German research institutes and served as an advisor to the Austrian National Bank and major private banks. He currently publishes his analyses of the Central European and post-Soviet socioeconomic developments in several European journals and newspapers.

Dr. Zwass is the author of eight books, translated into several languages, and of hundreds of articles published in Europe and in the United States. His most recent books in English are *The Council for Mutual Economic Assistance* (1989), *Market, Plan, and State: The Two World Economic Systems* (1987), and *The Economies of Eastern Europe in a Time of Change* (1984).

Printed in the United States
by Baker & Taylor Publisher Services